THE EVENT OF THE
DERRIDA'S POST-DECONSTRUCTIVE REALISM

MW01518500

Jacques Derrida's writings often embed the key themes of deconstruction in a notion of the thing. *The Event of the Thing* is the most complete examination to date of Derrida's understanding of thinghood and its crucial role in psychoanalysis, ethics, literary theory, aesthetics, and Marxism.

Arguing that the thing, as a figure of otherness, destabilizes the metaphysical edifice it underlies, Michael Marder reveals the contributions it makes to critiques of humanism and idealism. Subsequently, the new realism that emerges from deconstruction holds the possibility of an event that problematizes all attempts to objectify the thing. An illuminating analysis of Derrida and phenomenology, *The Event of the Thing* is an innovative and compelling study of a crucial aspect of one of the twentieth century's greatest thinkers.

MICHAEL MARDER is an assistant professor in the Department of Philosophy at Duquesne University and research fellow at the Centre of Philosophy, University of Lisbon, Portugal.

MICHAEL MARDER

The Event of the Thing:

Derrida's Post-Deconstructive Realism

UNIVERSITY OF TORONTO PRESS
Toronto Buffalo London

© University of Toronto Press Incorporated 2009
Toronto Buffalo London
www.utppublishing.com
Printed in Canada

Reprinted in paperback 2011

ISBN 978-0-8020-9892-4 (cloth)
ISBN 978-1-4426-1265-5 (paper)

Printed on acid-free paper

Library and Archives Canada Cataloguing in Publication

Marder, Michael, 1980–
The event of the thing: Derrida's post-deconstructive realism/
Michael Marder.

Includes bibliographical references and index.
Includes some text in French.
ISBN 978-0-8020-9892-4 (bound) – ISBN 978-1-4426-1265-5 (pbk.)

1. Derrida, Jacques. 2. Realism. 3. Ontology. 4. Deconstruction.
5. Intentionality (Philosophy). 6. Other (Philosophy). I. Title.

B2430.D484M345 2008   194   C2008-904903-9

This book has been published with the help of a grant from the Canadian
Federation for the Humanities and Social Sciences, through the Aid to
Scholarly Publications Program, using funds provided by the Social Sciences
and Humanities Research Council of Canada.

University of Toronto Press acknowledges the financial assistance to its
publishing program of the Canada Council for the Arts and the Ontario
Arts Council.

University of Toronto Press acknowledges the financial support of the
Government of Canada through the Canada Book Fund for its publishing
activities.

For Patrícia, without whom no-thing would matter ...

Contents

Acknowledgments

The Event of the Thing would not have been possible without the intense intellectual exchanges I've had in the United States and in Canada. I bear a debt of gratitude to the faculty and graduate students at the New School for Social Research, with whom I have discussed my work. Simon Critchley, Jay Bernstein, Claudia Baracchi, Alan Bass, and Edward Casey have commented on the various drafts of the project. Roy Ben-Shai and Keren Sadan remain my constant interlocutors. North of the border, my meetings with the members of the Toronto reading group, including Robert Albritton, Stefanos Kourkoulakos, and Nchamah Miller, as well as with Aniruddha Chowdhury have provided me with incredible intellectual stimulation. I would like to thank the Gulberg and Vieira families for the hospitality they have extended to me during the writing process on both sides of the Atlantic. I am grateful to the Philosophy Department at the New School for the fellowships that allowed me to dedicate my time to this project. The staff members of the Jacques Derrida Archives at the University of California, Irvine have greatly facilitated my archival research. Virgil Duff and Theresa Griffin, of the University of Toronto Press, have made the editorial process as seamless as possible, while two anonymous reviewers have supplied me with useful references and have helped me to sharpen some of my arguments. I am at a loss for words that could adequately express my appreciation for the unconditional love and support that my mother and brother, Marina and Lev Marder, have offered and continue to offer me. Finally, I dedicate this manuscript to my wife and intellectual companion, Patrícia I. Vieira, who enhanced the readability of the present text and whose mere presence is a source of light for my world and work.

Part of chapter 1 appeared under the title 'Différance of the Real' in *Parrhesia: A Journal of Critical Philosophy 4*, April 2008, pp. 49–61. The book as a whole developed from an article titled 'Sure Thing? On Things and Objects in the Philosophy of Jacques Derrida,' featured in a special issue of *Postmodern Culture, 15*(3), dedicated to Jacques Derrida and published in May 2005. Both texts are reproduced with the permission of the copyright holders.

Introduction:
Hoc nihil ad rem

The thing is eventful, the event happens in the thing itself: such will have been the dual provocation of this book. If we are to learn how to hear the pro-vocative challenge, how to attune ourselves to the calling forth that proceeds from and summons us to the eventfulness of the thing and the thinghood of the event, we ought to learn, in the first place, not to precomprehend the source of the call in terms of a fixed ontological entity vaguely synonymous with the object. The refusal to accept this traditional meaning uncritically implies that, perhaps, in spite of the long and overdetermined philosophical genealogy of *onta* and *pragmata*, *res* and *causa*, *Ding* and *Sache*, what we know of and about the thing has nothing to do with the thing, *hoc nihil ad rem*, because we no longer or still do not know whether the thing has anything to do with knowledge. Such 'meta-not-knowing,' which touches not only this or that particular thing but also the relation or the non-relation of knowledge and thinghood, precipitates the event that shirks the mechanisms of recognition and conceptual identification. The futural coming of the unrecognizable event retraces the past of the thing that precedes subjective memory and repeatedly escapes from every stage of the philosophical genealogy that names it. In other words, the event reiterates the fugal iteration inherent in the thing and expresses itself as the event *of* the thing, whose escape is not wholly negative but generative and abundant.

The rejection of preconceived, unexamined notions is a hallmark of post-Kantian philosophy, with its methodological emphasis on critique, negation, and reduction, which informs all quests for the true objectivity. This emphasis goes hand in hand with the necessary detour through the true (transcendental, intersubjective, bracketed, purified) subject on which the success of such quests hinges. Yet no amount of critique will be sufficient if the value of truth itself comes into question and becomes irrelevant to the thing itself. In Kant's system, where the critical impulse delimits the absolute claims of knowledge, while the 'thing in itself' circumscribes the epistemological purview of critique and the ontology of objectivity alike, there is a dawning awareness of this insufficiency. Kantian awareness, however, fades as early as Hegel's dialectical philosophy, which prompts, inter alia, a gradual determination of the thing in itself for us. Even Husserlian phenomenology, with its anti-psychologist agenda, exempts the immanent structures of pure consciousness – but not the 'transcendence' of the thing – from the relentlessness of reduction.

Without rehabilitating the pre-Kantian innocent illusion of objectivity indifferent to subjective organization and arrangement, the deconstructive retrieval of the question of the thing in Derrida dethrones the 'primacy' of consciousness and overturns the claims it lays on the actual, present, real being. This retrieval suggests that, in contrast to the irreducibility of the thing, Husserl's pure consciousness is thoroughly reducible (chapter 2); that the interiority of the Hegelian subject turns inside out, consumes itself, and thus defers to the movement of the thing (chapter 3); and that, prior to and below the lines of demarcation between the subject and the object, this movement constitutes the differential of forces before and below its Kantian determination and ontologization (chapter 4). A crucial aspect of Derrida's tendency to think 'prior to and below' Kant is the tacit acknowledgment that any attempt to disentangle the thing from the object is *necessarily* preliminary and provisional, since it threatens to restore the absolute divide between the empirical and the transcendental, by stabilizing, objectivizing, and therefore incorporating into the object the distinction thus outlined. Still, the yardstick (if there is one) for distinguishing the object from the thing is the specific kind of difference each of them entails: whereas the former emerges in opposition to the subject, the latter signifies non-oppositional otherness and non-identity (chapter 1).

Deposited within the Heideggerian discourse on the epochal donation and withdrawal of being and substituting 'being under erasure,' the deconstructive thing appears only in retreating or withdrawing. That is to say, it subtracts itself from what it gives, makes appear, and at the same time expropriates, including space, time, the phenomenological world, and the process of signification that, in vain, strives to remark the thing's own self-remaking routine. Unlike Heidegger's being, however, the Derridian thing is both disseminated and disseminating, such that it evades the strictly conceptual grasp and any efforts of gathering into a totality. Its self-dissemination derives from its originary doubling or splitting – between the 'who' and the 'what,' the animate and the inanimate, the living and the dead, the phenomenological and the abstractly scientific – which precludes the possibility of synthesis, prevents the thing from assuming an objectively oppositional stance (against the subject *or* against the non-thing in general), and welcomes *différance* as well as the event in the virtual interiority opened by the split. While the thing is that which happens when the event happens, the poetics of the event analyse and re-synthesize language and discourse in the thing itself, which remains impervious to analysis, synthesis, and hence the order of knowledge. In acknowledging this imperviousness, one accepts the unbinding of the thing from the subject. This is the argumentative thread of chapter 1.

Chapter 2 brings together Derrida's modification of the Husserlian intentionality thesis and his deconstruction of the categorial/existential divide in Heidegger. Although, for Husserl, intentionality is unthinkable without its 'real' elements (*noema* and *hylē*), the fragments of subjective intentions are inevitably lost in the opaqueness of the intended thing. The return of these lost fragments defines the thing's own spectral intentionality, which aims at and obsesses us well in excess of the circumspective concern accompanying our being-in-the-world. Despite its inherent self-dissemination, the thing directs itself to us, investing 'our' collective subjectivity. Inscribed onto the body *proper* or, more specifically, onto the senses of seeing, hearing, and touching, the inversion of intentionality both enables and defies the functionality of sense as such. Finally, in the act of reading, the text reads us before and while we face it. Its intentionality anticipates and pre-empts the activity of consciousness and, in so doing, deflates all claims of primacy.

In chapter 3, I consider the role of the thing in Derrida's account of psychoanalytic and commodity-economic fetishisms. As an extended-psychic thing, as a juncture between *res extensa* and *res cogitans*, the unconscious is internally divisible and analysable: that is the sine qua non of psychoanalysis. On the side of the thing, psychoanalysis resists both the metaphysical belief in psychic undifferentiation and its corollary, the disavowal – registration and repudiation – of difference that leaves no space for analytic activity. But, on the horizon of negativity, the thing itself both invites and resists analysis as its impossible condition of possibility. One version of this resistance is the subsumption, in the thing itself, of the distinction between the fetish (what replaces the absent thing) and the thing, which, in its 'proper' non-oppositional otherness and non-identity, is the very figure of substitution and sup-plementation ('generalized fetishism'). Consequently, to love the thing is to leave enough room for its resistance and to allow the chain of sub-stitutions that makes up generalized fetishism to continue indefinitely in the thing itself.

The dynamism of this chain reflects the way in which the thing sets itself to work, but capitalist valorization harnesses the work of the thing for the purposes of profit-making when it abstracts its social di-mension and confines it to the law of value. As a result, economic fe-tishism utilizes the commodity as a 'sensuous non-sensuous' object-thing and objectifies the qualities of the thing as such, presencing and capitalizing on its virtuality. It is, then, possible to graft the features of the thing (self-supplementation, giving and demanding time, etc.) onto the bodiless body of the commodity, keeping in mind that the latter represents the process of the becoming-thing of the thing, which, in a phenomenological perversion, sustains what Derrida calls *mondiali-sation*, the becoming-world of the world, or the idealized projection of reified sociality writ large in the form of value.

The hypothesis of chapter 4 is that Derrida's writings on aesthetics charge art with the task of setting free the alterity of things that, in turn, deconstruct the work of art. For instance, the aesthetic style is a kind of signature that releases the work from the author/artist, by ab-sorbing and identifying the residue of its bearer's idiosyncrasy (that which is 'proper') and thereby signalling his or her death. The first idi-omatic signature lodged within the art-work is doubled by the coun-ter-signature of the art-thing that materially supports and resists – confirms and betrays – the work, both offering and denying the possi-bility of hypostasis. The release of the thing also transpires thanks to the aesthetics of the 'subjectile' which is Derrida's name for the subter-ranean movement of the post-Heideggerian hurling and falling under-neath the congealed objective and subjective forms. The unknown, unpredictable destination of the subjectilian trajectory sweeps away the artist, the art-work, and the art-thing in a certain purposeless pur-poselessness, which radicalizes Kantian aesthetics. Finally, the par-ergon undoes or, at least, complicates the dualisms of the thing and the work, the inside and the outside, the necessary and the incidental, and so on. It designates the mutual fall of the thing into the work and of the work into the thing, which, in this alteration or alterization, regains its non-oppositional otherness and non-identity.

If the 'thing' is one of the most inconspicuous terms in Derridian philosophy, then its inconspicuousness should be taken literally as the muteness at the bottom or at the heart of speech, as the muteness, also, of the written word, of materiality without materialism, the muteness that, finally and paradoxically, permits the conceptual equipment overlaying deconstruction to instrumentalize, idealize, and transfigure it either into textual analysis and criticism, or into a purely formal and secretly idealist exercise. But (and here is the brink of an aporia) to make the thing speak directly, programmatically, conceptually of itself and for itself, in its self-identity as 'the thing itself,' is to lose it all the more surely, given that neither the thing nor the written word operates in the medium of the voice, in which they would coincide with themselves. It is in the double bind of the approach to the thing that deconstruction risks arriving at what has nothing to do with the thing – *hoc nihil ad rem* – when it lets what or whom it approaches speak and, simultaneously, respects the irreducible muteness to which we shall now attune our ears.

Abbreviations of Titles of Works by Derrida

A   *Aporias.* Trans. Thomas Dutoit. Stanford: Stanford University Press, 1993.

AF   *Archive Fever: A Freudian Impression.* Trans. Eric Prenowitz. Chicago and London: University of Chicago Press, 1996.

AL   *Acts of Literature.* Ed. Derek Attridge. New York and London: Routledge, 1992.

AR   *Acts of Religion.* Ed. Gil Anidjar. New York and London: Routledge, 2002.

ARF   *The Archeology of the Frivolous: Reading Condillac.* Trans. John P. Leavey, Jr. Lincoln and London: University of Nebraska Press, 1987.

B   'Biodegradables: Seven Diary Fragments.' Trans. Peggy Kamuf. *Critical Inquiry 15*, Summer 1989, pp. 812–73.

C   (with Catherine Malabou) *Counterpath: Traveling with Jacques Derrida.* Trans. David Wills. Stanford: Stanford University Press, 2004.

CI   'Circumfession.' In Geoffrey Bennington and Jacques Derrida, *Jacques Derrida.* Trans. Geoffrey Bennington. Pp. 3–315. Chicago and London: University of Chicago Press, 1993.

CIN   *Cinders/Feu la cendre.* Trans. Ned Lukacher. Lincoln and London: University of Nebraska Press, 1991.

D   *Dissemination.* Trans. Barbara Johnson. Chicago and London: University of Chicago Press, 1981.

DE   *Demeure: Fiction and Testimony.* Trans. Elizabeth Rottenberg. Stanford: Stanford University Press, 2000.

DP   *Déplier Ponge: Entretien avec Gérard Farasse.* Villeneuve d'Ascq: Presses Universitaires du Septrentrion, 2005.

E   'Economimesis.' Trans. R. Klein. *Diacritics 11*, Summer 1981,
        pp. 3–25.

EO   *The Ear of the Other: Otobiography, Transference, Translation.*
        Trans. Peggy Kamuf. Lincoln and London: University of
        Nebraska Press, 1988.

ET   (with Bernard Stiegler) *Ecographies of Television: Filmed Inter-
        views.* Oxford and Malden: Polity, 2002.

EU   *Eyes of the University: Right to Philosophy I.* Trans. Jan Plug et al.
        Stanford: Stanford University Press, 2004.

FWT   (with Elisabeth Roudinesco) *For What Tomorrow: A Dialogue
        with Elisabeth Roudinesco.* Trans. Jeff Fort. Stanford: Stanford
        University Press, 2004.

G   *Glas.* Trans. John P. Leavey, Jr, and Richard Rand. Lincoln and
        London: University of Nebraska Press, 1986.

GG   *Geneses, Genealogies, Genres, and Genius: The Secrets of the
        Archive.* Trans. Beverley Brahic. Edinburgh: Edinburgh
        University Press, 2006.

GT   *Given Time: I. Counterfeit Money.* Trans. Peggy Kamuf. Chicago
        and London: University of Chicago Press, 1992.

HC   *H.C. for Life, That Is to Say …* Trans. Laurent Milesi and Stefan
        Herbrechter. Stanford: Stanford University Press, 2006.

HQ   *Heidegger et la question: De l'Esprit et autres essais.* Paris: Flam-
        marion, 1990.

IOG   *Introduction to Edmund Husserl's* Origin of Geometry. Trans.
        John P. Leavey, Jr. Lincoln and London: University of Nebraska
        Press, 1989.

JDP   Jacques Derrida Papers. MS-C01, Special Collections and
        Archives, University of California Irvine Libraries. [All transla-
        tions of these materials are mine. The first number following
        the abbreviations is the box number, and the second is the
        number of the folder in the Derrida archive.]

L   *Limited Inc.* Trans. Samuel Weber. Evanston: Northwestern
        University Press, 1988.

LO   'Living On: Border Lines.' Trans. James Hulbert, in Harold
        Bloom et al., *Deconstruction and Criticism.* New York: Contin-
        uum, 1979. Pp. 62–142.

MB   *Memoirs of the Blind.* Trans. Pascale-Anne Brault and Michael
        Naas. Chicago and London: University of Chicago Press, 1993.

MC   'My Chances / *Mes chances*: A Rendezvous with Some Epicu-
        rean Stereophonies.' In J.H. Smith and W. Kerrigan, eds, *Taking*

Chances: Derrida, Psychoanalysis, and Literature. (Baltimore and London: Johns Hopkins University Press, 1984. Pp. 1–32.

MJ   *Marx en jeu.* Paris: Descartes et Cie, 1997.

MO   *Monolingualism of the Other, or the Prosthesis of Origin.* Trans. Patrick Mensah. Stanford: Stanford University Press, 1998.

MP   *Margins of Philosophy.* Trans. Alan Bass. Chicago and London: University of Chicago Press, 1982.

MPD   *Memoires for Paul de Man.* Rev. ed. Trans. Cecile Lindsey, Jonathan Culler, Eduardo Cadava, and Peggy Kamuf. New York: Columbia University Press, 1989.

N   *Negotiations: Interventions and Interviews, 1971–2001.* Trans. Elizabeth Rottenberg. Stanford: Stanford University Press, 2002.

OG   *Of Grammatology.* Trans. Gayatri C. Spivak. Baltimore: Johns Hopkins University Press, 1997.

OS   *Of Spirit.* Trans. Geoffrey Bennington and Rachel Bowlby. Chicago and London: University of Chicago Press, 1987.

OT   *On Touching – Jean-Luc Nancy.* Trans. Christine Irizarry. Stanford: Stanford University Press, 2005.

P   *Positions.* Trans. Alan Bass. Chicago and London: University of Chicago Press, 1972.

PA   *Parages.* Paris: Galilée, 2003.

PC   *The Postcard: From Socrates to Freud and Beyond.* Trans. Alan Bass. Chicago and London: University of Chicago Press, 1987.

PF   *Politics of Friendship.* Trans. George Collins. London and New York: Verso, 1997.

PG   *The Problem of Genesis in Husserl's Philosophy.* Trans. Marian Hobson. Chicago and London: University of Chicago Press, 2003.

PM   *Paper Machine.* Trans. Rachel Bowlby. Stanford: Stanford University Press, 2005.

PSY   *Psyché: Inventions de l'autre.* Paris: Galilée, 2003.

PTT   *Philosophy in the Time of Terror: Dialogues with Jürgen Habermas and Jacques Derrida.* Chicago and London: University of Chicago Press, 2003.

R   *Rogues: Two Essays on Reason.* Trans. Michael Naas and Pascale-Anne Brault. Stanford: Stanford University Press, 2005.

RP   *Resistances of Psychoanalysis.* Trans. Peggy Kamuf, Michael Naas, and Pascale-Anne Brault. Stanford: Stanford University Press, 1998.

S   *Spurs: Nietzsche's Styles*. Trans. Barbara Harlow. Chicago and
        London: University of Chicago Press, 1978.

SI   *Signésponge/Signsponge*. Trans. Richard Rand. New York:
        Columbia University Press, 1984.

SM   *Specters of Marx: The State of the Debt, the Work of Mourning, and
        the New International*. Trans. Peggy Kamuf. New York: Rout-
        ledge, 1994.

SP   *Speech and Phenomena and Other Essays on Husserl's Theory of
        Signs*. Trans. David B. Allison. Evanston: Northwestern Uni-
        versity Press, 1973.

SQ   *Sovereignties in Question: The Poetics of Paul Celan*. Trans.
        Thomas Dutoit and Outi Pasanen. New York: Fordham Univer-
        sity Press, 2005.

TP   *The Truth in Painting*. Trans. Geoffrey Bennington and Ian
        McLeod. Chicago and London: University of Chicago
        Press, 1987.

US   'To Unsense the Subjectile.' In Jacques Derrida and Paule
        Thévenin, *The Secret Art of Antonin Artaud*. Trans. Mary Ann
        Caws. Cambridge and London: MIT Press, 1998. Pp. 59–160.

USC   *Université sans condition*. Paris: Galilée, 2001.

V   *Veils*. Trans. Geoffrey Bennington. Stanford: Stanford Univer-
        sity Press, 2001.

WD   *Writing and Difference*. Trans. Alan Bass. Chicago and London:
        University of Chicago Press, 1980.

WM   *The Work of Mourning*. Trans. Pascale-Anne Brault and Michael
        Naas. Chicago and London: University of Chicago Press, 2001.

THE EVENT OF THE THING:
DERRIDA'S POST-DECONSTRUCTIVE REALISM

1 The Event of the Thing: 'Ereignis *in Abyss*'

Would that the letters might arrive. In arriving, the letters are the events, the very figures of the event, like the *arrivant*: like the letter, the event is a thing '*made to* arrive.'

H.C. for Life, That Is to Say ...

Les mots que tu viens de détacher (par exemple *blanchâtre* ou *eau)*, sans aucun droit, peuvent bien ressembler à des *éléments* de son nom: aussi bien des parties du nom (indivisibles) que son milieu élémentaire (indivisible). Mais l'élément est aussi infiniment divisible, anonyme, dans les choses et dans les syllabes.

Parages

Everything that will transpire below will waver and hesitate between the event of the concept and the impossibility of developing a concept of the event, between philosophy and poetry, between *the* thing and things. Such hesitation and wavering do not stand for the symptoms of provisional indeterminacy, but evince the idiosyncrasy of the thing that remains to come, promised in and as itself, outside any immediate or deferred presence of those things that give or present themselves to us. But undecidability becomes decisive for the event of the thing and for the eventhood of any event in at least two ways: 1) as that which tinges phonic identity (homophony) with graphic difference and non-identity, and 2) as the place before the distinction between 'who' and 'what,' where making and letting come, activity and passivity pass into each other. Neither a subject nor an object, neither the same as nor wholly other than itself, the thing makes and lets the event happen virtually, immanently, poetically.

1.1. Protocols of the thing: That the event will have been possible

The protocols of the thing are not the enumerations of its attributes; they are the thing's own dictates or 'laws' enjoining the subject prior to any intentional activity on her part. These protocols illuminating the thingly side of Heideggerian thrownness specify the conditions of possibility for the occurrence of the virtual (impending and spectral) event. Their overarching theme is the thing's non-identity with itself, its doubling into the qualitative and the quantitative, the living and the dead, the giving and the withdrawn, the spoken and the written.

1.1.1. It's virtually happening …

Before beginning in earnest, before *really* making a start and binding a starting place to a thing (*res*), let me indulge in a virtual thought experiment with the subtitle of this section. A singular speech-act, or an event of saying that elucidates the general dynamics of any event, 'It's virtually happening' makes, at the same time, a host of heterogeneous claims. To translate: 'It's almost happening; it's on the verge of happening,' or 'It is already (always already) happening but "only" virtually,' or again, 'It's as though the event is happening, while nothing really arrives; de jure but not de *facto*, it feigns its own occurrence,' and so on. Neither of these alternative renditions is more appropriate or more correct than the others, which would deserve to be eliminated on the pretext of causing 'white noise' that prevents the adequate transmission of meaning and sense. Rather, the event will have been possible only in the midst of the irreducible multiplicity and aporetic coexistence of all these possibilities with their eventful confusions and cross-contaminations. In keeping with Derrida's thinking of the event as the impossible arrival of something or someone who/that cannot be recognized as the *arrivant* she, or he, or it is, these confusions and cross-contaminations madden those who put their faith in the mechanisms of identification and recognition, the mechanisms whose inefficacy disseminates the exact time, place, and meaning of arrival.

If I now say that I am *really* beginning, I repeat and reaffirm, without idealizing or formalizing, the first beginning that did not count as such; across a barely perceptible delay of the paragraph break, I dispense to the first beginning its thingly character on the model of the Derridian repetition of 'perhaps, perhaps' and *'oui, oui,'* where the second, the other, the thingly affirmation or possibility, infinitely echoed and lodged in the first, props up, shores up, supports, but also counter-signs and reifies the first, infecting it with im-possibility.

Before coming back to this counter-signature, it is worth noting that the event of the thing draws sustenance from the uncertainty of every-thing that has to do with the time, place, and possibility of arrival of the one who or of that which comes. The event could have been possi-ble only if we were no longer certain that it is merely possible or even probable, if we were to forsake the absolute conviction that the thing arrives in the time-place for which the subject destines it (the preroga-tive of idealism) as much as the belief that the reality of *res* tirelessly and banally unfolds itself in those innumerable impersonal 'occur-rences' of which we have the undeniable empirical and phenomeno-logical evidence (the prerogative of realism). Or, in Derrida's own words: 'One can think sense or non-sense only by ceasing to be sure that the thing ever occurs [*on ne peut penser le sens ou le non-sens qu'à cesser d'être certain que la chose advienne jamais*], or – even if there is such a thing – that it would ever be accessible to theoretical knowledge or determinant judgment' (PF 39/59).[1]

The abeyance of assurances and of the transcendental surety for knowledge into which the thing has been converted at bottom, at *the* bottom, in the abyssal pit extending below the pyramidal edifice of the metaphysics of presence (comprised, on the Aristotelian model, of the thing, the animal defined as a living thing, and the human conceived as a political animal), is the initial step toward its virtualization. The virtuality of the thing is a prerequisite for the eventhood of an event in *Specters of Marx*, where the thing's refraction into use- and exchange-value is attributed to a certain mathematization, a rendering-numerical of the thing that turns ghostly: 'It is number itself, it is numerous, innu-merable as number, one can neither count on it nor with it' (SM 138). In overtly discussing Marx, Derrida covertly references Heidegger,[2] who detects in the rendering-numerical of things a vulgarized version of the Greek mathematical project, which, at its source, broadly equates *mathesis* with 'learning' and *mathemata* with 'what is learnable.'[3] The metonymic reduction of *mathemata* to numbers, as well as the steady abstraction and divorcement of the learnable from the phenomenologi-cal, lays the foundations for the impoverishment and forgetting of the Greek beginning. At the extreme, this forgetting results in the claim that 'every thing ... has a double': the table of the scientist comprised of atoms and empty space is a ghostly twin of the table one has known since one's childhood.[4]

From Derrida's vantage point, the thought of Marx and Heidegger alike unfolds as an uneasy synthesis of critical maturity and nostalgic naivety, precisely with reference to the 'real.' While the critical element is all too obvious, their naivety is expressed in mourning, lamenting, and thus ontologizing the same event of 'the loss of childhood,' if not 'the loss of innocence,' of the immemorial time when the thing was intact and could count as one. In both cases, this loss stems from the virtualization of the world, the symptoms of which include the splitting of the thing and the relegation of something like its 'truth' to the numerical aspect or, broadly speaking, to its non-material facet. To counterbalance this ostensibly deplorable development, the former insists on work and its use-value, which gives 'an account of reality as practical actuality' (SM 131), and the latter envisions a 'rigorous non-contamination' of the thought of essence with the technological (OS 10–11). But what is the fate of the event and of the thing in these mournful reactions? Do not both thinkers desire, in a daring but rather infantile fantasy of omnipotence, as Freud would say, to behold the unity of the thing, the unity that becomes actualized in accordance with the hand and the work of the human? Don't they desire to receive some reassurance, both practical *and* theoretical, that whenever the thing occurs, it is always ready to hand, prepared to be worked upon and to work for us? In other words, in different ways and despite themselves, Marx and Heidegger will attempt to conjure away the *dunamis* or the virtuality of the thing by way of conceptualizing it – at the limit of the concept's conceptuality – as actual, non-enigmatic, non-mystified.[5]

Although these pious attempts presuppose the existence of a solid line of demarcation between the fetish and the thing, they overlook the phenomenon of general or generalized fetishism,[6] where the thing is already – virtually – a fetish, and hence its own replacement, its own prosthesis, its own double: '*Two times at the same time*, originary iterability, irreducible virtuality of this space and this time' (SM 163). The very eventhood of the event promising, without any guarantees, the arrival of something or someone hinges on this iterative replacement of oneself, or itself, as the other 'according to the law of the double, of the substitution of the unique for the unique, which aims for its own specter and for itself [*qui se vise en son spectre et en soi-même*]' (HC 63/ 59). One could interpret the act of aiming for one's own spectre and for oneself as the harbinger of the auto-affective closure of intentionality betrayed by the use of the verb *viser*, to aim. I will have occasion to elaborate on this later. For now, suffice it to say that to aim for two things at once is to lose the target. As long as the chain of such substitutions *in the thing itself* is ongoing, the thing will not be 'itself,' will not arrive at itself or – this amounts to the same thing – will not reach its 'proper' limit and will frustrate all desires for unity.[7] What happens here is that the thing does not happen in concrete occurrences cathected by realism, nor arrive at a fixed identity with itself invested by idealism, but constantly slips away, such that this very slippage constitutes the event of its non-arrival and destabilizes the metaphysical identities of the animal and the human it undergirds. The elusive happening of non-happening deserves the appellation 'virtual,' since it does not touch its own limit, which is nothing but 'this thing without a thing [*cette chose sans chose*]' (OT 103/121).

Ever since Plato,[8] the replacement of the unique by itself, characterizing the event, has been the kairotic moment of everything that lives and enlivens (even from the other side of life) by way of extracting the infinite from the finite. It is the unmoved movement of this auto-supplementarity as and by the other that allows Derrida to situate life in the thing itself: 'At the same time Life, Thing, Beast, Object [*tout à la fois Vie, Chose, Bête, Objet*] …, the animal Thing, the animated-inanimated, living-dead Thing [*la Chose animée-inanimée, la Chose mort-vivante*] … gives birth' (SM 152/242). Life as the process of othering is no longer other to the ostensibly inanimate thing. The ensuing hybridization of the animal and the thing not only transgresses the traditional metaphysical boundaries, but also establishes a razor-thin difference between the virtual and the ideal, that is, between the virtuality of the spectral thing that proliferates, gives birth, gives place without taking any, and the ideality of spirit that formalizes and lives on the suppression of the virtual *dunamis* and possibilities of the thing.

Spirit as such is a formalized virtuality subjected to the demands and the order of the actual.[9] But before and beneath this subjection or subjecthood, the animated-inanimated thing breathes, inspires and expires, animatingly engages with spirit and spirits away. Older than any 'spiritualism,' the breath of the virtual thing spirits away spirit itself.[10] This does not mean that what I call its virtuality is exactly equivalent to the spectral. Rather, it 'is' the very difference between the spirit and its spectres, the pre-originary principle of the inexorable dissemination of the former in the latter and an ironic wink with a side-glance at Heidegger's ontico-ontological difference.[11] The intricacy of the relation between the spectres and spirit requires the incorporation of the animate-inanimate thing (as that which ensouls and, simultaneously, that which is ensouled) in the best traditions of associating *psyche* and *anima* with the element of air and, particularly, with breath. Needless to say, such incorporation will erode these traditions from within, and it will confirm that the event and its risk, superseding the most daring fantasies of idealism, depend upon letting the thing 'breathe *without me* [*la laissant respirer* sans moi]' (SI 20/21).[12]

To put it differently, the event of the thing deconstructs the partitions Heidegger has erected between the existential and the categorial analytics in *Being and Time*.[13] Mirroring the virtual doubling of the mathematized thing, the author, who is 'someone,' is doubled with the stylistic marks that authorize his text, for instance with 'the stroke of genius [*le coup de génie*]' in 'the signature of the Thing "Shakespeare" [*la signature de la Chose 'Shakespeare'*]' (SM 22/47). With the capitalization of the thing and confinement of the proper name in quotation marks, Derrida advises us that the death of the author is not the final verdict; that the author continues to survive, to outlive his death in the guise of a virtual thing that indeterminately abuts the proper (name) and the improper (multiplicity of possible translations it approves a priori, in advance); that this death is, strictly speaking, that kind of thingly after-life which Walter Benjamin isolates in the work of literature meriting translation. What Derrida calls 'the stroke of genius' is the event of generation, generativity, and life *offered from the side of death* – not a resurrection, but the spectral doubling of the author in the breathing *and* breathless Thing.[14] Thus, to return to Heidegger, the existentialization of the categories and the categorization of the *existentiales* is the twofold feat of the virtual animated inanimation of the thing.

The thing that sutures the two moments of life and death facilitates the exemplary event, which Derrida explores in his meditation on Blanchot titled *Demeure*. This event is 'an encounter between what is going to arrive and what has already arrived,' the 'encounter of death as anticipation with death itself' (DE 64). In the chasm between the author himself, the voice of the narrator, and the character of the short story who outlives the instant of his death, the Thing 'Blanchot' is not just double but triple. The impossible testimony that ensues from the event of the triple split revolves around something that virtually happened, something that was on the verge of happening, something that happened without happening, in the 'deferred immanence' of my death.[15] In the syntagma 'deferred immanence,' we ought to hear the overtones of the eventful and eventalizing path Derrida charts between idealism and realism,[16] between the mark of the thing and the

infinite deferral of its empirical inscription. It implies that the immanence of death is always accompanied by the indispensable but non-
immanent supplement, equally rid of all transcendental connotations,
'the added delay preceding the "thing" that is pending because it cannot be long in coming [*le délai supplémentaire avant la 'chose' qui est en instance parce qu'elle ne saurait tarder à venir*], to the point of being *on the
point of* arrival' (DE 46/56).[17]

Any thing that will have arrived despite its failure to arrive will have
happened in the virtual time-place,[18] which has nothing to do with the
glitter of virtual reality. The virtuality of the thing's place pre-dates the
distinction between the 'who' and the 'what' – which is why it gives
place without taking any. The name of this receptive spacing is the pa-
laeonym *khōra*, which migrates to Derrida's work from Plato's *Timaeus*.[19]
In this place nothing happens (actually) and everything happens (virtually), because it is the very condition of possibility for the event.[20]

A text that has arisen from the lecture Derrida gave at the Cerisy-la-
Salle Colloquium in 1975, *Signsponge* questions the opposition between
the 'who' and the 'what,' with reference to the thing, the name of the
thing, the name of the name, and the name of the person, Francis Ponge.
The crucial outcome of this exercise, which takes shape in the proposition 'Francis Ponge will be my thing today,' is that 'you will not be able
to decide whether the thing or the person I am speaking of is *one*, or
what it is or who it is [*Vous ne pouvez pas decider si la chose ou la personne
dont je parle en est* une, *ce qu'elle est ou qui elle est*]' (SI 10/11). The thing,
therefore, inhabits and haunts the undecidable place named *khōra*,
where the differentiation into 'who' and 'what' has not yet taken place,
or where it has taken place too rapidly, shuttling between the one and
the other in the blink of an eye and without respite. This place without
place of the thing, the person, *or* both – one *or* two – is the locus of the
event, whose eventhood is predicated on the interchangeability or the
undecidability of the disjunctive 'or'; Derrida refuses to determine 'the
arrival or coming of "*what* comes" and of "*who* comes" [*l'arrivée ou la
venue de* 'ce *qui vient*' *et de* 'qui *vient*']' (R *xii*/11) either in terms of the
content, or in terms of the form proper to such a receptive opening.

An exceptionally strong temptation to render determinate the virtuality of the thing's place is motivated by the conclusion that it may, on
occasion, precipitate the rise of the symbolic order. In no circum-
stances, however, will it completely merge with this order, as it does in
Lacanian and post-Lacanian psychoanalysis. Only an approach enam-
oured of the primacy of recognition will attempt to reduce the virtual

to the symbolic, because 'it [recognition] gives back, in the place, let us say, of the thing itself, a symbolic equivalent [*parce qu'elle rend, à la place, disons, de la chose même, un équivalent symbolique*]' (GT 13). Derrida discerns that recognition does not recognize the thing itself, but already something – the generalized fetish – that flourishes in its place, something that takes the place it has occupied, or the one it has ensconced within itself. To be sure, this is a problem only from the perspective of recognition, because the identity of the thing is nothing but a fictive cover for the endless proliferation of generalized fetishes. What flourishes in the virtual place of the thing is the symbolic equivalent that partakes of the infinite deferral of the thing itself, in its place: this is the logic of general fetishism. But the violence enacted by recognition (for which the 'real,' thingly overabundance of the virtual will always remain empty, bare, and formal) is that it simultaneously benefits from and annuls the thing and the gift, the given thing and the thing *as* the giving withdrawal of *khōra*.

What does one mean when one says that the thing's time, too, is virtual? The thing is always dated, interlaced with time in a modified version of ecstatic temporality, but the date refers itself to a particular thing: the ring, the band, or the annulus that inaugurates *Shibboleth*. The structure of datability, which, in Heidegger's text, gives evidence for the pre-interpretation of the meaning of temporality,[21] remarks the anniversary of the event with a return, a turn of the band that signals both the necessity and the impossibility of repeating the unique and the unrepeatable. Signing with a date is tantamount to a 'repetition without idealization' – these three words could furnish a definition of the virtual in a nutshell – that does not produce an ideal object, but resists, among other things, 'every objectivation' (SQ 5).[22] The date is, accordingly, a temporalizing, proliferating *khōra* for the events it receives. It is a receptacle, which frees itself from idealized objectivity and eschews enchainment to the autistically idiomatic body of the thing: 'This mark that one calls a date must nonetheless be *marked off* [démarqué], in a singular fashion, detached from the very thing that it dates, and must, in this very de-marcation, in this very deportation, become readable' (SQ 15/31). The date should be able to accommodate any events other than this singular anniversary, but in order to do so it must unbind itself from the same thing to which it bound itself through a unique instance of reception; it should come detached from (and hence partake of) the thing as the very figure of detachment that breathes on its own. Then, and only then, will it become, at once,

readable *and* unreadable, that is, iterable and repeatable outside all idealization, more independent of and more reliant on the freedom of the
thing itself.

1.1.2. Double affirmative, double perhaps

There are two telling examples of the non-idealized, non-idealizing repetition in (Derrida's own) language bearing a curious relationship to the
thing. In both cases, the same short word repeats itself after a small but
indispensable punctuation break, a comma. In *Politics of Friendship*, the
word 'perhaps' demands to be thought together with that which is possible qua possibly impossible and, therefore, together with the coming
of the event. 'Perhaps' welcomes the event.[23] Nonetheless,

> one can talk endlessly about ... possibility without ever coming close to
> the thing itself in its coming [*De celle-ci on peut parler à l'infini sans jamais
> effleurer la chose même en sa venue*]. It may be [*Il se peut*], then, that the order
> is other [than that of 'good sense,' following the itinerary from the possi-
> ble to the real – M.M.] – *it may well be* [cela se peut] – and that only the
> coming of the event allows, after the event, *perhaps* [peut-être], what it
> will previously have made possible to be thought. (PF 18/35)

The repetitive multiplication of the 'perhapses' – *on peut, il se peut, cela se
peut, peut-être* – touches precisely on the thing and its coming, its advent
and event. In Bennington's interpretation, which departs from Gasché's
investigations, 'perhaps' is a 'transcendental motif' that makes the
event possible.[24] And yet the element that Gasché brings out and that
Bennington puts aside is the 'quasi-' of the 'quasi-transcendental,' the
qua si or the 'as if' of indeterminate transcendentality, as Derrida would
say. Why 'as if,' and where does the thing enter?

In the passage before us, Derrida conjectures that perhaps one cannot insist on the 'perhaps' as the *necessary condition of possibility* for the
coming of the event. Perhaps, he would add, despite what 'good sense'
dictates, the priority of 'perhaps' does not unavoidably give way to a
transition from the possible to the real, from indeterminate potentiality
to the actuality of things. And, vice versa, it might be possible to rethink the possible based on the real, to come 'close to the thing in its
coming' after the event, after the advent of the virtual thing that es-
caped recognition in its first apparition. As if the event has not occurred, the future remains open and still 'possible to be thought,' but

this futural possibility itself relies on the coming to pass of the event, on the pastness of the event that will have been 'futurally' possible without being present. (Let us, then, venture a hypothesis that the difference between the virtual and the ideal is folded into or reflected in the difference between 'as if' and 'as such.' Repetition is at work across the lines separating the two conditions, but while the first comes to terms with the non-identity and non-presence of that which is repeated, the second persists in unsuccessfully aiming at the self-identity and self-presence of an ideal object.)[25] The thing (*res*) neither realizes a past potentiality nor remains presently indeterminate. Rather, it is as if the thing has already occurred and is, virtually, yet to come; its forever-suspended quasi-transcendental 'causality' is neither a priori nor a posteriori, since it operates perhaps before *and* perhaps after the event.[26] Immemorial past, the future to come: perhaps, perhaps.

Derrida writes 'Perhaps, perhaps [*Peut-être, peut-être*]' as a freestanding sentence in his 1995 Eulogy for Deleuze, whom he represents as a thinker of 'serial singularity' (WM 193–4/238). Behind the scenes, he repeats Deleuze by reiterating the word 'perhaps' in 'serial singularity,' which means that it happens serially, twice, but also singularly, as the first and as the second, as heterogeneously auto-supplementary, as the other in the same. The second comes first, and the first – second: this logic of the supplement, which precludes 'the adequation between the concept, the name, and the event' and which occurs 'once and only once, therefore for the first and last time (perhaps, perhaps)' (PF 66), has been in place since the earliest of Derrida's writings (*Speech and Phenomena, Of Grammatology*). But what if a term supplements itself, and what if, moreover, it is 'perhaps' that strikes twice? Who can come up with 'the right order' in dealing with its insistent yet indeterminate iteration? Perhaps the simultaneous precedence and antecedence of the 'perhaps' is a key to this order, while everything that is not merely virtual but effective and effectual is a detour from its first to its second instantiation – the detour that is as minuscule as a comma in the planetary order of things.

However minuscule, a comma is a mark of *punctuation*, ergo of interruption. Between the two 'perhapses,' it micrologically condenses within itself everything that unfolds outside presence, in the uncertain delay at the heart of repetition. Where the second instance of the 'perhaps' seems to reinforce the first, it in fact disrupts it, by beckoning the stoppage and recommencement of breath and remarking this punctuation mark in diction: 'If no decision (ethical, juridical, political) is possible without interrupting determination by engaging oneself in the *perhaps*,... the same decision must interrupt the very thing that is its condition of possibility: the *perhaps* itself' (PF 67). Repetition counter-signs and thereby reifies, transforms 'perhaps' into a thing[27] – 'this very thing' – which cannot be a condition of possibility outside the quasi-transcendental dimension because of the mutual interruption Derrida recounts. At the same time that the 'perhaps' makes a decision possible by interrupting its determinacy, the decision itself interrupts the indeterminacy of the thing that makes it possible (the *'perhaps* itself'). The 'perhaps' disrupts its own order so as to disallow its ossification into the certainty of transcendental causation. It makes the event possible only by virtue of something other than possibility: 'One would have to know of what this supposed cause, the thing, the "real" itself [*cette cause supposée, la chose, le 'réel' même*] will have been *capable*' (PF 82/100).

If the event is possible only when there are no more assurances that it might be possible, then the quasi-transcendental 'as if' that resonates in the 'perhaps' is no longer a condition of possibility for the event (à la Kant), but rather a part of what Derrida calls the 'unconditional impossible [*l'inconditionnel impossible*].'[28] Allowing the risk that inhabits the logic of repeating 'perhaps' to permeate one's speech, one could say that the condition of possibility itself becomes unconditional and impossible in its attachment to the event of the thing, to the thing's freeing up, absolution, or disengagement from the world in which it may be found, as well as from its 'causal' function. Evidently, the thinghood of the thing that as something 'un-conditioned [*un-bedingtes*] ... conditions the thing as thing' in Heidegger[29] may explain the unconditionality of the gift, forgiveness, and hospitality in Derrida, who glosses over the issue in *Given Time*: 'That is why the condition common to the gift and the event is a certain unconditionality (*Unbedingheit*: let us leave this German word suspended here; it says something about the thing [*Ding*] and the non-thing ... [*il dit quelque chose de la chose (Ding) et de la non-chose*])'(GT 123/156–7).

Now, the event of this quasi-transcendental unconditionality that conditions all empirical occurrences in the world in the form of the double 'perhaps' describes 'a "thing," an autonomous "cause," unconditionally free in its institution, in its speech, in its writing, in its thought [*une 'chose', une 'cause' autonome, inconditionnellement libre dans son institution, dans sa parole, dans son écriture, dans sa pensée*]' (USC 33). The hint for the freeing up of the thing from itself[30] is in the quotation marks that cut it loose from itself and suspend its causal function. Neither the mechanical necessity of inner causality nor the theological notion of the uncaused cause defines the thing's unconditional liberty. Instead, the repetition of 'perhaps' is the place where the thing breathes autonomously, on its own power, with the uncertainty that surrounds everything that is living.

I am still circling around the comma in 'perhaps, perhaps,' where a new beginning hatches from the broken flow, and where a spacing for the event imbues the repetitive auto-affection of the same word with the disordering of hetero-affection.[31] This comma, taken as a station or a transitory stop that prescribes to the reader the act of drawing a breath in the course of the locutionary reproduction of a written text, syntactically mimes the performativity of the 'perhaps,' where one holds one's breath in expectation, in a spatio-temporal suspension that cannot rest assured that something else, even another 'perhaps,' would come in the footsteps of its in-de-terminable delay. Derrida utters these words with a sigh, with the expiration that could always be one's last, such as in the beginning of the second chapter of *Politics of Friendship*: 'Someone sighs; a wise man has uttered his last breath, perhaps. Perhaps. Perhaps he is talking to his sons ... [*Quelqu'un soupier, un sage expire peut-être. Peut-être. Peut-être parle-t-il à ses fils ...*]' (PF 26/44). '*... peut-être. Peut-être. Peut-être ...*' – although two tentative periods supplant the comma, what else could this be if not the very rhythmicality of living in the midst of that uncertainty that even the strongest *conatus essendi* will not quell? More pertinently to the event I am considering here, the thing's own autonomous breathing pulsates in this virtual repetition of the 'perhaps.'

This repetition doesn't *merely* repeat the same word twice, but also allusively resonates with the repetition of affirmation ('yes, yes'; '*oui, oui*'), which dwells, among other places, in *Parages* and in 'Ulysses Gramophone.' On the one hand, Derrida contends that without a certain, if inaudible, yes-saying there is no signature,[32] but on the other hand, this initial acceptance or, to use Kant's word, receptivity extended to that which or the one whom I cannot really accept or contain eventually constitutes experience itself: 'The event is another name for that which, *in the thing that happens*, we can neither reduce nor deny (or simply deny). It is another name for experience itself, which is always experience of the other' (ET 11).[33]

Note, in the first place, that the event transpires 'in the thing that happens.' More will need to be said on the subject of this eventalizing interiority of the thing. Second, what transpires in the thing is not negative (neither reducible nor deniable). That is to say, it is something given that one cannot decline but can only affirm with a yes-saying strong enough to withstand the assaults of the phenomenological machinery of reduction and the dialectical mechanisms of negation. What happens when the thing happens – not alongside it, but right within it – is experience as the experience of the other. One would be unable to say 'no' to this event of the thing, which immemorially receives the other and alters (both transforms and 'others') itself in spectrality and virtuality. Even the kind of self-forgetting, or an unconscious lapse that functions as a minimal and minimalist precondition for such reception, will not be negative, will not be a 'non-experience,' because in the event of the gift 'some thing must happen or arrive [*il faut que quelque chose arrive*] in an instant, in an instant that no doubt does not belong to the economy of time'.[34] One of the crucial consequences of this insight is that the key to the thing's absolution from us is time, since the thing removed from 'the economy of time' is not itself atemporal, but arrives 'in an instant' that temporalizes, that is, in an instant both tied to and untied from temporality. Thus, the immediate reaffirmation of the affirmative – *oui, oui* – mirrors simultaneously the ligature and the detachment of the thing from time.[35]

In addition to this redoubling, many of the protocols that have been already established in the discussion of the double 'perhaps' are applicable to the double affirmative, but the uniqueness of this repetition is that it opposes the Nietzschean eternal return to Hegel's negation of the negation. The repetition, whose goal it is to '*affirm, finally, without a possible return ... the eternal return of the other* [affirmer enfin sans retour possible ... le retour éternel de l'autre]' prepares for '*the chance (or failure) of the event* [la chance (échec ou échéance) de l'événement]' split between the 'who' and the 'what' of arrival: '*Some thing (other) who/ which would arrive (to himself) finally* [quelque chose (autre) qui (lui) arriverait enfin]' (PA 65). To affirm unconditionally is to say 'yes' to the thing that or to the one who arrives, as well as to the chance and the eventful failure of the event. The affirmative is, therefore, completely enveloped in the possibility of the 'perhaps,' which does not offer any guarantees for the event's coming about.

If the first 'yes' is a signature, then the second stands for the signature of the signature – its intended confirmation, self-relation, and authentication – which accomplishes the exact opposite of what it intends, namely, counter-signs, repeats the unrepeatable, transforms the signature into the response of the thing dated as the 'modern multiplicity of *signatura rerum'* (SI 50).[36] While the first 'yes' opens unto the experience of alterity in the thing itself, the second risks the formalization of this gift, testifying to the impossibility of receiving it without the originary repetition, without difference and hetero-affection, without the spectral fissuring of the thing itself and of the thing's 'self.'

The performativity of the 'yes,' like that of the perhaps, is responsible for a certain stoppage or suspension: this time, the suspension of clarity in the telephonic reception and emission of messages presumed in the double affirmative. The event of this suspension undermines the claims of recognition and supplies the conditions of possibility for any event, but it is inconceivable without a particular relation to the thing: 'Such a word ["yes"] says but says nothing in itself, if by saying we mean designating, showing, describing some thing to be found outside of language, outside marking' (AL 297). To be sure, in the logic of the speech-act to which Derrida refers here, yes-saying is not a constative utterance, corresponding to and describing the way things are, yet that does not mean that it is absolutely detached from the thing. The thing will not be found either 'outside of language, outside marking,' or wholly inside the empirical use of language, provided that it is the 'first' archi-written, self-remarked mark, the impossible condition of possibility, which drives and drives to the point of despair all the other 'firsts' that intend to cite, recite, or remark it.

Methodologically, this indeterminate position gives rise to what 'Ulysses Gramophone' terms, with and against Kant and Heidegger, the 'quasi-analytics of the "yes."' First, Derrida implies that this monosyllable is and is not a part of the "transcendental analytic' because, although it transcendentally gives experience (and, perhaps, the ethical grounding for thought), it is not a condition of possibility for concepts accessible to pure understanding. Second, the 'quasi-analytics of the "yes"' cannot fall decisively within the purview either of the categorial analytic of the world or of the existential analytic of Dasein, because it is a mark that does not belong to an object and is not appropriable by a subject (PSY 648).[37] It is, nevertheless, a mark of the thing affirmed in every signature and in every subjective experience only belatedly, *after* one says 'yes' to the initial (mute) 'yes' of the thing that is no longer present 'in person.'

1.2. In-to the things themselves!

In introducing this chapter, I wrote that 'the thing makes and lets the event happen virtually, immanently, poetically.' Here, I wish to focus on the second of the three adverbs: the 'immanently' occurring event that arrives in the thing itself. This focus requires a modification of the phenomenological slogan To the Things Themselves!, such that the 'interiority' of the thing would come to the theoretical foreground. After outlining the *différantial* qualities of the thingly interiority, I will discuss how it shelters the event of expropriation in a reconfiguration of the Heideggerian *Ereignis*.

1.2.1. 'What' 'is' 'inside' 'the' 'thing'?

The event occurs 'inside' the thing itself, but how to approach the question of interiority at the level of effective virtuality, in the 'place without place' of the *khōra*, where 'the distinction between phantasm and the so-called actual or external reality does not yet take place and has no place to be' (HC 108)? The quasi-noumenal interiority of the thing is indistinguishable from its exteriority, from its adumbrated (i.e., forever incomplete) phenomenal appearance and fleeting apparition, which gives one a sense of 'the so-called actual or external reality' without being identifiable and without appearing as such. Nor is the posing of the ontological question 'what is …,' *ti esti*, completely justified in this context, since 'what' the thing harbours precedes the distinction between 'who' and 'what.' As regards its spatiality, if the thing 'does not yet take place and has no place to be,' it is u-topic in a very precise sense of *utopia*, signifying the non-place of the *khōra* that might (perhaps) give birth to the category of space within the thing itself. Finally, with reference to temporality, the 'not yet' that pertains to the pending division between interiority and phenomenally external reality is a forerunner of the possible engenderment of time in the same placeless site, and thus points toward something like the thingly *différance*.

  Couched in terms of a receptacle, the thing 'is' a fold effectuated and inhabited by *différance* – the differing, differed, deferring, and deferred spatialization of time and temporalization of space – which lets it abide in its non-identity and otherness to itself.[38] As Derrida himself puts it, '*Différance*, which (is) nothing, is (in) the thing itself. It is (given) in the thing itself. It (is) in the thing itself. It, *différance*, the thing (itself) [*La différance, qui n'(est) rien, est (dans) la chose même. Elle est (donnée) dans la chose même. Elle (est) la chose même. Elle, la différance, la chose (même)*]' (GT 40/59). To translate: the emptying of *différance*, 'which (is) nothing,' virtually fills the thing to the point of merging with it above and beyond the copula, but the identity of the thing and *différance* – 'It, *différance*, the thing (itself)' – is a non-identity, the 'congenital' splitting of the thing that is never, strictly speaking, itself. The successive bracketing of the copula (is), the preposition (in), and the evidence (given) that culminates in the parenthesizing of identity (itself) draws inspiration from phenomenological reduction whose goal it is to extract from the thing itself its very essence, which, for Derrida, is nothing but non-essence, the nothing.[39] In this sense, the thing denotes a pre-ontological figure of the expropriation of essence and prepares the event of such expropriation in everything it receives, welcomes, suffers, undergoes, experiences.[40] Thus, *différance* affects and infects both the seemingly vacuous concept of the thing, which retains non-identity and the impossibility of arriving at the 'thing itself,' and concrete things that present themselves in the manner of adumbration (or what Nietzsche terms 'perspectivalism') without becoming fully given or present.

Différance is a mark of the mark or of the sign, and the problem of *différance* is, first and foremost, a problem of signification. According to the conventional model of signification outlined in *Margins of Philosophy*, the 'sign is usually said to be put in the place of the thing itself, the present thing, "thing" here standing equally for meaning or referent [*Le signe, dit-on couramment, se met à la place de la chose même, de la chose présente, 'chose' valant ici aussi bien pour le sens que pour le référent*]. The sign represents the present in its absence. It takes the place of the present' (MP 9/9). But when the thing no longer secures the production of meaning, when *différance*, which (is) nothing in actuality, internally afflicts it, when it gives place without occupying any, then the old model of signification becomes outdated and the thing supplants itself as other, signifies and remarks itself, disseminating the functions of 'meaning or referent.' As long as the sequence of its self-remarking is ongoing, the thing will not coincide with itself, will not arrive at its proper, self-identical limit.[41] The thing impregnated with *différance* will contain, without delimiting it, the principle of signification. The bracketing of givenness, which instantaneously gives and withdraws the given, will allow itself to be internally supplanted, welcoming and non-synchronously coexisting with that which supplants it: '*What broaches the movement of signification is what makes its interruption impossible. The thing itself is a sign* [La chose même est un signe]' (OG 49/72). The thing in itself is ecstatic, outside itself in itself, other (even) to itself.

Whereas the thing remarks and retraces itself, it remains, for us, a '*sujet intraitable*' (JDP 13/1), an untreatable, untraceable subject, or, colloquially, someone or something one finds impossible to deal with.

Augmenting the deconstruction of the existential/categorial dualism, Derrida argues in a text as early as 'Violence and Metaphysics' that what 'the things share here with others, is that something within them too is always hidden, and is indicated only by anticipation, analogy, and appresentation [*que les choses partagent ici avec autrui, c'est que quelque chose en elles se cache aussi toujours et ne s'indique que par anticipation, analogie et apprésentation*]' (WD 124/182). Because both things and human others partake of this inaccessible, secret interiority[42] infinitely deferred in time and space, Derrida levels a criticism against Levinasian 'transcendental violence,' which, despite Levinas's own philosophical commitments, circumscribes the field of alterity to the otherness of another person.[43] The alterity of the thing that remarks itself prior to the intervention of any 'external' system of signification implies that the latter can indicate things only obliquely if it is to respect its own quasi-transcendental condition of possibility, namely, that which is hidden and withdrawn in the thing itself (*différance*). As a result, the Kantian word 'respect,' the deference before the humanity of the other person, a word that frequently crops up in Derrida's writings on Levinas, will describe, among other things, one's practical, relational attitude to the alterity of the thing. The thing in itself is not a noumenal 'dead-end,' but an end in itself.[44]

That is not to say that, mutatis mutandis, the other is reducible to a thing, let alone to a transcendental Thing. The other is both a thing and not a thing: 'The other as *res* is simultaneously less other (not absolutely other) and less "the same" than I [*l'autre comme* res *est à la fois moins autre (non absolument autre) et moins 'le même' que moi*]' (WD 127/187). From a strictly phenomenological perspective, the quality common to others and to things is that, unlike objects, they do not – indeed, cannot – expose themselves to me in their entirety. The volume of the thing eclipses a considerable portion of its surface from my view and necessitates a completion of the given 'by anticipation, analogy, and appresentation' of the yet invisible outlines. To continue in the same argumentative vein, the interiority of the other is inaccessible to me from the unique standpoint available to this interiority alone, regardless of the exposure of his denuded face. It will be objected that, whereas I can turn the thing around or change my spatial position in relation to it in order to inspect some, though not all, of its temporarily hidden dimensions, the other's interiority defies all provisional visibility. But, having registered this objection, one would be unable either to exclude the thing from or to include it in the field of alterity without fatefully altering and contravening this field. Less other than another person, the alterity of the thing might provide the materials for the operations and manipulations of consciousness. More other, or, in Derrida's words, 'less "the same,"' it is not another 'I,' but something foreign to *the formal structure of consciousness* that, in each case, is filled with an infinite variety of heterogeneous contents, however inaccessible they are from the standpoint of a single subject. Both less other and less 'the same,' the thing is the indwelling of *différance*.

Decades later, the 'a' of *différance* will silently resurface in connection with the thing and its other who/that inhabits it. In *Specters of Marx*, Derrida writes: 'Nominalism, conceptualism, realism: all of this is routed by the Thing or the Athing called ghost [*Nominalisme, conceptualisme, réalisme, tout cela est mis en déroute par la Chose ou l'Achose nommée fantôme*]. The taxonomic order becomes too easy, at once arbitrary and impossible' (SM 138/220).[45] The 'Thing or the Athing' impregnates with difference and non-identity the three mutually exclusive '-isms' that respond to the problem of universality. But how does it guide or direct them, if they branch off in contrary directions (e.g., nominalism could be justifiably called the 'opposite' of realism)? The secret is that by properly routeing these currents of thought, the thing – in its interchangeability with the athing – re-routes, diverts, and disconcerts them, makes them flee. And indeed, the most noteworthy feature of this passage is that the thing is interchangeable with its other, with the athing that fetishistically substitutes for it thanks to the disjunctive conjunction 'or' reminiscent of the 'or' that has stood between the thing and the person on the indeterminate fork of the event of Francis Ponge. The ingenuity of this substitution is that it is, literally, imperceptible to the ear, since, in French, *la Chose* sounds exactly like *l'Achose* the moment the '*a*' of the definite article migrates into the privative '*a*' of the noun. Hence, with the phonic self-annulment of the article, the conceptual unity of *the* thing dissipates. 'The' thing is not the thing itself; it, itself, is a non-thing.

We might ask what it would take to follow Derrida's indeterminate thing / athing emancipated from the order of knowledge there, where another indeterminacy comes to inscribe itself into the verb 'to follow' (*suivre*), rendering it indistinguishable from the verb 'to be' in the first person singular. How do we (how do I) come to accommodate *différance*, following or indeed becoming the double movement of thingification and a-thingification? In the *La Chose* seminar, Derrida playfully undermines the traditional humanist-idealist contention, '*je ne suis pas une chose*' (JDP 13/1). This statement may be translated as 'I am not a thing,' but also as 'I do not follow a thing,' or 'I cannot keep up with the thing.' I am unable to keep up with it because it constantly escapes from me by becoming other to my intentional grasp, but also because it includes me in its virtual interiority, which accommodates the 'who' and the 'what,' the animate and the inanimate. In line with the logic of de-distancing, the thing stands for the absolute nearness and proximity that remain the farthest – which means that the closer I come to it, the more briskly it flees from me. And, vice versa, the one who attempts to absolve or separate oneself from it, uttering, for instance, 'I am *not* a thing,' is immediately incorporated into the thing, which is interchangeable with its other.

In the aural and conceptual registers, where *la Chose* is *la Chose* and *la Chose* is *l'Achose*, the opposition between the thing and its other assumes the veneer of a tautology.[46] It does not subsist as an opposition, for if it did, it would have immediately transformed the thing into another object standing against and available to consciousness.[47] At the same time and all the more imperceptibly, the thing, indistinguishable from its opposite, loses itself, disseminates the 'principle' of its thinghood (e.g., causality) in objectivity and subjectivity alike. The non-identity of the Thing 'itself' exposes itself only graphically, but the price paid for this exposure is a ghostly incarnation of the name in the nameless (the routeing of nominalism) and, again, of the thing in the subject-object dyad. Cited directly, without detours, head on, the indeterminate spatiality of thinghood passes into the most rigid and determinate opposition of objectivity.[48]

The singular event of the thing that virtually happens in these pages citing or naming the thing by the word 'phantom' holds together but avoids synthesizing homophony and heterography, phonic sameness and graphic difference. Consequently, this event places its bets on – to paraphrase Hegel's enunciation of the identity between identity and non-identity – the difference between difference and non-difference, on the same and the other said or uttered in the same breath, pronounced as the same and inscribed as the other. Circumventing and routeing the *principium contradictionis* that subtends conceptualism, nominalism, and realism, the thing continuously turns inside out and outside in to the extent that it internally accommodates its other (or even substitutes the athing for itself), and to the extent that it exteriorizes this internal unrest, producing virtual, phantomatic effects in the noematic reality of thought (the three '-isms') and in the real actuality of the world. That the taxonomic order, which, at the most basic level, is charged with the task of distinguishing between things and non-things, becomes 'at once arbitrary and impossible' may be explained by the dual effects of such an unrest demanding, simultaneously, the graphic acknowledgment of the thing as the other of the thing and the phonic acceptance of its tautologous identity.

The annulment of opposition between the thing and its other (the athing) that perpetually supplants it does not amount to the disappearance of difference, but to its proliferation within the inopposable thing itself. Derrida lays out this logic opposing opposition in *Politics of Friendship* apropos of the Schmittian enemy-friend dyad: 'What is true of the enemy (I can or I must kill you, and vice versa) is the very thing that suspends, annuls, overturns ... friendship, which is therefore, at once, the same (repressed) thing and *an altogether different thing* [*l'amitié qui est donc à la fois la même chose (refoulée) et tout autre chose*]' (PF 122/ 144).[49] In other words, enmity is born in the *différance* – delay, deferral, resistance – of friendship, which is a thing at the same time (*à la fois*) the same as and completely different from enmity. The enemy-friend dyad is more than an example because it stands for any and every thing, which is always the same as and completely other than its other, thanks to *différance* immanently operative in it. Such *différantial* non-oppositionality charges the thing with the task of providing the very opening for hospitality that receives the same as much as (and as) the other. The dehiscence of welcoming is thus a thing irreducible to 'an object of knowledge': 'If we do not know what hospitality is, it is because this thing which is not something is not an object of knowledge.'[50]

1.2.2. The event of expropriation, or how the thing 'spirits away'

In the light of the non-coincidence with itself of the thing wherein *différance* dwells, the syntagma '*Ereignis* in abyss,' which has furnished the subtitle to this chapter, ought to be read not, so much, in terms of the placement of the event in an abstract bottomless 'place without place,' but in terms of its concrete consummation in the thing itself. It is, Derrida would ask us to imagine, as if the abyss opens in the thing that eventfully appropriates everything in the spacing that constitutes it as other, the spacing to which its 'interiority' testifies. The fictional reality of the 'as if' renders the thing virtually indeterminate when it yields the 'effect of language (*fabula*), but such that only by means of it can the thing as other and as other thing come to pass with the allure of an inappropriable event (*Ereignis* in abyss) [*effet de langue* (fabula) *telle que par elle seule la chose en tant qu'autre et en tant qu'autre chose peut advenir dans l'allure d'un événement inappropriable* (Ereignis *en abîme*)]' (SI 102/103).[51]

Let us unpack this dense conditional statement. First, if the event of the thing is inappropriable, that is due to the fact that the thing itself is the immemorial (non-principle) of appropriation virtually operative before and after any activity on the part of intentional subjectivity. The reality of *res* is the enabling limit of human possessiveness. Unlike its counterpart in traditional realism, though, Derrida's thing and the event it announces come to pass thanks to and 'only by means of' the 'effect of language,' when the 'as if' of fabulous and fabulating (i.e., ineluctably literary and textual, not purely conceptual) signification affords us a glimpse into and an approximation of the self-remarking itinerary of the thing. But the thing remarks itself as other and as the 'other thing,' that is, without gathering itself up in the present. In coming to pass it bypasses the present, disperses and disseminates itself, and rejects the claims of self-identity that 'brings home' and assimilates the other to the same.

Derrida links such bypassing of the present to the historical development of 'tele-technology,' which speeds up or even makes phenomenologically accessible a 'practical *deconstruction* of the traditional and dominant concepts.' Elaborating on this term, he writes,

> I say 'deconstruction' because, ultimately, what I name and try to think under this word is, at bottom, nothing other than this very process [of the tele-technological], its 'taking-place' in such a way that its happening affects the very experience of place, and the recording ... of this 'thing', the trace that traces (inscribes, preserves, carries, refers, or defers) the *différance* of this event which happens to place [*qui arrive au lieu*]. (ET 36)

Before the experience of place, there is a tracing, inscribing, preserving, carrying, and so forth, recording 'this "thing"' that affects the taking-place of the place and, by implication, anything that might happen *to* it and *in* it. In other words, what pre-exists experience, not in actuality but in virtuality, entails 1) the *tele-* of distancing (diametrically opposed to the 'proper' in the sense of 'proximity') and, therefore, detachment, separation, but also a possibility of relationality across the divide, 2) technique or originary artificiality (*techne*)[52] and, therefore, nothing 'natural,' and 3) the function of tracing, which is compatible with 'the effect of language,' and which recovers the grammatological notion of archi-writing.[53] These three criteria – relational distancing, originary artificiality, and archi-writing – outline the trajectories whereby the inappropriable event of the thing bypasses the present and escapes manipulation on our part.

Second, given that *Ereignis* is Heidegger's word, his writings on the 'event of appropriation' must inform any reading of Derrida. For instance, *Contributions to Philosophy* enframes the epochal withdrawal and donation of being within the context of such an event: 'Be-ing as enowning (*Ereignis*) is hesitant refusal as (non-granting). Ripeness is *fruit* and *gifting* ... Be-ing holds sway in *truth* and is clearing for self-sheltering.'[54] Derrida's event analogously activates the 'hesitant refusal as (non-granting)' *and* the "gifting" of meaning when it shelters and encrypts *différance* in the thing itself and, at the same time, clears the space or the spacing for 'natural languages' that attempt, failingly but eventfully, to retrace the self-remarking, self-expressive routine of the thing.[55] The inappropriability of the thing, which virtually appropriates everything, de-subjectivizes *Ereignis* and constitutes its negative moment, which is more Heideggerian than Heidegger's own critique of Husserl's residual psychologism would warrant.[56]

Conversely, 'gifting' appropriation is the positive dimension of the event, in which 'the thing itself always escapes [*la chose même se dérobe toujours*]' (SP 104/117),[57] leaving in its wake, behind itself (and hence around us) a trail of what might constitute our environing 'world.' This fugal movement, the flight of the thing itself, is its flight *from itself* (*la chose* flees from *le même*; it subtracts itself from its sameness, self-coincidence, or identity with itself)[58] and, equally, an instant of the thing's self-appropriation and self-realization. The thing becomes other and renders itself inaccessible when it strips itself of its self-identity *and*, more interestingly still, when it is most 'itself' in the internal unfolding of its otherness and *différance*. In both cases, the thing's giving withdrawal spirits away a solid foundation, a fundamental basis, from the edifice that metaphysics predicates on it and on the distinction between the same and the other. 'Cette chose *même* étant la chose *autre* en tant qu'elle se dérobe ... son silence nous commande [*This thing itself being the thing other as far as it escapes ... its silence commands us*]' (DP 66):[59] in other words, even though our approach to this non-ontological entity is always belated, even though it escapes from us as the other, what we inevitably stumble upon is not pure absence but the *after-event*, the *après-coup* of the thing's being-there expressed in the pregnant silence that resonates for us as a 'command.'

Third, the escape of the thing is a direct consequence of the event's placement *in abyss*, but it would be necessary to understand what Derrida means by this syntagma in order to flesh out the sense of thingly appropriation. A preliminary analysis will reveal that the placement of *Ereignis* in abyss does not annul the effects of the appropriative event, but merely turns them against themselves in the spirit of what will later be called 'auto-immunization.' The prime example for this development is the self-referential performativity of Ponge's *Fable*, whose first line proclaims, 'With the word *with* begins, therefore, this text [*Par le mot* par *commence donc ce text*]' (qtd in PSY 19). What Ponge places in the abyss of a singular repetition is, certainly, nothing other than the small, monosyllabic word *par* – 'by,' or 'with.' To repeat, he deposits in abyss this tiny word, not a thing. In 'Psyche: Invention of the Other,' as well as in *Signsponge*, Derrida reads this utterance as a speech-act that, in Austin's felicitous terms, knows 'how to do *things* with words.' Indeed, Ponge's performative seems to have eliminated the thing qua a referent supplanted by the word '*par*,' which is something other than the thing, if not the other *of* the thing. But, since the thing itself 'is' its (own) other and the other thing, its withdrawal modulates the eventhood of *Ereignis* and projects outward, into the realm of self-referential signification, the spacing of *différance* encrypted in it.[60] Hetero-affection ensconced in auto-affection, the thing is concealed in the 'fabulous' repetition, folding, or complication (PSY 58) of a single word – whether it is 'yes,' or 'perhaps,' or any other – that infinitely reflects itself. This ostensible tautology is the primal scene of signification, which detaches itself from the alterity (and, by implication, from the detachment) of the thing, all the while straining to retrace its 'proper' non-identity.

The two elements of the abyss – singular repetition and tautological dissemination of sameness – grafted onto the event give it the structure of calendarizable datability and virtuality. *Ereignis* in abyss is a unique event 'always already' handed over to iterability; mourned in the unique loss of its uniqueness, it retains the possibility of a surprising return. But in what sense does Derrida insert the thing into these abyssal dynamics? And how does this affect the thing's dispossession?

It is imperative, once again, to begin with the de- or ex-propriation of the word, the signifier, the *representamen* whose property 'is not to be *proper* [*propre*], that is to say absolutely *proximate* to itself (*prope, proprius*). The *represented* is always already a *representamen*' (OG 50). This 'properly improper' property of the signifier, which, at a distance from itself, stands for the other, is the key function of the signifying relation.

But assuming that this self-distancing connotes *différance*, which (is) (in) the thing itself, the non-proximity of the *representamen* to itself is a borrowed property projected out of the depths of the thing. The act of making meaning, which, as Derrida comments in the next sentence, is 'nothing but signs,' does not shed eidetic light onto the thing, but transports, contrabands, shuttles, carries over, and, thus, translates and metaphorizes bits of non-identity that emerge out of its spacing before they recede back into the abyss of the thing. To place the event of signification in abyss is to assign and consign it to the thing itself without erasing the distance between the two cases of 'self-distancing': that of the sign and that of the thing. In the latter, the former accomplishes its telos and, at the same time, loses itself as a conventionally understood sign operative in a 'natural language.'[61]

The second moment of the word's expropriation has to do with its analysability into letters, syllables, graphemes, and phonemes that circulate within and between texts and create a different, subterranean economy of meaning, which sometimes erupts only to create friction with the explicit, programmatic, conscious sense of the text.[62] It is well known that Derrida's own engagements with texts utilize this analysability, but where does the thing fit? Playfully dividing his proper name into letters and syllables *Ja, Der, Da* in *Limited Inc.*, Derrida asks, 'Is my name still "proper," or my signature, when, in proximity to "There. J.D." (pronounced in French, approximately Der. J.D.) ... they begin to function as integral or fragmented entities [*corps*, body], or as whole fragments of common nouns *or even of things*?' (L 33).[63] The iterability of the fragmented entities or bodies that temporarily come together to form a particular word underpins the expropriation of its synthetic unity in a feat whose consequences are all the more dire when the proper name itself is pulverized or disseminated. But what is the rationale behind the ostensibly insignificant addition of 'or even of things' at the end of the question?

According to Derrida, the 'fragmented entities' are already something other than words (he uses the term *corps*, body, to describe them) once they have undergone the process of fragmentation. It is conceivable that they could be transfigured into other units of sense 'as whole fragments of common nouns,' but before achieving this transfiguration, they must be dispensed to the abyss of the thing that interiorizes their remains and temporarily holds them back prior to projecting a new *différantial* unit. As usual, the supplementary option ('or even of things') for the engenderment of word fragments must come first in order for that which is supplemented ('common nouns') to materialize. But, more important, the treatment of the word's divisibility achieves two interrelated objectives: 1) it proves that this semantic unit is incapable of sustaining the ideal unity of a concept,[64] and 2) it betrays the materiality of language as a body, *corps, res extensa*. This twofold achievement, then, deflates the metaphysical claims of language, exposes the divisible nature of its non-formal, material substratum and, with this, reveals its mortal, finite core.

The process whereby the word falls apart is not autotelic; from the ruins of a word 'whole fragments of common nouns or even of things' may be reborn. Regenerating out of the abyss of the thing, a new, post-deconstructive synthesis of the synthetic ('whole') and the analytic ('fragments') arises, such that it would be no longer possible to decide whether the surviving entity is a word or a thing.[65] Such indecision constitutes the eventhood of the event. For example, the fragment *gl* that traverses the field of ruins speckling *Glas* survives its extraction from a myriad of words such as *glycines, sanglot, seigle, Gleichgewicht, gladiolus, glaviol* and *glas* itself, as well as in a modified form of *cloche, éclosion, gicle, clou,* and so on. Derrida, nevertheless, refuses to situate this remainder squarely within the limits of speech, signification, and writing:

> I do not say either the signifier GL, or the phoneme GL, or the grapheme GL. Mark would be better, if the word were well understood ... That has no identity [*Cela n'a pas d'identité*], sex, gender, makes no sense, is neither a definite whole nor a part detached from the whole
>   gl remain(s) gl [*gl reste gl*]
> falls (to the tomb) as must a pebble in the wate. (G 119/137, right)

The impossibility of saying or writing this combination of consonants is not empirical but quasi-transcendental: 'gl' belongs on the side of archi-writing (of a 'mark ... if the word were well understood') at the same time that it makes an appearance in a determined system of writing. Incompletely detached from particular words, empirical languages, and systems of inscription, it ceases to name some thing and, thanks to this cessation, claims for itself the properties of things. The assemblage of these two letters thus possesses a certain material gravity, a certain thingly heaviness that draws it down, makes it fall, onomatopoeically, 'as must a pebble in the water.'[66] The downward movement warrants the mark's *falling away* from the metaphysical fiction of language,[67] from the dream of a word 'properly' intended (in the phenomenological sense of empty 'intentionality') for a particular thing, which will have been conceptually subsumed in the word's unity and unicity without a remainder.

Counteracting such metaphysical thrust, the heavy, thingly residue *gl* remains inappropriable by linguistic ideality: 'gl remain(s) gl' devoid of identity and bereft of an identifiable reference.[68] This free-standing proposition – 'gl remain(s) gl' – marked off or detached from the rest of the text in *Glas*, is untranslatable into a logical expression of identity in 'S is P,' or its tautological expression, 'A is A.' In its proximity to itself (the proximity that the formally tautological character of the proposition and the word 'proper' itself indicate), *gl* remains forever distanced and detached from itself by the word and the thing 'remain(s),' *reste*, which is by no means synonymous with the purely synthetic function of the copula. 'Neither a definite whole nor a part detached from the whole,' it indeterminately mimes the ecstasis of the thing itself, substantiates the reference to 'whole fragments' in *Limited Inc.*, and thereby preserves the openness of a spacing in the 'new synthesis' of the synthetic and the analytic. This complex gesture of binding and unbinding, or, if one could refer to it thus, of post-deconstructive synthesis, motivates the self-remarking iteration of the thing.[69]

The regenerative event of thingly survival, drawn from the abyss of the unsayable and the un-inscribable, expropriates the ideality of the phenomenon, breaking the unity of sense and sound and preventing a particular linguistic entity from becoming a 'master-word.'[70] In the Husserlian vein, the ideality of the phenomenon depends on the subject, who, in the absolute proximity to himself, hears himself speak: 'The phenomenon continues to be an object for the voice; indeed … the ideality of the object seems to depend on the voice' (SP 78). But, faced with the mark *gl* (which is not a vocable), who would be able to hear himself speak this non-ideal non-object, whose non-objectivity does not veer on the side of pure subjectivity, whatever it may be, but ought to be conceived as 'language without language, the language become the thing itself [*le langage sans langage, le langage devenu la chose même*]' (MP 106/125)?[71] In and of itself, the sundering apart of the auto-affective sound or sounding of the voice signals an event of expropriation, because I can no longer find myself close (proximate, *proprius*) to myself as soon as I do not hear myself speak.

Despite the adjournment of the reference to a particular kind of externality – to the fiction of a non-textual signified – the expropriation of the voice admits language into the realm of the thing. Exteriority survives *within* the word's disintegration and dispersal into a non-totalizable multiplicity of other 'common nouns or even things,' each of which is a 'whole fragment' (like *par*) *and* 'neither a definite whole nor a part detached from the whole' (like *gl*). But, instead of succumbing to the temptation to interpret this adjournment of reference in terms of Derrida's textual hyperidealism, it would be productive to locate the margin right in the text, that is to say, to pursue the material residue of exteriority (the thing) within language itself: 'In my view, language has an outside ... I do not call this, with ease, the "real," because the concept of reality is overloaded with a slew of metaphysical presuppositions ... Something really exists beyond the confines of language ... [namely] ... the matter of traces derived from various texts.'[72]

1.3. The literary and the poetic: A name without the thing and the things without a name

The poetic dimension of the event of the thing encompasses both the conventional notion of poetry, which is one of many literary genres, and a more 'originary' sense of *poiesis*: the force of making, creation, 'bringing-forth,' which, within language, evinces the need for analysis and post-deconstructive synthesis. The starting point for the analytics of the poetic event is that there is no simple, unmediated, identifiable starting point, but only scattered, dispersed, multiple *things* in the absence of *the thing* (in the singular).[73] Among philosophical discourses, descriptive phenomenology yields the closest approximation to the analytics of dispersed things, which is not crassly empiricist and which, as a rule, is the birthright of literature, especially of poetic witnessing: 'These "things" that are not only "words": the poet is *the only one who can bear witness of them*, but he does not name them in the poem' (SQ 67).

These things without a name, these poetic miracles of bringing-forth or creation divorced from the act of naming and from all active comportment, refer themselves to particular dates and events that, in the case of the poet Celan, spell out historical trauma. In so doing, they elude the mastery and intentionality of the witness's conscious subjectivity.[74] Such elusiveness taken to the extreme will result in the transformation of the things themselves into witnesses who/that transgress the boundaries between the categorial and the existential analytics of Dasein – the 'humanist' boundaries within which 'a thing or an animal, *a fortiori*, a body could never attest to anything [*une chose ou un animal, a fortiori un cadavre ne sauraient jamais attester*], even if it does attest in the loose sense of being a clue or evidence' (D 81/106). In another traumatic, wartime narrative – that of Blanchot – this humanist logic implodes when in the course of the 'return to the real' (*retour au réel*) the things themselves, the corpses of horses, testify, as the only witnesses to the horrors of war, death, and destruction.[75] The things speak mutely; their testimony brought forth, at once 'poetically' and passively, from the decomposing remains virtually addresses us from the unnameable side of death.

Now, in contrast to the poetics of things without names, literature is, for Derrida, a *'name without the thing* [le nom sans la chose]' (D 20/ 17).[76] It follows that poetry no longer stands for a literary genre, since, with regard to the event of the thing, it is almost opposed to the genus of which it is, presumably, a species. What does Derrida mean, then, when he says that literature is the 'name without the thing'? Even on the most literal surface of the text, this statement is not redolent of nominalism or idealism,[77] since it arises in the context of questioning the *institution* of literature attached to its Latin and European provenance with its aspiration to universality or globality. Despite this aspiration, there is no 'world literature,' even if 'such a thing is or remains to come' (D 21). The thing 'world literature' is a Latin-European promise to the world, the thing to come, and hence an impending event, which, in the meantime, persists only in the shape of a name. Because the literary thing is not identical to itself, its name is not correlative to one fully realized entity (*'without the thing,'* in the singular). I wrote that the literary and the poetic are *'almost* opposed' to one another in Derrida, precisely because this apparent opposition occludes a necessary succession, whereby before speaking of the dispersed and plural things without a name (poetry), one would have to invoke a name no longer imbricated with a single, self-identical thing (literature). The poetic things occupy the vacated space of the latter, reiterating and re-marking the non-identity of the literary thing to-come.

And yet, in line with the logic of non-opposition, the *without* (*sans*) of the 'name without a thing' does not cut 'literature' loose from all reality effects. This thingless name is not unrelated to the reality of things and events; it conjures up a situation in which 'it is impossible to decide for the reader between the fictional, the invented, the dreamt event [*l'événement fictif, inventé, rêvé*] … and the event held to be "real" [*l'événement tenu pour 'réel'*]' (GG 17/26). That is perhaps why in his discussion of the fictional status of literature, Derrida contends that 'literature can say anything, accept anything, receive anything, suffer anything, and simulate everything' (D 29). With this, he not only reasserts the quintessentially democratic disposition of this institution that embodies the 'freedom of speech,' but also transposes onto it the receptivity of the *khōra*.

Like the *khōra*, the literary thing functions as a receptacle, the dehiscence of an opening welcoming the event in its virtual interiority. Paradoxically, the thingless name comes to contain, undecidably, 'the event held to be "real,"' the so-called reality of *res* inscribed in the virtuality of literary fiction. The *khōra*-like 'suffering,' 'passion,' and receptivity of literature may even supply the conditions of possibility for experience and subjectivity in general, but at the same time they schematize the outlines of a virtual, minimal experience articulated with the bareness of the trace that erases itself 'from the moment that the possibility of fiction has structured – but with a fracture – what is called real experience' (D 92). Thus, the genitive in the expression 'the experience of the thing' portends a lasting ambiguity, in that it indicates both the way one could experience the thing *and* the experience of the thing itself, accessible only from its 'side,' from its own standpoint.[78]

The structuring self-erasure, the giving withdrawal of the literary thing preceding, pre-empting, and outpacing the first act of *poiesis*, leaves in its wake nothing less than the world (albeit a fictional one) and poetic 'things without a name.' If literature is 'the most interesting thing in the world, maybe more interesting than the world' (AL 47), then it is neither a fully immanent – 'in the world' – nor a truly transcendent – 'more … than the world' – thing, but the very (phenomenological) origin of the world *in* the world. As such, the ecstatic literary thing conducts itself in the same fashion as the 'other ego' in Husserl's *Cartesian Meditations*. The difference, cast in Heideggerian terms, is that literature transgresses and spans the categorial and the existential analytic of Dasein, or, more precisely, that, analogous to the animal in the *Fundamental Concepts of Metaphysics*, it both lacks and does not lack the world. In this sense, the literary thing meets human Dasein 'half-way,' when, like him, it originates a rich phenomenological world, and when, like it, he becomes *weltlos*, worldless, in his capacity as a survivor:[79] 'The survivor, then, remains alone … At the least, he feels solely responsible, assigned to carry both the other and *his* world, the other and *the* world that have disappeared, responsible without world (*weltlos*), without the ground of any world' (SQ 140). A certain degree of thingification accompanies every survival that expels the survivor from the horizon of the bygone world, just as a certain measure of egoity is associated with the interest that every new literary thing provokes in us, promising something like '*poiesis* before *poiesis*,' the opening of a 'new world.'

As a consequence of the active exchange between the two analytics, it is not far-fetched to speak of the literary and poetic things' life, death, and survival.[80] In *Demeure*, Derrida asks, 'What if a manuscript cannot be reconstituted?' and immediately adds, 'It is a mortal text' in opposition to the metaphysical claim that 'these things [the manuscripts] are immortal [*ces choses sont immortelles*]' (D 100/135). In *The Ear of the Other*, he complicates Benjamin's definition of the text's originality: 'A text is original insofar as it is a thing, not to be confused with an organic or a physical body, but a thing, let us say, of the mind, meant to survive the death of the author or the signatory' (EO 121). And in *Acts of Literature* he shares with the reader his sense of 'marveling bewilderment at remains as a written thing' (AL 37).

In all three instances, the mortality of literary and poetic things positively betokens their capacity to live and to survive in the light of their enabling finitude. To recall, the life (the life-death, or the after-life) of the thing begins with its autonomous breathing 'without me.' Adding another twist to the expression of the thing's animation, Derrida's meditation on Celan's definition of poetry as 'a turn of the breath' includes the observation that 'breath remains in some living things, at least, not only the first but also the last sign of life, of living life' (SQ 110). It might appear that in this turn of the phrase Derrida has reinscribed the conventional distinction between the living poetic voice and the dead, neutral space of literary writing, when in fact he subjects this distinction to a merciless interrogation. First, breath resides 'in some living things,' that is, not in pure life but in animate-inanimate entities: those that are provisionally alive, constantly receiving reminders of the ephemeral nature of their existence from their thingly dimension. A locus of breath and of its spatio-temporal turns, poetry will therefore fall in the category of such finite, mortal, provisionally 'living things.' Second, breath is simultaneously 'the first but also the last sign of life'; it stamps all beginnings and ends, as much as all the traversals between the predicament of the living and that of the non-living. Apropos of the breath and breathlessness of poetic language, the massive problematic of 'living speech' in its entirety suggests itself along with its obverse, which consists of those punctuating, puncturing, spacing moments within speech where the drawing of breath precariously anticipates a new locutionary act and symbolically coincides with absence and death.[81] With this, the breath of 'some living things' accentuated, turned, and twisted in poetry disperses and autonomizes them on the edge of their finite life.

Another consequence of trafficking things across the existential-categorial divide is the substitution of names – the proper for the common and the common for the proper – in a procedure defining literary acts. Francis Ponge, for example, 'disguises every proper name as a description and every description as a proper name … You never know whether he names or describes, nor whether the thing he describes-names is the thing or the name, the common or proper name [*ni si ce qu'il décrit-nomme est la chose ou le nom, le commun ou le propre*]' (SI 118/ 119). Derrida's explication of Ponge plays with various layers of ambiguity: besides questioning whether the referent named is a thing or another name, a 'what' or a 'who,' he tells 'us' (his readers whom he will never know) that we will 'never know whether he names or describes.'[82] Let us, then, frame this passage between, on the one hand, the notion of literature as a name without the thing and, on the other, poetic things without name. In lieu of the alliance of naming and mastery, the description that refuses to name endows one with a peculiar attitude toward anonymous things – the attitude that is devoid of mastery and that therefore cultivates a poetic receptivity to the world.[83] Note, however, that, contrary to all expectations, Derrida does not privilege the poetic way. Instead, he couples description and naming in a hyphenated verb ('describes-names'), thereby leaving room for literature's thing-less name. His reluctance to 'choose' the poetic over the literary, description over naming, and again, powerlessness over sovereignty resurfaces in *H.C. for Life*, where the coming of the event bridges the gap between the passive 'letting come' and the active 'making come' (HC 66).[84] The event of the literary thing is possible only in the night of not knowing ('You will never know …'), when description looks like naming and naming resembles description, when receptivity and activity are indistinguishable from one another, when the event has already occurred and is yet to come, when the thing passes itself as the name and the name puts on the camouflage of the thing.

The work of expropriation is that which is required in order for the name to put on this camouflage, or to transmute itself from a proper into a common name. Just as it happens in post-deconstructive synthesis, the event of the thing burgeons in a named word thanks to a triple confusion: 1) that of one proper name with another, 2) that of proper and common names, and 3) the confusion of the first two confusions. Reading Juliet's supplication of Romeo, 'O be some other name,'[85] as a metonymy for literary expropriation, Derrida writes,

> But that can mean two things: take another proper name (a human name, this inhuman thing which belongs only to man); or: take another kind of name, a name which is not that of man, take the name of a thing then, a common name which, like the name of the rose, does not have that inhumanity which consists in affecting the very being of the one who bears it even though it names nothing of himself. (AL 428)

The contrast between these two options seems straightforward enough. Were he to take 'another proper name,' Romeo would be able to extricate himself from the influence of his family name, which inscribed him in the history of animosity between the Capulets and the Montagues. Were he to take 'another kind of name,' a common name of the thing, he would disentangle himself from all human imperfections and would live up to Juliet's idealization of him. Nonetheless, each of these options fatefully includes the other.[86] The purely human name (assuming that such a thing exists) stands for 'this inhuman thing' responsible for strife and hatred, this thing whose inhumanity is definitive of the essence of man ('which belongs only to man'). But the name of the non-human thing 'does not have that inhumanity' that threatens to annihilate the being of its bearer. Heeding Juliet's admonition, Romeo could adopt another human name and disguise himself as another person, *or* he could borrow a non-human name from another thing, from the thing qua other, in an a priori doomed attempt to live up to the demand of loving idealization.[87] Derrida's point, however, is that the italicized disjunctive '*or*' is at work *within* each choice open before Romeo, who may swap the inhumanity of the human for the humanity of the inhuman. And if this narrative really metonymizes literary expropriation, then it keeps in store two other substitutions: of Juliet for the critic, and of Romeo for the literary thing itself.

2 'This Thing Regards Us':
The Promise of 'Reified' Intentionality

Intentionality is no longer, then, an aiming at being and the noetic synthesis of its different moments, operated by a pure subject. The intentional lived experience is no longer a simple 'unreal' constituting the meaning of the 'real.'

The Problem of Genesis in Husserl's Philosophy

L'amitié politique est attentive à l'égalité comme à la chose (l'affaire, *prágma*), à l'une autant qu'à l'autre, à l'une pour autant qu'elle se rapporte aussi à l'autre. C'est là ce que l'amitié politique 'regarde' (*blépei*) et ce qui la regarde.

Politiques de l'amitié

2.1. The real of intentionality and the intentionality of the real

Ever since his first systematic study of Husserlian phenomenology, which has resulted in *The Problem of Genesis in Husserl's Philosophy*, Derrida has channelled his efforts toward an auspicious and fecund modification of the 'intentionality thesis'.[1] In its earliest form, this modification depends on the argument that, owing to its ambiguous position neither entirely within nor entirely outside consciousness, noematic representation makes possible and, at the same time, derails the subject's intentional acts. At a later phase of rethinking this fundamental phenomenological concept, Derrida will theorize the ghostly as the excess of the real that, evading the conceptual categories of consciousness, affects the latter with the intentionality of the thing itself.

2.1.1. *The real of intentionality:* Noema *and* hylē

Derrida stages his reading of Husserl against an invariable backdrop in which the critique of idealization uncovers multiple cross-contaminations between the empirical and the transcendental.[2] In the process of phenomenological idealization, just as the pure ego displaces the empirical subject, so the intended object of sense (*noema*) supersedes the rich, potentially sense-less, but ultimately inexhaustible material thing. The message of deconstruction, however, is that this displacement and this supersession are never complete, and that their incompletion is a prerequisite for the 'normal' functioning of consciousness. More specifically, a reassessment of the second moment of phenomenological idealization (*noema* supplanting the thing) testifies to the way in which the thing both obfuscates and clarifies the intended object of sense, turning it into a detached attachment, a supplement, and, hence, a fetish of consciousness.

As soon as one focuses on this critical backdrop, one will be sure to recognize in it a colossal challenge to the noetic-noematic correlation, which guarantees the 'making' of meaning and sense exclusively for the pure, ideal subject who is preoccupied with a purified, idealized object. According to Derrida, in the wake of innumerable phenomenological reductions that disclose the conditions of possibility for the constitution of meaning, Husserl loses sight of something irreducible, namely, the non-idealizable materiality, barely indicated in the Aristotelian word *hylē* and tacitly subjugated to, or subsumed under, the demands of form (*morphē*) in the Gordian knot of a non-constituted, originary correlation.[3] Despite, for the most part, evading Husserl's phenomenological gaze, this category both partakes of and transgresses the structure of intentionality.

The crucial pages in '"Genesis and Structure" and Phenomenology' that situate the two correlations under the heading of 'transcendental intentionality' are worth quoting at some length:

> Transcendental intentionality is described in *Ideas I* as an original structure, an archi-structure (*Ur-Struktur*) with four poles and two correlations: the noetico-noematic correlation … and the *morphe-hyle* correlation … That this complex structure is the structure both of intentionality, that is, the structure of the origin of meanings and of the opening to the light of phenomenality, and that the occlusion of this structure is non-sense itself, is indicated by at least two signs: (A) Noesis and noema, the intentional

moments of this structure, can be distinguished in that the noema does not belong to consciousness in a *real* way. *Within* consciousness, in general there is an agency which *does not really* belong to it [*Il y a* dans *la conscience en général une instance qui* ne *lui appartient* pas réellement] ... (B) While the noema is an intentional and non-real element, *hylē* is the real but not intentional element of the experienced ... It is the pole of pure passivity, of the non-intentionality without which consciousness could not receive anything *other* than itself. (WD 162–3/242)

The centrepiece of this passage and of the essay as a whole is the circumscription within consciousness of what it doesn't immanently include, or transcendentally exclude: '*Within* consciousness, in general there is an agency which *does not really* belong to it.'[4] This necessarily maladjusted agency or, rather, these agencies are indispensable to any subjectivity that is not monadic, closed off to the world of others and of things. As margins that furrow the very core of the system, they exist in various degrees of distance and proximity to consciousness *within* consciousness, governed, as they are, by the thing that evades the subject's intentional grasp. *Noema* and *hylē* are, therefore, the supplements – and this will be the Derridian take on Husserl's 'correlations' – of the privileged noetic and morphic poles of transcendental intentionality. But because the supplements are always dangerous, their immanently transcendental and transcendentally immanent loci threaten the originality of this 'archi-structure' and the ideal sense that germinates in it.

On the one hand, the noematic ideal object is a detachable part of consciousness that 'does not belong to it in a *real* way,' given that it borrows the quality of detachability from the thing itself, which, in its autonomy, breathes on its own, without the subject who would appropriate it. Since it both belongs and does not belong to the transcendental mental processes that strip the real object down to ideal objectivity, *noema* forms a spectral (non-real *and* non-ideal) detached attachment, the subject's mode of existence in self-transcendence[5]. In the last instance, when the pure ego intentively relates to a noematic object, instead of discovering the things themselves, it finds, at best, an objectified and, at worst, a fictionalized version of itself, of what belongs to it, but not 'in a *real* way.' A general consequence of this unintended 'self-discovery' is that Husserlian intentionality is meaningful solely in the context of the subject-centred search for ideal meaning and sense, that is, as the 'structure of the origin of meanings and of the opening to the light of phenomenality.' It tells us nothing about that which or the one who, de-centring the subject, endeavours to *make sense of us*, let alone about the initially sense-less material thing from whose abyss meaning and sense are born, eluding the so-called 'originary' structure of consciousness. From a strictly phenomenological point of view, an 'occlusion of this structure' succumbs to 'non-sense itself,' but, as a real part of the material thing, this non-sense will be more fertile for the exercises in meaning-making than the delimited sense of transcendental intentionality.

On the other hand, the pole of *hylē*, materiality, or simply 'stuff' is part and parcel of the fourfold structure identified by Derrida, but it is even closer to the thing itself than *noema*: '*Hylē* is the real but not intentional element of the experienced.' While *noema* lays out the path for the percolation of consciousness into the exteriority of the world without granting consciousness a chance to reach the thing itself, the hyletic aspect of the archi-structure encourages the breach of interiority by the exterior order of the real, without being fully identified with an element of that order[6]. It is here that Derrida locates the opening of phenomenology onto the sense-less, onto the receptivity of consciousness that, in moments of respite, does not engage in intentional activity but becomes 'purely passive' and welcomes the alterity of everything that is other to it.[7] With this, he accepts the Levinasian proposition that all experience is the experience of alterity, provided that this alterity is, at first, inseparable from the thingly, material substratum that imposes itself on consciousness before being conjugated with *morphē* in an 'original' correlation.[8] In this respect, like the dark halo of 'determinate indeterminacy' that surrounds the active sphere of consciousness in Husserl, non-intentionality is a sine qua non 'without which consciousness could not receive anything *other* than itself,' indicating the passivity of the subject, who may become an object of another intentional regard, or who may let the sense-less abyss of the thing breathe enigmatically. Thus, the hyletic pole moderates the diluted alterity of the noematic object through which consciousness receives only an alternative version of itself.

Derrida's interest in *hylē* extends as far back as *The Problem of Genesis in Husserl's Philosophy*, where it forms the non- or pre-intentional part of lived experience: 'The sensuous *hylē*, as such and in its purity, that is to say, *before* being animated by intentionality, would *already* be a piece of lived experience ... It is thus a non-intentional piece of lived experience that the *hylē* is animated by intentional form' (PG 86).[9] In other words, before I aim at or direct myself to a thing, bestow sense upon it and thereby animate it with intentionality, or, conversely, before I make a decision that would let the animated thing breathe independently, on its own, without me, I am compelled to avow the pre-intentional, not yet thematized, or non-thematizable aspect of lived experience independent of the subject who has it. Such would be the experience we 'have' without first taking possession, appropriating, or choosing it, the experience without which no intentional directionality will have been conceivable. Animated by a force other than intentionality, *hylē* nonetheless furnishes the conditions of possibility for the latter inasmuch as it protects consciousness against a lapse into absolute idealism, and, in so doing, takes up a prosthetic, ancillary position vis-à-vis the pure ego. That is to say, the intentional grasp toils to repeat, reiterate, re-live a piece of experience that has already been lived non-intentionally, and, with this, to re-mark the thing that has already animatedly marked itself and has been *internalized but not incorporated* in psychic life.[10] Intentionality includes something 'real' despite itself, non-intentionally, belatedly, and in the mode of the present perfect ('*before ... already*').

As the 'real' of intentionality, *hylē* compensates for the fissure between the empty intention and intuitive fulfilment that produces meaning in 'the absence of any object given to intuition [*l'absence d'objet donné à l'intuition*]' (SP 92/102). That the intentional act of aiming at an object does not have to find fulfilment in, or to arrive at, its intended destination is a proto-formulation of Derrida's views on *destinerrance*, the eventful errancy of the missive, the non-arrival of the letter at the correct address. To be more precise on the sense of such compensation, *hylē* does not take over the functions of intuitive fulfilment, nor does it seal the fissure between the absence of the intuited and the presence of the intended. Rather, it countervails the idealist thrust of signification and sense-bestowal, when, in 'the absence of an object given to intuition,' intuition itself is given, handed over, meted out to something other than the object – for instance, to the opaque body of the sign from which it never emerges (the same): 'But the "animation" cannot be pure and complete, for it must traverse, and to some extent lose itself in, the opaqueness of the body' (SP 38). We have already designated this transformative opaqueness as the abyss of the thing.

If one could somehow recuperate this loss, if one could find the means to reverse the traversal of the body by the animating spirit that falters in its effort to reproduce the wonder of its homecoming, then one would not witness a spiritual or spirited 'resurrection' of ideal intentionality,

but its return in spectrality that clings to the memory of corporeal traversal and loss. In the conversion of spirit into spectres, the transition
from the real of intentionality to the intentionality of the real is looming
on our theoretical horizon. In a preview of this transition, I would argue
that the living-dead spectre is the side-effect of the incompletion and impurity of intentional animation. Having absorbed the remainder of conscious directedness,[11] the 'opaqueness of the body' refuses to dissolve in
pure phenomenal light, but, alternatively, acquires an intentionality of
its own – the intentionality of the real, of the thing that aims at us. Thus,
in keeping with the peculiar logic of the supplement, the thing itself
forms a residuum of the intended object of sense, which is no longer ide-
ally constituted by a pure subject.[12]

2.1.2. *The intentionality of the real:* Res nostra agitur

Derrida takes hyletic 'animation' literally and, responding to the Husserlian postulation of the unavoidably adumbrated appearances of the
physical thing, writes, 'The hyletic lived experience as such does not
give itself through a variation; *it is the place or the moment where the per-
ceived thing is varying itself'* (PG 87, emphasis added). Let us foreground
three interrelated consequences of this 'programmatic' statement.

1) If, following *Ideas I*, 'hyletic lived experience as such does not give
itself through a variation' or through a series of successive adumbra-
tions, and if, moreover, Husserl reserves the non-variational mode of
givenness solely for the immanence of mental processes that are present and transparent to themselves, then hyletic lived experience is not
given at all, either immanently or transcendentally. But the non-givenness of pure *hylē* is not purely negative, in that it motivates the interminable approach of intentional consciousness to its forever-incomplete
object, which never fills, in toto, the place of the thing's self-variation.
What remains non-given or withheld, therefore, is this thingly place
from which the adumbrated objects emanate, with the proviso that its
very non-givenness or withdrawal governs the subject's approach to
such objects.

2) To say that in the place withdrawn from intentionality 'the per-
ceived thing is varying itself' is to insist on the thing's self-animation,
self-variation, in a word, auto-affection: 'The Thing touches itself, is
touched, even there where one touches Nothing [*La Chose se touche,
même là où l'on ne touche Rien*]. Henceforth this is what we shall have
to try to understand, as well as how touch and non-touch are *really*

touched and self-touching [*comment le toucher et le non-toucher se touchent*, réellement] – with infinite tact' (OT 46/60). It goes without saying that the thing must come detached from itself and from us in order to relate back to and affect itself. The signs of this self-detachment are abundant, be it the difference between the topos of the thing and everything that ensues from this withdrawn place, the non-included inclusion of *hylē* under the rubric of transcendental consciousness, or the gaping interval at the heart of 'lived' experience. But what happens the moment the thing reconnects with itself, ecstatically, in a bond of auto-affection? Although it would appear that auto-affection confirms the closure of intentionality translated into self-directedness, one would need to turn to models other than that of autotelic consciousness in Aristotle's mind thinking itself, or in Husserl's subject hearing itself speak. When the thing itself touches itself, it does so '*really*' ('réellement'), restoring a non-idealized and non-identical substratum to the sense of touch. In this self-relation the thing is never fully present to itself; it maintains its detachment or absolution from itself, which allows it to commune with itself 'even there where one touches Nothing,' there where one abuts the athing or the effect of its non-self-presence and withdrawal.

3) The thing's non-givenness and self-variation preclude its recognition by the subject of intentionality – which means that the 'originary,' 'non-constituted' correlation *morphē-hylē* comes undone. Specifically, the first element of the correlation undergoes the kind of bracketing (radical reduction) that hurls the thing beyond the orbits of recognition and transcendental intentionality: 'But since the relation between the hyletic lived experience and the thing is not intentional, it is only the *morphē* which makes us "recognize" in the *hylē* the figuration of one thing and not another' (PG 87–8). By no means does this imply that *hylē* de-individuates the thing and its 'figuration,' which, in each case, precipitates its difference from another thing standing out against the same neutral background. Instead, it leaves just enough breathing space for the individuation of the thing, unfettered from its delimitation in conscious recognition that subordinates all uniqueness to the homogeneous and *objective*, spatio-temporal and conceptual background from which it is called forth. The thing remarks itself so that its 'individuality' is never depleted, so that it remains inexhaustibly other to itself and to the subject, who relies on the mechanisms of recognition to comprehend it. In an upshot of its self-remarking, the thing ceases to 'make sense' for us but continues to generate sense at another register,

for exemple, in availing consciousness of its material conditions of possibility, in making sense *of* us and so on.[13]

The scene is set for the inversion of intentionality, whereby the thing, at once, reroutes the directionality of consciousness and aims at me.[14] But, before I cite the evidence for this inversion in Derrida's text, a few methodological observations are in order. To repeat, the exploration of the thing's intentionality does not invalidate Husserl's own discoveries, but picks up an argumentative thread already present in his work, where the non-intentionality of the sensuous gives rise to 'concrete intentive mental processes.'[15] In other words, although, methodologically, what I call the 'inversion'[16] of intentionality issues a posteriori, through the reduction of intentive mental processes and a confirmation of the thing's irreducibility, the ontological sequence is more complex. On the one hand, this primordially 'inverted' structure foreshadows – if not supplies the a priori material conditions of possibility for – the regular functioning of consciousness. But, on the other, it is a residue of objectivization, a trace of psychic animation, which consists of the fragments of intentions and unfulfilled intuitions lost in the density and opaqueness of the thing they have not surpassed. Both quasi-transcendental and supplementary, the 'inversion' of intentionality is not a watershed theoretical and practical event that occurs once and for all, but the unrelenting obverse of consciousness whose directedness toward the external things and toward itself is always warped, bifurcated, oblique, and indirect. The subsequent enunciation of post-deconstructive realism will have to attend to this intransigent anachronism.

As a trace of psychic animation trapped in the impenetrable materiality of the body and released with the thing itself, the virtuality of the ghostly moment prevalent in Derrida's later writings is not a surreptitious effect of ideality. On the contrary, it articulates the excess of the real in terms of the thing's self-animation, which no longer belongs to the order of knowledge. In *Specters of Marx*, the ghostly thing comes to embody this excess on the obverse side of intentionality:

> Here is – or rather there is, over there [*Voici – ou voilà, là-bas*], an unnameable or almost unnameable thing: something, between something and someone, anyone or anything, some thing, *'this thing'*, but this thing and not any other, this thing that looks at us, that concerns us [*quelque chose, entre quelque chose et quelqu'un, quiconque ou quelconque, quelque chose, cette chose-ci, 'this thing', cette chose pourtant et non une autre, cette chose qui nous regarde*], comes to defy semantics as much as ontology, psychoanalysis as

much as philosophy ... Nor does one see in flesh and blood this Thing that is not a thing [*Cette Chose qui n'est pas une chose*], this thing that is invisible between its apparitions, when it reappears. This Thing meanwhile looks at us and sees us not see it even when it is there [*Cette Chose nous regarde cependant et nous voit ne pas la voir même quand elle est là*]. (SM 6/26)

In addition to explicitly quoting Shakespeare on 'this thing,' the allusive richness of this passage cites without citing a host of pivotal figures in the history of philosophy, from Hegel to Husserl, Heidegger, and Levinas. While it calls for an interminable analysis, I will limit my interpretive remarks to the problematic of intentionality. In response to Hegel, Derrida maintains that when the 'thisness,' the empirical singularity, of the thing escapes its sublation into higher conceptual forms, it defies philosophy. The dialectical procedure is doomed from the start because the enunciation of a positive or 'positivizing' negation misses the thing which is 'this ... and not any other' and, at the same time, 'not a thing' whatsoever, an unlimited positivity and an unconditional negativity.[17] That which philosophy is unable to detect is the amorphic non-identity barring conceptual recognition and resonating with the most rigorous sense of negative theology.

Derrida draws our attention to such 'amorphousness' in his invocation of the in-between space in which the thing dwells ('between something and someone, anyone or anything'; 'invisible between its apparitions'). In the light of the rejection of figuration as the model for the thing's appearance, and, by implication, for the appearance of God,[18] its spectral apparition pertains as much to the one who or to that which is locked between the outlines of a figure, as to what lies beyond these confines. The event Derrida furtively sketches here reveals that, outside its figuration, the thing aporetically conjoins the non-identifiable (because non-figurative) singularity of the 'this' and the seemingly indifferent generality of the 'any,' some thing and something. The emphasis on the second polarity is a part of the retort he addresses to Heidegger, whose critique of the indefinite alterity of the 'they' – idle talk, publicness, and so on – in *Being and Time* is ultimately a condemnation of the scholastic category of something, *quodlibet ens*, the unappropriated thing superficially beheld and known in common.[19]

The promise of vagueness is that it liberates the thing from the clasp of possessive subjectivity and places the Heideggerian *Ereignis* 'in abyss.' Both the distension of the thing beyond its figural outlines, whose irrelevance renders it simultaneously too precise and too imprecise, absolutely concentrated and utterly dispersed, and its conversion into a receptacle of *différance* indicate that it is not a signified entity of which we can make sense, but a signifying (or proto-signifying), sense-making process. The impossibility of 'figuring out,' of pointing out and recognizing, the thing is, then, symptomatic of its exemption from the order of knowledge, but not from the pre-ontological faith that underpins this order.

As Derrida contends in the unpublished 1970s seminar *La Chose*,[20] we summon or name the thing, which is not an object, exactly there where all knowledge claims fail and become irrelevant, fall by the wayside:

> *The word 'thing' does not merely have several meanings, or a great richness of meaning. One quickly appreciates that its meaning is without limit and that, as a result, the thing may be put in place of anything* [chose peut être mis à la place de n'importe quoi]. *It is a universal substitute, anything whatsoever, the X* (etwas, quelque chose). *When one cannot name or does not want to name something, one says, 'the thing.' When one cannot or does not want to name – some thing – one says,* 'the thing' [Quand on ne peut nommer ou ne veut nommer quelque chose, on dit, la chose. Quand on ne peut ou ne veut nommer – quelque chose – on dit, *la chose*]. (JDP 13/1)[21]

The disbanding of the thing's conceptual limits emulates the dissolution of its phenomenological figuration; 'meaning ... without limit' is a correlate of an entity without outlines. It is this positive lack of a limit that turns the thing into 'a universal substitute,' which, in a prefiguration of *Specters of Marx*, enters into a constellation with every singularity, for example, that of the secret: what one does not want to name, what one conceals behind the common name of 'the thing,' or again, what one does not know how to name. To invoke the name of the thing is to linger on the edge of the ineffable, to dissimulate and disseminate some other thing that does not phenomenally appear thanks to the invocation of this common name. Short of not saying anything about a singularity, one says, in the most general fashion imaginable, 'the thing.' Thus, a double haunting accompanies the overturning of intentionality, first, where the thingly universal but non-identical substitute inhabits or spectrally animates anything whatsoever, and second, where the singular disseminated thing displaces and transforms us into the objects of its invisible regard.

To return to the Heidegger-Derrida nexus: a constant referent in the attack Heidegger launches against public things filling the world of *das*

Man is that they disallow the attitude of solicitation because they concern everyone and no one in particular. Above all, this is a veiled political assault on the key underlying assumptions of communism and its efforts at instituting communally held property, which would amount to a *res nullius*. Derrida nonetheless repudiates the deduction of an indifferent comportment toward a public thing from the indeterminacy and vagueness of some thing (*quelque chose*) that populates Heidegger's world of 'inauthenticity.'[22] The stakes of this virtual response, appropriately enough featured in a book preoccupied with the legacies and spectres of Marx, are high. It would be sufficient to return to the first pole of the event of the thing, its complete singularity, which does not succumb to its indeterminate character, in order to dispel the conclusion of *Being and Time*. But, as though this were not enough, Derrida also touches upon the thingly dimension of care via 'this thing that looks at us, that concerns us [*cette chose qui nous regarde*].'[23] He elaborates on the intricacy of the French verb *regarder* – which means 'to look,' 'to concern,' and 'to keep' – with the purpose of establishing an overdetermined relationship between the specularity of the 'reified' gaze and a concernful ethical stance.[24] In the eventful inversion of intentionality, the thing directs its own gaze toward us. We are the objects of the regard of this thing, which is interchangeable with any other. Derrida thus casts the old Latin syntagma *res nostra agitur* in a new light. The thing looks at, concerns, agitates, and keeps together the plural 'we' (*nous*), which betokens a multiplicity of human and non-human entities (the 'we' is left indeterminate), a whole community situated on the horizon of the thing.

Before its appropriation by an individual or by a number of individuals, the detached, absolved thing itself establishes a social bond between everything and everyone that appears in its visual field. What are the implications of such reified specularity for the attitude of concern? As a consequence of the inversion, the thing attains a certain degree of intentionality and ceases to function merely as an object of our concern (Heidegger's *Besorge*). Henceforth, it would be possible to attribute a certain fascination to the thing itself, since to regard is to look without indifference, to study carefully and attentively.[25] Regarding us with enthralment, '*the thing is engaged … We are before it: that is the cause of everything* [La chose est engagée … Nous somme devant elle, voilà la cause de tout]' (DP 18).[26] It is wholly engaged (with 'everything') after its initial disengagement or absolution from consciousness that intends it and from the straitjacket of the principle of identity that defines it.

Moreover, if it is engaged or concerned in a causal mode, this is owing not only to the etymological connection between *cause* and *chose*, but also to the thing's remarkable capacity to bring together disparate entities in a non-totalizing, disseminative key.[27] The first person plural that appears before the thing (but how can one, or more than one, appear before something that is not an ob-ject, something that perpetually slips away, falls apart, or hides behind the act of looking? The impossibility of accomplishing this feat, which nonetheless enjoins us, holds the promise of a disseminated sociality) echoes, without a doubt, the community that congregates under the gaze of the thing in *Specters of Marx*. One might surmise that this 'we,' too, is an effect of the thing, before which we struggle to gather ourselves as a plurality.

Politically, the social generativity of the thing plays a lead role in Derrida's attempt at re-evaluating the meaning and the tradition of a 'democratic republic' in the sense of 'a *res publica*, a republic where the difference between the public and the non-public remains an undecidable limit' (R 92).[28] The isolation of the thingly aspect (*res*) of the public recaptures the whole realm of phenomenology, which we have never left and which, in a revised form, is no longer restricted to the entities that appear publicly in the broad eidetic daylight. The undecidable limit between the public and the non-public, between politics and ethics, now passes through the thing itself, which beckons us to come together and – privately, though not privatively – withdraws in the same gesture. To the extent that its giving withdrawal is interminable and to the extent that our intentionality still directs itself toward the elusive thing, the concern it evokes rises to the boiling point of an obsession[29] that relentlessly keeps us on the edge because, in the absence of a recognizable figure, the definite-indefinite outlets for channelling it are infinite. Indeed, even the colloquial expression 'it concerns me' retains something of this ambiguous back-and-forth between passivity and activity, where I become a grammatical object of the sentence, while the 'real' object of my concern acts as though it were a subject. With this ambiguity, the 'thing seems to defy any grammar' (OT 176) whose goal is to provide the basic rules for meaningfulness and to set clear parameters for logic.[30]

With regard to the overdetermined meaning of 'regard' in Derrida's book on Marx, a step back to Plato will not go too far afield, since, on one level, *eidos* connotes 'looking,' the mere look of the things as they present themselves.[31] The eidetic look inscribes ideas on the very phenomenological surface of the appearance of things, but it also describes the fashion in which the things themselves look or gaze *at* us. That is why, in his approach to the thing, Derrida adds to its being-here, which is characteristic of the categorial presence-at-hand or readiness-to-hand, the existential term par excellence, being-there, 'over there' ('*Voici – ou voilà, là-bas*'), that explains how it might become the subject of a look. Now, what the thing sees when it looks at us is that we do 'not see it even when it is there [*ne pas la voir même quand elle est là*].' In other words, it receives the specular evidence of our blindness both to the fact that it sees us and, especially, to the fact that it is there, that it is existentially self-animated and that this thingly self-animation or self-remarcation lets it see (our blindness) in the first place. The underside of intentionality is, therefore, imperceptible to the phenomenological apparatus. Regardless of the perspective it assumes or feigns to assume, intentionality can aim neither at the other *of* intentionality nor at the other, thingly intentionality. There is no exchange of glances between the thing that remains equally invisible 'between its apparitions' *and* 'when it reappears,' on the one hand, and the human subject on the other. The inversion of intentionality, the laying bare of its reverse side, is irreversible. To elucidate this radical auto-critique of phenomenology, Derrida relies on the Levinasian idea of an asymmetrical, anachronic relation to the other, for whom he substitutes the thing: 'A spectral asymmetry interrupts here all specularity. It de-synchronizes, it recalls us to anachrony' (SM 6–7). Not only does that which looks at us dissimulate itself behind the act of looking, but this very act is not available for identification because the two gazes, the two specularities and the two intentionalities, never cross paths.

The expression Derrida reserves for the non-coincidence of the two gazes is 'the visor effect': 'To feel ourselves seen by a look which it will always be impossible to cross, that is the *visor effect* on the basis of which we inherit from the law [*Que nous nous sentions vus par un regard qu'il sera toujours impossible de croiser, voilà l'*effet de visière *depuis lequel nous héritons de la loi*]' (SM 7/27). Visor, *visière*, originates from the French verb *viser*, 'to aim at,' which relates directly to phenomenological intentionality and its inversion. Concealed behind a visor, the invisible thing gazes at me, regards me, aims at me.[32] In an analogy to the Levinasian face (*visage*: etymologically close to *viser*) that addresses me before, below, and beyond spoken discourse, the thing places on us a mute demand, a proto-law, 'on the basis of which we inherit from the law.'[33] Moreover, the visor is an artefact, a cover and an effect of the cause or *chose* that displays how a community constitutes itself around the presence-absence (the trace) of the thing. When we 'feel ourselves seen [*nous nous sentions vus*],' we are passively and sensuously related to ourselves – one to the other and each one to everyone – by that which or the one who, akin to law itself, sees us without being seen. The reflexive form of '*nous nous sentions*,' then, is a grammatical symptom – indeed, a reflection – of this relatedness.

2.2. The thing of the senses

Vision or lack thereof is not the exclusive avenue for the haunting experience of being targeted by the thing. Broadly construed, the inversion of intentionality invites a reconsideration of the other senses and sense organs in its aftermath. In this section, I turn to the senses of hearing and touch – the ear, the hand, and, eventually, the rest of the haptic body – and discuss their appropriation by the intentionality of the thing.

2.2.1. Not-hearing-oneself-speak

Contributing to the closure of intentionality, Husserlian ideal subjectivity is born in the channel of an auto-affective vocal mediation, where I hear myself speak. Rather than disrupt such closure, the ideal object that co-originates with the subject is wholly included in it qua infinitely repeatable, retraceable, iterable. What hearing oneself speak excludes, however, is the exteriority of the thing, which will erupt only when my own speech does not reach my ear, thereby fracturing the perfect *noema-noesis* correlation: when either my muteness or my deafness to myself blocks the medium for idealization.

The efficaciousness of the *noema-noesis* correlation is doubtful, especially in those cases where the indefinitely repetitive production of ideal sense, subjectivity, and objectivity appears to enjoy the highest degree of success. It is not by a pure coincidence that the famous Husserlian example of the inner voice, 'You've gone wrong,' which Derrida cites in *Speech and Phenomena* (70), is above all a protest, a remonstration, an objection the subject raises against itself as the object of reproach. The subject's guilty consciousness, which turns against – objects to and objectifies – itself, holds the key to its relation with other objects. But why do I need to repeat this accusation? Repetition elliptically signals the reiteration of objectivity and objection, *as though* I did not hear myself speak the first time, *as though* my discourse were useless and irrelevant, *as though* it did not criss-cross the non-translucent inner space of difference between my mouth and my ear and between *noema* and *noesis*. Husserl's subjectivity, hearing one's own speech, is virtually deaf and ineducable, or, at the very least, it must feign (Derrida's word) these qualities to keep itself intact with the assistance of 'the voice that keeps silence.' One implication of this fissuring in the subject is that its mental processes are not immanently transparent to themselves, or, differently put, that hyletic lived experience and, with it, the thing itself generate a sort of insurmountable opaqueness and density *within the phenomenological subject*.[34]

A strange allegiance is thus forged among the muting of the phenomenological voice, the silent milieu of writing, and the muteness of the thing that delivers the law: 'Inscription can require the muteness of the thing. It gives orders while remaining silent [*inscription peuvent requérir le mutisme de la chose. Elle ordonne en se taisant*]' (SI 14/15). The density of the untraversable space between the subject's mouth and ear, between speech and hearing, arrests auto-affective intentionality in its tracks and maintains a trace of lost intentions that hauntingly return to us in the commanding silence of the thing that has absorbed them. The self-address comes to us from the other (the thing) in us and by means other than speech, such as the pregnantly silent order. The same silence of the thing is characteristic of the written mark, which, in the deferred interval between its inscription and its decoding, mutely aims at us,[35] but also regulates all repetition in inner speech. As a nonsaying, writing keeps the secret it would be unable to divulge or to narrate, the secret of the thing's independence from the one who speaks, and lets it speak for itself: 'To leave, or to allow, speech [*Laisser la parole*] ... To let it speak all alone [*La laisser parler toute seule*], which it can do only in the written form' (WD 70).[36] Left alone as writing, speech parallels the thing that breathes without me.

Finally, partaking of this secrecy, the idealized phenomenological voice that feigns its own superfluity amid the plentitude of inner discourse speaks without speaking, without being ready to relinquish its hold on silence. To name it 'the voice that keeps the silence,' *la voix qui garde le silence*, as Derrida does in the title of a chapter in *Speech and Phenomena*, is to stress the mechanism by which it preserves and maintains, perhaps even nurtures, the absence of sound in the economy of inner discursivity and, at the same time, endeavours to encompass and neutralize, detain and contain within itself the muteness of the thing.[37]

Its 'saying without saying' that borders on writing is, of course, the crux of the essay on Joyce that constructs a gramophone, or a phono-gram – which is to say, an indeterminate amalgam of speech and writing, voice and line, *phonē* and *grammē*. The interchangeability of dictation and inscription figures the law of the thing in its gramophonical aspect, said or written in the spacing of the mute affirmation that precedes any empirical utterance or inscription. Before and between saying and writing, *res ipsa loquitur*.

Besides Husserl, the other great proponent of the ideality of hearing is Hegel, for whom, according to Derrida, 'if sight is ideal, *hearing is even more so*' (MP 92). Hegel couches the advantage of ideality in terms of the predominance of theory over desire, where the ideal, theoretical sense 'suspends desire, lets things be [*laisse être les choses*], reserves or forbids their consumption' (MP 92/106). But it 'lets things be' only on condition that they are stripped bare to their abstract materiality, translated into a series of vibrations or tremblings (*Erzittern*) inside the ear, and reconciled with the ideal subjectivity to which idealized objects are never *really* antithetical. Faced with this simulation of receptivity to things, Derrida's dual task will be to restore the material substratum of hearing – by re-imagining the thing or the organ of sensory perception we call 'the ear' – and to quit the Hegelian contest of theory and desire, in which the degrees of interiorization vary without affecting the principled, intentional activity of the subject who aims at the thing.

Derrida undertakes and, to some extent, accomplishes the restoration of the thingly substratum of hearing with the help of 1) Nietzsche, for whom the ear is a figure of attunement, receptivity to and discernment of differences, a double 'yes-saying' to the other, and 2) Freud, who reaches the conclusion that it is 'the most tendered and most open organ, the one that ... the infant cannot close' (EO 20, 33). Before empirically saying 'no' to the other, I respond in the affirmative, without audibly uttering anything, simply because my interiority is breached. Through this primordial unhinging of the subject, through the ear that as an infant I cannot shut, things beyond my control intrude. These things aim at me, have me by the ear: 'You open wide the portals [*pavillons*] of your ears ... you transform yourself into a high-fidelity receiver, and the ear ... dictates to you what you are writing' (EO 35).[38] The thingly receptacle, the embodied *khōra*, the concentration of the unconscious in a bodily organ that is a part of the subject she is unable to control early on in life, is what dictates, prescribes, gives a law in accordance with the speech of the other or the silent command of the thing.[39] Yes, yes.

Do I still hear myself speak? On the one hand, in dictation, I receive something from myself as soon as the hand with which I write registers an impulse proceeding from my ear. On the other hand, it is no longer the sound of my own voice that sets the process in motion, but the dictating voice or, perhaps, the dictatorial silence of the other who/ that imparts things to me while keeping its distance and refusing to forge any theoretical and desirous ties with me. I do not hear myself speak. Doubly passive, *I hear myself hear*,[40] or *I hear myself not speak*, as the detached thing attaches me to myself, rivets my ear to another ear (which is also the ear of the other) and to my hand, thus facilitating a practical attitude Heidegger calls 'attunement.'

Putting to one side the inversion of intentionality in hearing, we might observe that the reflexive construction of the subject is, likewise, indebted to the exteriority of the thing in the structure of the address I offer to the other. This thing is precisely the ear of the other 'that signs': 'The ear of the other says me to me and constitutes the *autos* of my auto-biography' (EO 51). The homology between the ear that 'says me to me' and the invisible gaze of the thing that makes us 'feel ourselves seen' is perspicuous enough: both correspond to the detour I am obligated to make through the thing in my relation to myself.[41] But why does this mysterious organ, the overextended ear, take over the signing role of the hand and the vocal function of the mouth? In the apparent Babel of the senses, I entrust to the other the empty intentionality of my discourse, which can hope to reach fulfilment but in her ear. At the end of the temporal delay with which what I say arrives – if it arrives – the event of my signature and of my 'ownmost' self ('*autos*,' homophonous with '*ōtós*,' the Greek word for 'ear') happens in the thing itself, in the ear of the other from which I do not return to myself in a long Hegelian or a brief Husserlian odyssey. I do not hear myself speak. It is the other who finally hears me, and in so doing heteronomously 'says me to me' from the outside. To sum up, not-hearing-oneself-speak permits me to escape the monotonously repetitive noise of inner discoursivity and to lend an attentive ear to the others, to hear the things themselves and to lay the groundwork for a non-solipsistic subject-formation, while hearing-oneself-not-speak elucidates the way in which the new subjectivity is set to work, or practically animated by the alterity of the thing.

And yet the thing that animates the new subjectivity is not only a natural, bodily organ – the ear – but also what Freud calls a 'prosthetic' device, an invented artifice, namely, the telephone that infinitely extends the frontiers of the hearing-heard body.[42] The lines of tele-phony, or 'distant voice,' form an intricate knot in Derrida's texts. In a nutshell, it would be too facile to say that Derrida's early project of deconstructing Western phonocentrism consisted in a simple re-valorization of writing over speech, *graphē* over *phonē*. A more nuanced approach will discover that in so far as it is repeatable, every voice and every spoken utterance already contains that distance or difference from itself which writing unavoidably introduces into it. If *graphē* inflects every *phonē*, then all speech is tele-phonic,[43] distant from itself, owing to the breach that affects it 'from within and from the very beginning' (OG 56–7), forcing it to call for a reaching out and reconnection across the distance.

In addition to equipping Derrida with a paradigm for reading Heidegger's ruminations on conscience and 'the call [*der Ruf*] of care,'[44] the telephone is a thing in which one loses one's voice as a metonymy of intentionality:

> There, I have just hung up in the little red booth, I am in the street, I hold on to your voice [*je garde ta voix*], I don't know where, I am losing myself in it too, such is [*telle est*] … The chance of the telephone – never lose an opportunity – it gives us back our voice certain evenings, at night especially, even more so when … the device blinds us to everything. (PC 10/14)

The receiver that imperceptibly passes into the ear and ever deeper into memory, which holds on to the voice of the other long after the actual communication is over ('I have just hung up … I hold on to your voice'), is the indeterminate place outside the sphere of knowledge ('I don't know where'), the thing that absorbs all vestiges of subjectivity and equates me with 'a certain network of telethings' (PC 38). When one is on a telephone that cannot be hung up since it continues to work before and after the circumscribed vocal interaction with the other, holding on to alterity coincides with losing oneself. This thing disconnects me from myself and gives me a chance to reconnect to myself differently; rebinding us to ourselves with a thingly bond, 'it gives us back our voice.' Once again, the first person plural is not insignificant. Bereft of the hope of regaining my old voice, I am unable to differentiate it either from the voice of the other, which I still keep (*garde*) even though it has been deposited in the same indeterminate locale as my own voice, or from the receptive muteness of the telephone-thing, whose powers of transmission come at the price of altering my voice, for no one sounds the same on the phone. Conversely, the plural subjectivity recovers its voice in a community of the 'I,' the other, and the thing. In the night of phenomenology, when all claims of recognition and identification such as 'such is [*telle est*] ...' (repeating an abbreviated version of the telephone, tele-) cannot be complete and absolute,[45] the thing itself 'blinds us to everything,' incapacitates our intentional acts, aims at us – literally, calls us – and dispenses back to us a reified intentionality, a natural-artificial voice.[46]

Ultimately and in this very voice, it is the thing itself that speaks so that one is unable to make out, to tell, or to hear what it says, what it means or intends to say, and even whether it says anything or is said by something/someone else. An example from *Glas* will illustrate the inaccessibility of thingly intentionality. Whereas the Saussurian 'authentic onomatopoeia' presupposes that, in language and according to 'a very simplified structure of imitation,' certain sounds reproduce particular noises emitted by the things themselves, Derrida questions this authenticity and places under scrutiny the 'original instant' when the onomatopoeic sounds merely imitate these noises before being drawn into the phonetic-etymological evolution of language (G 92–3, right). In the absence of a clear delineation and teleological unfolding of the sonorous sequence extending from the noise of the thing, through the same noise merely reproduced in a word, to the evolved word that bears an indirect relation to the sound of the thing, there is no certainty as to where the thing ends and the word begins in an authentic onomatopoeia, whether it is the word or the thing itself that speaks, and precisely what resonant emission of the thing (for instance, the tolling of a bell) underlies an evolved word such as *glas*.

Better yet, one is structurally unable to hear what the thing says not because of the refined sense of hearing that the sublimated onomatopoeia, the prerogative of a few 'certain ears,' demands of us, but because '*mimesis* no longer allowed itself to be arraigned, to be compelled to give accounts and reasons, to subject itself to a verification of identity within such a frame' (G 93–4, right). In this context, *mimesis* is the imitative relation between the word and the thing, but since the latter exceeds itself and, overflowing its figural outlines, is more than it is, it includes the mimetic relation 'within' itself. This inclusion bestows on mimesis the qualities of the thing that similarly eschews arraignment and 'verification of identity.' Is it a thing or not a thing that sonorously addresses itself to us? Do I hear the noise of a thing or the sound of a

fragment lifted from the non-arbitrary, motivated system of signification? Short of giving a determinate response, my hypothesis is that
these questions stem from the thing itself that contains *différance* and is interchangeable with the athing.

2.2.2. *The imperative for thinking the hand*

The inversion of intentionality would not be complete without the tactile sense of the thing that touches me but cannot be touched, the thing
beyond my reach, foreign to the onto-epistemological grasp that ori-
ents itself toward the value of truth:

> By virtue of this strange verdict, without truth, without veracity, without
> veridicity, one would never again reach the thing itself, one would above
> all never touch it. Wouldn't even touch the veil behind which a thing is
> supposed to be standing, not even the veil before which we sigh together,
> before which we are together sighing … We'll have to give up touching as
> much as seeing and even saying. (V 23–4)

The thing's withdrawal behind a veil renders it unavailable to vision
and clothes it with a kind of inaccessibility that is not provisional, one
that does not leave any space for the theatrical raising of a curtain and
phenomenological revelation of the thing itself in its truth as *aletheia*,
unconcealment. Were the thing to hide behind a veil in a sort of provisional unavailability, its outlines, the contours of its figure would still
be anticipated both visually and in a tactile manner: by examining the
uneven creases of the fabric that retrace the shape of the thing and by
stroking this textile screen interjected between it and my hand. Yet
Derrida is saying, 'one would not even touch the veil'; what is *behind*
will obstinately maintain its distance from us as long as it refuses to be
reduced to an ob-ject, that is, something projected, thrown, or standing
before us in the sense with which Husserl imbues the German *Gegen-
stand*. At the same time, if we recall that one of the incarnations of the
veil in Derrida is his prayer shawl (*tallith*), then what hides behind it is
the body *proper* of the one who wears it: a thing wrapped in a thing.

  Like and as the unique author whom we are reading here, the thing
stays behind the curtain, *derrière le rideau* – which is one of Derrida's
encrypted signatures in *The Postcard* and in *Glas*.[47] Conversely, we – a
certain sad, perhaps mournful and nostalgic, 'sighing' collectivity –
find ourselves before the veil behind which the thing dissimulates

itself. It is this 'we' that becomes the object of the thing in a strange economy of before and behind devoid of a point of contact, the economy that duplicates the lateral-dorsal conflation of Plato and Socrates, speech and writing. Following the investment and animation of a collectivity by the thing, 'we' have no other choice but to 'give up touching as much as seeing,' a practical comportment as much as a theoretical relation to the cause or *chose* of our coming together, which is, perhaps, nothing else than touch itself, 'this common thing termed *"le toucher"* [*cette chose commune qu'on nomme* le *toucher*]' (OT 136/158).

Only at the most superficial level does the retreat of the thing from the hand that intends to touch it resemble the veneration of something sacred, metaphysically 'safe and sound,' something that, keeping itself forever the same, resists all alteration and corruption. In the twentieth century alone, the intellectual itinerary of sacred untouchability passes from Benjamin (the untouchable originality of a text unattainable in translation) through Levinas (the 'holy' metaphysical separation of the other, the inviolability of the virgin, the injunction against murder inscribed on the fragile face of the other) to Nancy, who concerns himself with tact, with the challenge of 'touch without touching [*toucher sans toucher*]': 'In touching, touching is forbidden: do not touch or temper with the thing itself, do not touch on what there is to touch' (OT 66/98). (One will note, parenthetically, that within broader parameters this list would be incomplete without that which remains 'safe and sound' in Heidegger's originary withdrawal of Being and in Freud's a-temporality of the unconscious. For example, in *The Ear of the Other*, 'this untouchable something is the sacred, which says: Don't touch me. Thus, for Heidegger there would also be something untouchable' [p. 115]).

Nancy's tactful respect borders on the Kantian noumenal (and ethical) non-relation to the thing-in-itself replete with the mutual recoil of the tactile organ – the hand – and of that which is not handed over to touch – the thing that in its indifference to all affectations originating from the outside maintains sameness and self-identity. But the Derridian *mode of untouchability* diverges from its Kantian and post-Kantian modalities, in that the thing, in Derrida, eludes the clutches of intentionality when it falls apart, internally alters itself, becomes other to itself. Non-metaphysical untouchability does not stem from the transcendent purity of an enigmatic entity protected from all empirical accidents; it is beholden to nothing but the thing's impurity, the bastard auto-affection or self-remarking routine of a singular-universal supplement. A new figure for the sacred is, thus, the impure.

Indeed, that we have to give up touching does not entail a complete cessation of contact, as it does in the realm of the noumenal, but enfranchises the thing, something in or of the thing, to touch us in a unilateral, asymmetrical fashion. Contemplating a unique thing, a prayer shawl, Derrida asks himself: 'Do you wear this thing? ... Does it not carry off [*emporte*] before being worn [*porteé*]? ... I touch it without knowing what I am doing or asking in so doing, especially not knowing into whose hands I am entrusting myself, to whom I am rendering thanks' (V 44–5). The thing comports itself as though it were a subject who steals away and 'carries off' our intentionality. In the obscurity of not-knowing, my desire to touch the thing itself trustingly abandons me in the hands of something or someone I cannot reach.[48] Here, as in Husserl and Merleau-Ponty, the effect of extending my hand is that it is touched and enveloped by the hands of another, the hands of the other thing, when, for instance, 'my finger feels itself touched by the thing that it touches' (OT 163). Through me, thanks to the mediation of my desire, this thing touches itself, affects itself, remarks itself as the other, and, at the same time, deprived of an identifiable figure,[49] guards its untouchability at the limit of my intentionality.

One shouldn't forget, however, that the hand, which is a privileged organ of touch – and more needs to be said on the subject of this privilege – is neither a thing nor an object:

> Heidegger dit de la main qu'elle est une chose à part ... Il faut penser la main. Mais on ne peut la penser comme une chose, un étant, encore moins comme un objet. La main pense avant d'être pensée, *elle est pensée*, une pensée, la pensée [*Heidegger said of the hand that it is a thing apart ... It is necessary to think the hand. But one cannot think it as a thing, as a being, and even less as an object. The hand thinks before being thought, it is thought, a thinking, the thought*]. (HQ 190–1)

'Geschlecht II: The Hand of Heidegger' demonstrates how the sacralization of the hand, its designation as 'a thing apart,' determines the way it practically humanizes and defines what is unique about the human.[50] Instead of debilitating the subject, the severing of this organ from the rest of the body enables, following the example of an invigorating, empowering castration described in *Glas*.[51] In keeping with the Heideggerian emphasis on praxis, what humanizes is the hand that writes without the assistance of any technical mediations. Despite its 'apartness,' the hand, which is an embodied, extended thing that 'thinks before being thought,' does not form a separate substance (*une substance séparée*) in the manner of Descartes (HQ 191) but aporetically draws together *res cogitans* and *res extensa*.[52] Before human intentionality finds an occasion to aim at and to think this thing, the hand itself stretches toward and moulds consciousness.[53] The activity of a thinking (*une pensée*) that emanates from the hand itself always precedes the passive voice in '*elle est pensée*' by means of which the tactile sensory organ is thought.

How does Derrida himself think the hand? His preliminary comment seems to be simple and innocent enough – there is not one hand, but two – but its consequences are far-reaching. Bi-manualism sets to work the *différance* inherent in manual activity. What one hand makes appear, the other makes disappear; what one writes and inscribes, the other scratches off and ex-scribes.[54] In and of itself, human intentionality is split against itself, or, more precisely, each phenomenological act has, as a minimum, two (sometimes mutually incompatible) objects, *noemata* diverge from *noesis*, and, without any extraneous interference, the directionality of consciousness thwarts itself. The thing vanishes in the unbridgeable distance that geometrical spatiality does not calibrate and that separates *noema* from *noesis*, disconnecting the touching from the touched: 'It is necessary that the space of the material thing – like a difference, like the heterogeneity of a spacing – slip between the touching and the touched, since the two neither must nor can coincide if indeed there is to be a double apprehension' (OT 175).

In its excessiveness, double apprehension fails to seize anything whatsoever. The two hands reach out toward the *noema* (in this case, something touched) and get a hold of the void, that is to say, let the void or 'the space of the material thing' slip between them. When he thus interlaces the spacing between the two hands and the spacing within the thing itself, Derrida intensifies the logic of Husserlian intentionality, which is quite empty prior to its fulfilment in intuition. In Derrida, this emptiness reunites *noema* and *noesis* in a relation of nonfulfilment that could be extended from the thing to what Levinas calls the 'metaphysical desire' for alterity. Not only does the noetic grasp come out literally empty-handed, but it also corresponds, in a perverse sort of correlation, to the space of the material thing, which is not empirical *and* not transcendental, analogous but irreducible to 'difference' and 'heterogeneity.'

The imperative for thinking the hand turns into the aporetic injunction to think the hand*s* (with the hands, if not with Nietzsche's hammer, prior to the origination of conscious thought), along with everything that slips between them. That the dissemination of touch does not reach its limit with the postulation of bi-manualism is attributable to this slippage, as well as to the haptic sensitization of the whole body *proper* that signs for itself even when the hand does not hold a pen, nor intends to reproduce its deliberate signature. But what might appear to be a recovery of Freudian polymorphous perversity, where the infant experiences every region of her body as sexually charged without exception, is, indeed, a reductive re-discovery of that which enables touching, self-touching, affection, auto-affection, namely, a 'quasi-transcendental privilege' of spacing: 'No longer would the general haptology one constructed ... depend on a particular sense named touch ... This would presuppose interruption in general, and a *spacing* from before any distinction between several spaces, between psychical "spreading out" or "spreading into" (*Ausbreitung, Hinbreitung*) and *extensio* of the real [*reell*] thing' (OT 119, 180).

General haptology is the appellation of the thing itself that accommodates the modalities of the 'who' and the 'what,' psychic differentiation and spatial extension. *Le Toucher*, the original French title of *On Touching*, confounds the neat division between these two modalities, in that it means 'to touch him' when '*le*' is taken as a personal pronoun, *or* 'the touch' when '*le*' functions as a definitive article in combination with the noun. Provided that the thing touches and affects itself as other, the basic structure of directing-oneself-toward is always already inverted in the back-and-forth between *le* and *le*, 'him' and 'the.' It is this hetero-affection of auto-affection that yields, finally, untouchable things.

General haptology complements its strategic, deconstructive inversion with a certain genetic fluidity of intentionality 'before any distinction between several spaces,' as well as before any distinction between the spatial and the non-spatial, the extended and the cogitative. To the extent that it merely highlights the spacing constitutive of the various senses, the dissemination of touch in the entire body occurs before the moment of their differentiation. That is why vision freely passes into touch, touch into hearing, and hearing into the detection of a scent.[55]

2.3. Being read: Under the eye of the text

Above and beyond affecting various senses and the very sense of the senses, the inversion of intentionality pertains to other human activities, such as reading. The specular scene of reading is far from uncomplicated:

my gaze travels around, inspects, scans the body of the text that faces me, while the text itself stares back at me, perhaps blindly but, in any event, fixedly.[56] In the hope of deciphering its promise of meaning-making and sense-bestowal, my intentionality directs itself toward this obscure object, this nebulous referent that oversteps its limits, extends into 'general textuality' and ever further into a 'form of reality' no longer opposed to 'fictions.'[57] But the textual literary thing itself a priori delimits without determining my directedness toward it, and a posteriori faces me, returning my regard.

Delegating the authority of the text's intentionality to the signature, Derrida writes: 'In the morning, expecting to recognize familiar things, you find his [the author's] name all over the place, in big letters, small letter, as a whole or in morsels deformed or recomposed. He is no longer there, but you live in his mausoleum, or his latrines. You thought you were deciphering, tracking down, pursuing, you are included' (G 41–2, right). Let us begin to decipher from the last sentence, at the end from which everything begins with the inclusion of the interpreter in the interpreted that a priori inflects the act of interpretation, and in the full awareness that *we, ourselves*, are included. 'You thought you were deciphering ... [but] you are included' scathingly dispels all illusions concerning the cogency of the hermeneutical mission and the readers' transcendent position vis-à-vis the text. The readers dwell in the crypt ('his mausoleum, or his latrines,' containing his – the author's – remains or his waste) of meaning jealously guarded by the text,[58] such that our admission into this secret place of 'making sense' does not break the seal, but traps us in the space left vacant in the wake of the author-thing that/who has withdrawn and is no longer there. His uncanny, signed name alone survives in the place of 'familiar things' or objects we could still anticipate and identify ('expecting to recognize'), tracking down and pursuing their meaning. No longer comfortingly familiar, this withdrawn, Kafkaesque, uncanny thing tracks down, pursues, and aims at its inhabitants from all sides when it includes them in a way that disrupts the calm of the readers' indwelling in the textual domicile. In other words, the 'you' Derrida directly addresses in *Glas* (his reader, any reader of Genet-Hegel, Derrida himself as a reader of Genet-Hegel, and so forth) is something or someone the text makes sense of or detains in the catacombs of meaning. Therefore, any text taken as an object – however ideal or idealized – will remain obscure, illegible and undecipherable, because its objectification will inevitably lose sight of the inversion of intentionality, whereby we become the objects, the objectives, or the targets of the textual things themselves as soon as we commit ourselves to the act of reading.

It is this inversion that renders everything readable not only readable, but also, at the same time, unreadable. What stays secretive and withdrawn is the intentionality of the text itself that concerns or regards me, that is concerned *with* me in so far as it gives itself to be read, opens itself before I literally open a book, or prepares the ground for my approach to it without prescribing the exact manner of receiving it. As Derrida says apropos of Ponge, 'His signature also regards me. Is this possible? [*Sa signature aussi me regarde. Est-ce possible?*]' (SI 22/23). To avoid misunderstanding, it should be noted that what is at stake here is not the intentionality of the author, but that of his signature, of his writing, which alienates and reifies the marks of his idiomatic style and transmutes them into things even before they first pour onto a page. Neither Derrida nor Ponge himself regards me from the other side of directedness-toward. But their signatures aim at me in an asymmetrical fashion, so that I would be incapable of deciphering them and of disentangling the knot of the 'who' and the 'what' tied in them.

If the subjects of the regard are the signatures, whether they are 'whole or in morsels deformed or recomposed,' then I am targeted from the beginning to the end (as well as before the beginning and after the end) by language and by its proper elements, the letters of the signatures that disassemble and reassemble into other words. In their texts, the names 'Derrida' and 'Ponge' entrust themselves to language, to the chance of the textual production they undersign, which, like the door in Kafka's 'Before the Law,' is left ajar without giving any guarantees that the reader will ever cross the threshold.

But the letters of the reconfigured signatures are only the smallest units that regard us, for the same operation is performed by the sentence and the text:

Older than consciousness, older than the spectator, prior to any attendance a sentence awaits 'you' [*une phrase 'vous' attendait*]: looks at you, observes you, watches over you, and regards you from every side [*vous regarde, vous observe, veille sur vous, vous concerne de toute part*]. There is always a sentence that has already been sealed somewhere waiting for you … The text occupies the place before 'me'; it regards me, invests me, announces me to myself, keeps watch over the complicity I entertain with my most secret present, surveys my heart's core. (D 340–1/3789)

This sentence and this text allude to Kafka's door, intended for a singular and unique subject of the law. They do not invite a reader in general – any reader whatsoever – to approach, but aim at the singular 'you' that does not pre-exist them as such. What does this mean? First, in an analogy to the ear of the other that 'says me to me,' the textual thing that regards me constitutes my very subjectivity and interiority ('announces me to myself,' 'surveys my heart's core'). The thingly mediation in my relation to myself is unsurpassable. Second, 'older than consciousness,' the text exhibits the structure of intentionality before intentionality, the irreducible mode of conscious comportment that precedes my own consciousness as much as the consciousness of a transcendental subject. Which is to say: it presages the consciousness of writers and readers alike, who assemble in the passive bond uniting those who are written and those who are read by the text. The names of the authors are disseminated, alienated, and reified, not to mention the innumerable signatures of the 'cited sources' that continuously invest and undersign them. On the other side of the bond, the activity of the readers is subverted by the tireless vigilance of the text that regards them. Thus, in the economy of this passage, the textual thing has immemorially usurped the place of intra- and intersubjectivity, the prerogative of our writing and reading ourselves and others. It is more interior and subjective than any subject, but it, nonetheless, remains a thing.

In the section of *Dissemination* titled 'The Trigger' ('*Le Déclenchement*'), in the process of reading Sollers's *Numbers*, Derrida, once again, links the text with 'things':

> The text is remarkable in that the reader (here in exemplary fashion) can never choose his own place in it, nor can the spectator ... Because his job is to put things on stage, he is on stage himself, he puts himself on stage. The tale is thereby addressed to the reader's body, which is put by things on stage, itself [*Le récit dès lors s'addresse au corps du lecteur qui est mis par les choses en scène, elle-même*]. (D 291/322)

The inversion of intentionality crystallizes in the moment when, instead of controlling and arranging textual things, the reader is acted upon by them, 'put by things on stage.' The staged things include the text and the reader's body, a peculiar *res extensa* that invites '*le déclenchement*,' which, as the epigraph from Littré makes clear, signifies both a certain openness, unclenching, release and the engagement of a

weapon in the moment of aiming at a target. Indeed, the two significations go hand in hand where the non-prescriptive openness of the text
targets me so that, under its regard, subjected to its gaze and care, my
embodied consciousness would take form. The spectator is a part of
the spectacle but – we should not miss the nuance of this specularity –
the textual thing does not observe the reader from the outside, for its
'reified' regard radiates from within, from the deepest interiority of the
subject's 'most secret present.' It aims right at the heart, from within
the very heart it animates, whose beating it controls. If such a thing
were possible, the specularity of the thing is devoid of distance (in the
empirical sense of the term), because it circulates entirely in the spacing of difference that only anticipates measurable space. Hence, the illusion of the unmediated interchangeability between the spectator and
the thing on stage: the pure speed of the inversion that does not 'cover'
any distance between the two modalities of the same thing.

This interchangeability, whose technical name is 'a fold,' taints the
pure present of the act of reading: 'You: reading, seeing, speaking.
Numbers, reading you, seeing you, speaking to you in the process [*en
train*] of reading, seeing, speaking; "in the process" here meaning "at
the moment in which presently [*au moment où présentement*]" you read,
see, speak, etc.' (D 307/341). If the book reads us, looks at us and addresses itself to us in the 'present moment' when we read it, then this
very moment is a site for the non-intersection of two asymmetrical intentionalities and, therefore, the non-present or the no-longer-present
in the present. The inversion of intentionality is its internal perversion,
a violation of the phenomenological 'principle of principles' (the *archē*
of the 'living present') according to which the thing appears before the
faculty of intuition in flesh and blood.[59] What does not appear, what
does not give itself fully is the thing's (the book's) own intentionality,
which folds or remarks that of the subject, introducing spaced repetition into the pure present.[60]

Such will have been the breaking point between the quasi-transcendental a priori of the thing's directedness toward us and its a posteriori reflection of our own regard, since the fold is, at the same time, the
break, *la brisure*, the hinge that both articulates and disarticulates two
terms. The bookish thing returns our gaze, but the 'mirror in which
these *Numbers* are read, in its capacity for seeing you, will of course be
broken, but it will reflect that breaking in a fiction that remains intact
and uninterrupted [*Le miroir, tel qu'il vous verra, où se lisent les* Nom-
bres, *sera certes brisé mais il réfléchira la brisure dans une fiction intacte et*

ininterrompue]' (295/327). In other words, the thing's intentionality is not anthropomorphic, given that it does not a posteriori mime the activity of human consciousness. The metaphor of the broken mirror contributes to the sense of inadequation and divergence between the two parts of the fold, between the two intentionalities that neither parallel nor intersect with each other. The secret of this mirror, which stands for our intentionality so uncannily 'returning' to us from the thing, is that it works adequately and expresses the break only when it offers the image of inadequation. There is no speculative identity between the reflected and the reflecting, just as there is no meta-intentionality of which the conscious and thingly intentionalities would partake as *noema* and *noesis*, respectively. Rather, the two asymmetrical terms initiate an abyssal back-and-forth of reality and fiction characteristic of the event of the thing; where a work of fiction (*Numbers*) intimates the *reality* of the fracture in the thing itself, this reality produces nothing but the *fiction* of its own intactness and continuity, as though domesticating the rupture between the reflected and the reflecting.

Reflection, mimesis, imitation: if one rehearses the lesson of *Dissemination*, one will recall that these 'reproductions' are not the lesser, derivative forms of the original production of meaning and sense. In themselves, they are generative – which implies that the a posteriori return of our regard in the intentionality of the thing crafts and moulds human consciousness 'in the first place.' Engaging with the poetry of Edmond Jabès in 1964, Derrida records the engendering of the poet by the poetic thing he calls forth into being, or in-vents: 'In question is a labor, a deliverance, a slow gestation [*génération*] of the poet by the poem whose father he is' (WD 65/100).[61] Within the circularity of engendering and generation, which is an effect of the 'fiction that remains intact and uninterrupted,' as well as in the logic of performativity in general, the categories of a priori and a posteriori no longer make sense.[62] The reflected regard of the thing is not passive (but also not purely active), because it both precedes and succeeds the split between theory and praxis, the eye and the hand.

Performatively, the textual poetic thing gives birth to its progenitor, all the while observing and remarking its own production. For instance, 'Francis [Ponge] sticks ... to the thing that regards him as he acts [*tient ... à la chose qui le regarde faire*] even as it always says no, start over again' (SI 68/9). A figure for desire itself, the critical regard of the textual thing is never satisfied with the action of the subject who brings it forth. This other gaze, this other intentionality with its unwavering verdict 'it's not enough,' attends to and impels the activity of the poet, who, in his turn, 'sticks' and commits to the thing, binds himself and holds onto it, takes its side. It reads him even as he desperately strives to make it readable, to tear it away from unreadability, to solve the mystery of its intentionality, and to overcome the invisibility of its *act* of gazing. But none of this is ever enough.

3 Deconstruction of Fetishism:
The Love and the Work of the Thing

As a name or thing, would the sponge-towel form a sort of fetish (of the commodity or the penis) which one could then interpret according to a conventional reading of Marx or Freud?

Signsponge

Il faut *laisser* les choses se faire (il ne *faut* même pas, *ça laisse* de toute façon), et la scène se déployer toute seule; c'est très vieux mais cela ne fait aussi que commencer, voilà à quoi j'essaie de me résoudre.

La Carte postale

3.1. For the love of the thing: Derrida's psychoanalysis

My subject will be Derrida's psychoanalysis: the one he is attached to, the one he resists, the one he loves, the one he loves to resist and resists to love, the one he deconstructs. And the subject, the navel, the undeconstructable of Derrida's psychoanalysis (the event that has never taken place as such and thus deserves the title of the 'event') is the thing. A kind of shorthand reasoning would refer to the state or the status of the Derridian thing as something always already deconstructed, or more precisely, as the undeconstructable remainder of the ideal object, which fails to be integrated within the idealist framework. Debris of (*débris de*) and remain(s) (*reste*) that are deposited both at the very beginning and at the very end of *Glas* guard and modify, preserve by way of altering, the trace of self-consuming remains with which deconstruction falls in love. But this trace attracts a strictly objectless love in both senses of the word 'objectless.' First, even if its playing field is confined to the ruins and fragments of idealizing repetitions, the love of the thing does not transfigure that which it loves into an object that, as such, would be prone to the machinations of consciousness. Here, love and resistance to love are one and the same, in so far as one's passion for the thing resists the objected and objectifying approach to the beloved. At this point, the second meaning of 'objectless' is well within our purview. The love of the thing is purposeless to the extent that it rejects the structure of intentionality, whereby consciousness inherently directs itself toward noematic objects. A listless, detached attachment, it deprives itself of a destination and hence of a derivation from a unitary, originary source. The only option left at its disposal – obsessively wandering among the ruins – is not an end in itself, nor does it accomplish any externally posited goal. *As an activity*, it is wholly superfluous.

3.1.1. Who/what is analysed in psychoanalysis?

If the subject of Derrida's psychoanalysis is the thing – which is, strictly speaking, not a subject – and if the love aspiring to a thing is devoid of an intended object, then a question arises: Who or what is analysed in psychoanalysis? Or, in slightly different terms: When it comes to psychoanalysis, what is analysed in whom and who is analysed in what? To broach the question, we ought to recall that the opposition between the 'who' and the 'what' has been shaken, first, in the indeterminacy of the receptive *khōra*, and second, in the thing itself that has supplanted this Platonic palaeonymy. The next step will require grafting the psychic and psychoanalytic categories onto such thingly indeterminacy.

In psychoanalytic terms, the event of the thing is psyche itself and, especially, the unconscious conceived as an extension that 'has no measure in common with anything, and above all with any other extension.' 'This incommensurability,' Derrida goes on to say, 'passes through a thinking of *place*, as a place or locus that is reducible neither to objective extension, nor to objective space. This place must be *spacing* before it is space' (OT 24). The unconscious spacing cannot be subsumed exclusively under the heading of 'who' or of 'what,' since it represents the improbable intersection between *res cogitans* and *res extensa*, not to be confused with the Spinozan postulation of monistic substance.[1] In spite of the limitations that plague spatial metaphors of extension, 'psyche' is a hinge that articulates the extended/nonextended psychic thing, and that signifies both the name of a thing, and the name of a person, namely, the mythical character Psyche.[2]

From Aristotle to Husserl, this character has been identified with the principle of animation and pure life. But, Derrida observes, Nancy's Psyche, who 'sees herself treated as a dead woman' and gives birth to the very onlookers gathered around her – those who know that she does not know (it) – epitomizes a crucial exception to this monolithic philosophical tradition (OT 19).[3] The event of the psychic thing, the event of the unconscious (could there be any other, worthy of the name?), is that the ego is a spectre born of a dead woman, or of something or someone treated as such by her own progeny on the borderline between the living fecundity of generation and the peculiar fecundity of death.

The myth of Psyche, in Derrida's vernacular, is the embodied, ensouled, almost inspired myth of the metaphysics of presence portraying a non-constituted, originary psychic unity. In other words, it is the myth of the myth that posits her corporeal extension as absolute by depicting Psyche in the atomic simplicity of something utterly undifferentiated and fully present to others. Not surprisingly, in debunking this myth, one of the objectives of deconstruction is 'to analyze tirelessly the resistance that still clings to the thematic of the simple and the indivisible origin' (RP 35), such that the mere formality of the analytical approach would break through the simple, non-constituted indivisibility that is a *meta-symptom of resistance to analysis*. That is not to say, however, that other kinds of resistance to the purported psychic indivisibility would invariably call for analysis and impose its methodology on deconstruction.[4] For instance, the undecidability of the thing vacillating between the 'who' and the 'what' cannot be resolved by means of a clear-cut analytic delineation of its subjective and objective, inspiring and expired 'regions.'

The belief in psychic undifferentiation puts to work the entire metaphysical machinery of trace reduction,[5] whereas 'deconstruction of presence accomplishes itself through the deconstruction of consciousness, and therefore through the irreducible notion of the trace (*Spur*), as it appears in both Nietzschean and Freudian discourse' (OG 70). Resisting symptomatic, metaphysical resistance, deconstruction asks, not without a measure of sarcasm: But by what means should we analyse a non-synthetic unity? What is psycho-analysis, if the metaphysical thing 'psyche' is defined by the inherent impossibility of analysis? Does this entanglement motivate the occasional catachrestic operationalization of psychoanalysis as the analytic of things mediated by the discourse on psychic objects?

It follows that there must be a trace of differentiation in order for us to speak meaningfully of the psyche and in its proximity. Such a trace will be unlike any other, since the insertion of the dramatis persona and the thing Psyche in its place – in the place without place of the archi-trace – will fashion the caesura for memory, or the archival network for the inscription of traces:

> Freud made possible the idea of an archive properly speaking, of a hypomnesic or technical archive, of the substrate or subjectile (material or virtual) which, in what is already a psychic *spacing*, cannot be reduced to memory ... [This] trace no longer distinguishes itself from its substrate [*La trace ne se distinguerait plus de son support*]. (AF 91–2, 99/152)

The extension and extensibility of the psychic thing that is not coextensive with any other extension imposes on us the exigency to winnow spacing from space, and timing from time. First, in a proto-structure of the archi-trace (in a word, *différance*), psychic spacing gives room to archival space without claiming a proper place of its own. In terms that are both more formal and more political, the unconscious imposes its 'spaced divisibility [*la divisibilité espacée*],' 'hierarchized multiplicity,' and 'conflict of forces' on sovereign identity (R 54). But the spaced, quantitative, 'written' results of this imposition ought to be rigorously separated from the spacing, writing quality of the psychic thing that effaces itself from its own effects as soon as they are produced. Along with the thing that 'contains' it, *différance* names this rigorous separation when it touches, without bridging, both shores (the 'who' and the 'what') of the psychic event before it takes place in a determinate Freudian topography.

Why, then, does the extended psychic thing resemble a trace that 'no longer distinguishes itself from the substrate'? The unity of the substrate and the trace[6] materializes the psychic thing as the self-imprinted imprinting, the immanently divisible field haunted from the beginning by the possibility of fission (AF 100). The writings or the creases that emerge in the substratum are not inflicted on it from the outside, but evolve from the thing itself, which 'already remarks itself [*La chose se remarque déjà elle-même*]' (SI 6/7) as a 'container' of *différance.*[7] And yet to remark itself, the thing must become other to itself; technically, it must endure a separation-from-(it)self as the precondition for being-bound-to-(it)self.

Second, the operations of the archi-trace are immemorial. They are 'hypomnesic,' 'cannot be reduced to memory,' and therefore are not of the same order as the temporal memory-trace. Rather, they mark the temporalizing instants when the psychic substrate (still imagined or imaged topographically) divides itself into the furrows and creases that anticipate the activity of consciousness, and perhaps welcomes such activity in the space opened up by the seismic schisms where memories will inscribe themselves. At the same time, however, one should not conceive of the immanence of these furrows as something 'natural': the hypomnesic moment governing recollection is that of originary technicity, which characterizes the archive as well as writing itself.

In brief, the psychic thing is bound to itself as other to the extent that it unties itself from the spatiality it makes possible by immemorially dividing, imprinting, writing itself in the material substrate.[8] Consequently, the logic of analysis applicable to the psyche will aim to accomplish none of the tasks usually associated with the analytic exercise, that is, to untie or resolve the self-binding, self-remarked knot of the traumatic or traumatizing thing. Quite the opposite is true: it repeats and re-binds (with ineluctable differences) the psychic architrace modelled on writing that obeys the desire to retrace, up to a certain limit, the disquietude of archi-writing as the 'thing that can never be recognized as the *object*' (OG 57). Precisely as unrecognized and unrecognizable, the thing is a having-been-there in the mode of the trace targeted by subjective synthesis and its analytic corollary, which venture to erase *and* retrace it, as though for the first time.

The limit of the analytic procedure lies beyond our capacities of recognition, which only encounters objects and subjects, and never handles things:

> We do not know *what* is bound [ce qui *est ainsi lié*], unbound, banded together, contra-banded, disbanded. We know nothing of the nature of the excitatory process in the psychic system … Obviously it is in the place of this *thing X* [*à la place de cette* chose X] that the '*Vorbilder*,' the images, the models, the prototypes, and the paradigms, from whatever field they come try themselves out. (PC 349/370–1)

The differential quantities of psychic force do not determine its quality, do not shed light on the 'whence' and the 'whither' of the play of analysis-synthesis. However interminable, analysis halts in 'the place of this *thing X*' that stands on the threshold of the noumenal, where its unbinding or disbanding is interchangeable with the banding-together of synthesis.

Keeping in mind the genetic limitations of analysis, let us return to this section's guiding question, Who or what is analysed in psycho-analysis? In the matrix of *Glas*, where the twists and turns of Hegelian dialectics test the ligature of the thing, if 'desire is related to a living thing, thus to something that relates (itself),' then the 'dead thing ... it-self does not oppose itself, does not of itself enter into relation. The dead thing is in the relation without, itself, relating to [*dans le rapport sans, elle-même, se rapporter-à*]' (G 120/137, left). The border between life and death passes inside the thing[9] that relates and doesn't relate to itself. It is, therefore, not an accident that Derrida's rendition of the extended psychic thing spans the poles of both life and death, self-binding and detached absolution, a relation and a non-relation to one-self (or to itself). To relate to the unconscious one cannot avoid em-barking on the painstaking detour of non-relationality, a patient approach to resistance, an analysis mediated and interrupted by the self-binding of the trace.

From *Speech and Phenomena* to *On Touching*, Derrida has attended to the unavoidable contamination of pure living, auto-affection and rela-tionality with death, hetero-affection and the non-relational. In the psychoanalytic vein, *The Postcard* channels these motifs toward the task of rebinding (*relier*) 'precisely by means of the analysis of the notions of binding, *nexum*, *desmos* or stricture, the question of *life death* [la vie la mort] to the question of position' in the 'auto-bio-hetero-thanato-graphic' mode of writing (PC 259, 336). The latter economic notation stands for the event of *res cogitans extensa* – the extended psy-chic thing – along with its 'offspring,' the ego, which spectrally issues from a dead woman. But it also ties analysis, division, decomposition to what is most living in life itself, posited and de-posited in the inces-sant movement of repetition (of which the analytic situation or *position* is but a privileged example) that, in the spiral of survival, perpetuates the living of a life marked with death.

The time of survival is the thingly survival of time itself: 'It is neces-sary to give oneself time. Time's remain(s) [*Il faut se donner le temps. Le reste du temps*]' (G 226/252, left). In the aftermath of Heideggerian ex-traction of pure auto-affection of time from Kant's First *Critique*[10] and Levinasian derivation of time as pure hetero-affection from the en-counter with the other,[11] Derrida contextualizes temporality in the process of temporalization. Temporalizing *différance* is equally in-debted to Heidegger and to Levinas, whose conceptualizations it non-synthetically weaves into the hetero-affection *of* auto-affection, the time of the other in the same who gives it to himself, different and deferred, deferring and differing. In their turn, 'time's remain(s)' are the effects of *différance* that lag behind the reception of the temporalizing gift from oneself as other. They gesture toward the non-present, non-representable memory reserved for the future, the timing of the unconscious left over after the self-division of the psychic substrate into a temporal, archival thing. The fate of *différance*, where it denotes a certain tension between (or even a certain drive toward) the same and the other, time and timing, the present and the futural past, and so on is thus firmly anchored in the fate of the thing.

This tension will announce an event only when the thing, released from its ligature to the subject, begins to breathe without me.[12] After me, 'without me,' without the *différance* of my death measuring and measuring up against my life, there will be the thing entrusted with time. Already Hegel's 'living thing,' related to itself and targeted by desire, is no longer simply opposed to pneuma, anima, or spirit. But, significantly enough, for Derrida, the thing begins to re-spire, to breathe again as soon as I dissolve my living bond with it and, delimiting and effacing myself, give way to something like non-subjective, non-representable memory. This recommencement constitutes the affirmative end that the interminable work of mourning and psychoanalysis itself keep in sight.

Yet even the affirmative end discontinuously projecting a new beginning is not immune to analysis and, in particular, to the speculative weighing of psychic investments and returns. For example, in a late interview that, glancing back at *Signsponge*, revolves around the deconstruction of Ponge, Derrida links the gesture of signing the abbreviated version of his own name – Derrida Jacques, déjà, 'already' – with the affirmation of the mourned thing: 'Signer, c'est affirmer de façon fière, et triomphante, quelque chose dont on fait déjà son deuil [*To sign is to affirm, in a proud and triumphant fashion, some thing for which one is already mourning*]' (DP 54). What is or should be interrogated here is the trajectory of the subject's transcendence, which feeds on the newly regained freedom of the thing: Does this trajectory increase the chances for a more assured survival that the subject gains at the expense of a calculated pretence of losing herself in the thing to which her *absence* firmly attaches itself (through which it is remembered)? Is this 'loss' forever deferred in the negative structure of 'without,' which refuses to accommodate a more radical 'without *with*,' the non-relationality of relationality formulated as an injunction in *The Truth in Painting*, 'Write, if possible, finally, without *with*, not *without* but without *with*, finally, *not even oneself'* (TP 17)? Would consciousness abandon or strengthen its position supported by the metaphysics of presence if it were to admit to the fact of its birth from the hetero-affection of an extended psychic thing? In other words, are we confronted with the logic of auto-immunization, according to which 'a living being can destroy, in an autonomous fashion, the very thing within it that is supposed to protect it against the other' (R 123), or with an auto-immunizing trick that affects the same with a diluted version of the other, absence, and death so as to prevent itself from being surprised by their unannounced apparition?

3.1.2. *Psychoanalysis and resistance – of the (non-idealized) mother*

Doubling negativity without yielding negation of the negation, without dissolving in a higher synthesis, the question of resistance everywhere foreshadows the question of analysis, since 'the constitutive idea of psychoanalysis' is 'analysis of resistances' (RP 22). But the genitive form in 'the resistances of psychoanalysis' is not univocal. Aside from the resistances that psychoanalytic discourse thematizes and that Derrida's 1996 essay knots together, we must consider what psychoanalysis itself resists. Of course, the two senses of the genitive are not unrelated to each other; as a matter of fact, they are closely allied, bound together, even contra-banded – as Derrida would say –, across provisional limits and borders. Schematically, then, 1) what resists psychoanalysis immanently yet absolutely (i.e., with the force that defies analysis) is the psychic thing in its thingly or material element, and 2) psychoanalysis interpolates itself into the position of a thing in so far as it resists the idealized and idealizing pursuits of the psyche.

We have already spotted structural resistance in the *thing X*, whose 'whatness' eschews all analytic attitudes and conscious manipulations. Differently put, this resistance announces itself in the phrase 'The thing itself already remarks itself.' For our purposes, this means that the psychic trace that repeatedly retraces itself (as other) may not coincide with the procedures of retracing and recapturing it, by which psychoanalysis abides. As Derrida reiterates in *The Postcard* and in *Resistances*, such impasses as the non-coincidence of the two asymmetrical sets of marks or traces need not be paralysing, for they effectively convoke the differential of forces between psychoanalysis, with its strategies of counter-resistance on the one hand, and psychic-material resistance on the other.

The trace whose impression is inseparable from the gullies of the substrate itself, the archi-writing of the thing Psyche, the psychic temporalizing spacing in which memory takes place – these are the synonyms for the singular event concentrated in the image of the navel,[13] the navel-thing connected to the unknown, 'the knot-scar that keeps the memory of a cut.' Freud cannot do anything else but attempt to 'suture or sew the thing up [*bien suturer ou coudre la chose*]' (RP 11/24), in other words, to mime synthesis, *analytically recognizing the impotence of analysis* there where the deepening of the incision translates into a further growth of the obfuscating scar tissue and the entanglement of the knot. It is from this analytic predicament (which Heidegger might have included under the heading of *Ent-fernung*, de-severance) that deconstruction learns at once to analyse and to resist analysis, problematizing 'the possibility of recapturing the originary' synthesis and the very 'desire to do so' (RP 27).

The navel-thing is the trace of birth and, hence, of the mother, of the originary and irrecoverable attachment and separation. It would have been easy to dilute this trace in the singularity of the event of birth, had not another scar tissue reasserted itself in Derrida's oeuvre, which, to be sure, does not explicitly set up a correlation between the two. Circumcision carves out another memory of the cut, both unique and iterative of the umbilical detachment, in the way it repeats the circularity of the first scar. Between the two births, the two incisions, the two scars – the event of the thing. Admittedly, circumcision modifies the extension of the body *proper*, but, more remarkably, it provides the spacing whose circumference may contain psychic life and, above all, the tortuous turns and returns of memory permitting me 'to re-member myself around a single event [*pour me remembrer autour d'un seul événement*]' (CI 59/58). But – nota bene – this is a single event split into two and, therefore, disseminated into an infinity of virtual iterations that transpire between its instantiations.

The thing itself remarks itself as other, but the phenomenal (if not the phenomenological) vulgarity of circumcision is that it seeks to present and represent the self-remarked itinerary of the thing *as such*, tangibly, in flesh and blood. Circumcision is that 'which comes back to me without ever having taken place [*qui se rappelle à moi sans avoir eu lieu*]' (CI 14/16) precisely because this spacing thing, which gives place without taking it, serves as a condition of possibility for spatiality, festering in a boundless wound that pre-exists all synthetic and analytic activities. The call or the recall – *rappelle* – it addresses to consciousness triggers the impossible memory of the thing's self-remarking, for which we are invariably, until the time of our death, only eight days old.

What is the role of the mother and of the one (or that which), elsewhere, Derrida names 'the living feminine' (EO 16ff) between the two events of the same birth? Who or what will stand between Aristotle's purely living but impassive Psyche and Nancy's Psyche, who 'sees herself treated as a dead woman'? And what would she resist?

The non-idealized mother is not 'a mother' but 'the mother,' or better still, 'the mother of ...,' with all the risks and complications brewing in the possessive form. Let us amass these ostensibly unrelated concrete figures of the mother, who reappears across Derrida's writings. First, the Oedipal mother of Freud, or rather of the Freuds – of Ernst and Sigmund, the one and the other, the one as the other. Commenting on *Beyond the Pleasure Principle*, Derrida observes that in the course of analysing the *fort/da* play of his grandson, Sigmund, 'it will be said, recalls himself.' He continues: 'He recalls to himself that Ernst recalls (to himself) his mother: he recalls Sophie. He recalls to himself that Ernst recalls his daughter to himself in recalling his mother to himself [*Il se rappelle que Ernst se rappelle sa fille en se rappelant sa mère*]' (PC 323/344). The threads/sons (*fils*)[14] entwine with one another, as well as around the figure of the mother, such that no analysis will manage to cut them loose. Only the act of pulling the strings, as one does in the process of playing with a spool or with marionettes, might make them dance.

Furthermore, in this family drama, the mother is identified with a particular thing: the spool that Ernst, of his own accord, makes appear and disappear, as though cutting and re-suturing the umbilical cord: 'Ernst, in recalling the object (mother, thing, whatever) to himself, immediately comes *himself* to recall *himself*' (PC 320). Subsequent to the initial fetishistic send-off of the thing, the subjectivity of Ernst is constructed around the thing's successive gathering, dispersion, and calculated displacement. What determines this immediate recall of oneself on the part of the Freuds, Sigmund and Ernst, when it comes to the mother-thing? Isn't the immediacy of the recall a sign that the thing is not authorized to breathe on its own, 'without me'? Or – vice versa – can the psyche itself breathe and animate anything without recalling itself in proximity to the thing? Doesn't the purported play make the thing work incessantly, here, there, and everywhere in-between, animating *anima* itself?

The work of the mother-thing boils down to a sort of hyperbolic, repetitive, and, I would suggest, overworked and overinvested act of giving birth. Sophie bears her son *and* her father, gives birth even prior to being born. The matter is complicated by the fact that the scene 're-calls that Sophie is dead' – like Psyche, who gives birth beyond the door sill of her death – and enacts a compensation for the 'irreparable wound *as* a narcissistic injury' (PC 324, 329). Before any wilful send-off and return in which birth, love, and death playfully move with the ma-nipulated rhythm of kaleidoscopic psychic shards making up the sub-ject, there is the immemorial and irreversible departure of the uncontrollable thing itself (the moment of injury, circumcision, death), with which repetition compulsion desires to come to terms. The anach-rony of circumcision's 'irreparable wound' before the playful repeti-tion of birth(s) is, thus, the effect of the mother of Freud.

Second, the mother of Christ, who, in the wake of the Virgin Birth, is the mother without being a mother, the thing without a thing. Interro-gating the notion of absence in the Hegelian reading of the Holy Fam-ily, Derrida writes: 'Who can be *absent* within it [the Holy Family], and what does *absent* mean in this case? Is the father absent? Is the mother? Since Joseph is absent and Mary a virgin, the son is the son of the Fa-ther' (G 97, left). This vanishing trace of the maternal is reminiscent of Sarah's non-presence in the process of Isaac's circumcision and/or sac-rifice, but, above all, it governs, adumbrates, and modalizes everything that still falls under the rubric of 'presentism' when it comes to the earthly familial trinity. Across the Hegel-Genet columns in *Glas*, the withdrawal of the mother (the erasure of the navel-trace) portends the bifurcated yet hyphenated construction of Judaeo-Christianity.

On the one hand, the Judaic son will claim that he has given birth to himself, citing not the virginity of the mother but the possibility of re-birth announced by his circumcision, which he imagines as an absolu-tion and a drifting away from the 'natural' order of love toward the transcendence of the law (G 42, left and right). This side of the event may be properly called 'fetishistic,' because it projects and transplants the myth of the detached and self-sufficient thing into the sphere of 'autonomous' consciousness. On the other hand, the Christian son will reaffirm the principle of love in the newly regained plentitude ('this de-bordering fulfillment of synthesis') that exchanges castration ('the very principle of exchange') for the singular and non-exchangeable, thereby allowing Christ, at the same time, to suspend and aggravate this principle (G 58–9, left). As a consequence, the bifurcated construc-tion of Judaeo-Christianity stands for the son's circumcision and the circumcision of circumcision (for the literal and the figurative event inscribed on the foreskin and in the heart) that transpires after his birth without birth.

'Remain(s) – the mother [*Reste – la mère*]' (G 115/132, right): in this quasi-sentence the qualities of her thingliness and resistance intersect. The virgin mother persists outside all regimes: outside that of castration, whose paradigm case 'a mother' has always been, notwithstanding her temporary capacity to fill the void with the child, *and* outside that of the self-engendering plentitude that finally liberates her from the work of procreation, sets her aside – and therefore consecrates her – excusing the father 'from passing essentially through the mother, consequently engendering the son all by himself, self-inseminating himself' (G 104, left). Set aside (*fort*), the mother is detached, a relation with her is broken off, but, in the same instance, she is deified, fetishized (*da*), converted into a non-relational relation that defines the thing. Her superfluity resists analysis. Although she is no longer incessantly put to work, nor forced to go into labour with every repetitive send-off and return of the spool, the *empty form* of the throwing gesture is retained. Mother here, virgin there. This empty pendular form that saturates *Glas* to exhaustion is embodied in the image of the natural-artificial flowers[15] that depict love and law, the one sublated into the other and resulting in the law of love and the love of the law. Like the absent mother, these flowers are taken away *and* ritually offered; they are cut with the formality of what *The Truth in Painting* calls 'the *sans* of the pure cut,' bleeding[16] at the edges of the clipped stem and the hollowed maternal form.

Third, Rousseau's mother qua a supplementary replacement of the mother, a generalized substitution of the unique and, thus, a defetishized – self-deconstructed – fetish:

> Jean-Jacques could thus look for a supplement to Thérèse only on one condition: that the system of supplementarity in general be already open in its possibility ... and that *in a certain way Thérèse herself be already a supplement*. As Mamma was already the supplement of an unknown mother, and as the 'true mother' herself, at whom the known 'psychoanalyses' of the case of Jean-Jacques Rousseau stop, was also in a certain way a supplement, from the first trace, and even if she had not 'truly' died in giving birth. (OG 156)

The Derridian supplement, it will be recalled, not only adds to and replaces but also comes before what it supplements. The fetish is the

supplement of the thing that precedes the thing, or 'originarily' substitutes for its loss and withdrawal. Within the logic of generalized fetishism, that amounts to saying that the thing itself is its own substitute. It
is, nonetheless, insufficient to associate, as Spivak does, the mother
with the fetish and the father with the thing itself.[17] An additional step
awaiting us at the intersection of *Glas* and *Of Grammatology* is the su-
perimposition of the fetish/thing interplay onto the category of moth-
erhood itself. The so-called biological mother is already a supplement,
and it is this initial fetishization of the thing that authorizes the further
chain of supplementations, identifications, and slippages between the
mother, Mamma, and Thérèse in Derrida's reading of Rousseau.

The power of the supplement would have been nil, did it not replace
the irreplaceable in the manner of the thing itself, or generalize the
unique, 'for example and *par excellence* the mother, where there are
grounds to supplement the non-supplementable [*là où il y a lieu de sup-
pléer l'insuppléable*]' (MO 88/105).[18] I call Rousseau's mother (indeed,
all his mothers) 'a de-fetishized fetish' because she (or they, the 'they,'
das Man in her) internalizes, impregnates herself with, and thereby levels and neutralizes the fetish/thing distinction. All she retains from fetishism is the framework of substitution rid of the 'external' reference
to the present thing itself. Generalizing and projecting this framework,
resisting and deferring the presentation of 'the true mother,' the surro-
gate mothers of Rousseau infinitely give birth to themselves as others
as long as the chain of supplementations winds on, as long as, in the famous formulation of *Speech and Phenomena*, 'the thing itself always escapes.' In a self-proliferating fashion, they express the thing that
remarks itself as other, the thing that defers itself in 'the mirage of the
thing itself, of immediate presence, of originary perception [*le mirage de
la chose même, de la présence immédiate, de la perception originaire*]' (OG
157/226). This is the necessary (not the empirical) reason why 'the
known "psychoanalyses" of the case of Jean-Jacques Rousseau stop' at
his 'true mother,' analogous to the thing itself.

The Rousseauian substitution of mothers inverts, in an almost symmetrical fashion, the Freudian substitution of sons. Whereas the Freudian threads or sons (*fils*) found themselves inextricably entwined, in
Rousseau it is the very medium, the matrix of weaving,[19] that resists
analysis with its irresolvable entanglements that tie the maternal knot of
a fetish without fetishism, that is, without the enforced distinction between the fetish and the thing. Yet the supplement is both dangerous
and protective. Rousseau repeats the Christic suspension and aggravation

of castration (circumcision) by simultaneously allowing and disallowing the auto-erotic, masturbatory replacement of hetero-eroticism 'that cannot be separated from his activity as a writer' (OG 155). The activity of the writer circumcises the untenable fullness of speech, both undermining and reactivating 'the enjoyment of the *thing itself* [*la jouissance de la chose même*]' (OG 154/222). From now on, the *thing itself* enjoys itself as other; in a kind of auto-teleology, the mothers give birth to themselves, while the son mimetically participates and withdraws from their exuberant proliferation through the media of writing and masturbation.

Finally, the mother of Derrida: the phantom mother, who is both dead and alive;[20] the mother who is becoming-the-son by engendering him differently at the threshold of her death; the mother-thing who has nothing of her own and who is, thanks to this dispossession, in the position to appropriate (in Hartman's astute phrasing, 'to grow heavy with') every thing, to envelop all the remains and debris dialectics leaves behind.[21] In 'Circumfession' – a text, whose aural version was deposited in the Parisian branch of Voice Library (Bibliothèque des Voix) in 1993 and whose syntax resists the analytics of citation, proscribing the violence of cutting and pasting – Derrida confesses that he is writing 'for a living mother who does not recognize her son [*pour une mère vivante qui ne reconnaît pas son fils*]' (CI 25/27). That is, he is writing for (supplanting and supplementing, both 'in place of' and 'in honour of') a unique collage of Aristotle's and Nancy's contradictory portraits of Psyche. In spite of her incapacity to recognize and, consequently, to know him, the *living* mother does not see herself 'treated as a dead woman.' Saturated with herself, she enlivens her son from the brink of her grave, gives birth from death and non-recognition, and exchanges the act of speaking for him[22] for the supplementarity of his writing for her.

In addition to sketching the contradictory portrait of Psyche, Derrida tirelessly traffics bits of identity across generations and sexual differences. According to his protocols of reading (spelled out, above all, in *The Postcard*, where Socrates writes down what Plato dictates to him), everything is to be read in reverse, so the mother of Derrida becomes the son of her son, while the son becomes the mother of the mother. Within the economy of the countersignature, maternal speech supplants that of the son who writes instead of the mother. But if *Signsponge* has a message to convey, it is that the countersignature is the prerogative of the thing,[23] for example, of the paper that presses against the impression of the pen it receives, or of the psychic substratum that resists and, in doing so, bears and supports the memory-traces etched in it. Where there is a counter-signature, there is, unfailingly, the friction of thingly resistance enriched by the possible confusion of signatures from which the event may spring forth. Will this confusion be avoidable when one is no longer able to recognize (say, one's son, or one's signature), but also to 'name, foresee, produce, predict' things? In and of itself, the breakdown of recognition gives enough momentum for a conjuration of 'unpredictable things' (CI 31/32),[24] with which the mother is 'heavy' and through which the event of re-engendering the son will have taken place.

The reconstitution of the son is required because the living mother no longer recognizes him *as* her son. The dangerous supplement of this non-recognition is his re-memberance of himself around a single event of circumcision in a new kind of synthesis around and in lieu of the analysis of the body itself that bears the features of the thing's relational non-relationality. Nonetheless, something abides outside this reconstitution, slipping away from re-memberance and from the *fort/da* of analysis and synthesis. At the risk of a tautology that disregards the difference between a verb in the singular and a noun in the plural, what remains refers to nothing but the remains, namely, the umbilical cord and the ring of circumcised flesh that merge into the same thing, which the mother appropriates: 'Even the remains would belong to the mother [*le reste même reviendrait à la mère*]' (CI 68/68).[25] Were she standing in the place of radical exteriority, were her singularity irreversible, were it divorced from the iterative generativity of the son, his self-gathering around the two cuts would have been fixated on the loss, the pure absence, and the unknowable whatness of the *thing X* that supplies the building blocks for subjective synthesis, all the while lingering outside this noumenal construction site. The only trace of such fixation in Derrida's corpus is his inordinate love of the 'double bind' mirroring and compensating for the 'double cut,' of the umbilical cord and of the penis, that splits the event of splitting in two.

3.1.3. How to love the thing, or what does psychoanalysis resist?

Deconstruction shares with psychoanalysis the desire to trace the trace that translates into the love of the thing as the insubstantial – incompletely withdrawn – *remains, ruins,* or *cinders* of a 'consumed' substance.[26] On the one hand, this shared attraction binds deconstruction to psychoanalysis with the bonds of friendship, in 'the freedom of an alliance' (FWT 167) that sanctions their joint resistance, on a veritable front, to the idealized and idealizing perspectives on the psyche (Hegel, Husserl, etc). But instead of separating the 'allies' from psychic idealism once and for all, the common front runs in the heart of what is inimical to them. In the repetitions and returns of the same and in the consummation of the thing without remains, idealism resists idealism. On the other hand, 'this "yes" of friendship assumes the certainty that psychoanalysis remains an ineffaceable historical event, the certainty that it is a *good thing*, and that it ought to be loved, supported' (ibid.). To affirm the 'friend' as a 'good thing' that, in a Spinozan style, evokes the affect of love is to locate her among the remains *of* 'an ineffaceable historical event' she names.

To repeat: in Husserlian phenomenology, the infinite retracing of the outlines of the ideal object depends on the intra-subjective capacity to hear oneself speak in a struggle to re-present, expressively, an absent referent. But, Derrida wonders, what if the object of speech is the word 'I'? 'When I say *I*, even in solitary speech, can I give my statement meaning without implying, there as always, the possible absence of the object of speech – in this case, myself?' (SP 95) The answer to this question is negative, and the immediate implication is that the expressive meaning of the ideal object 'I' is indifferent to whether or not I am alive. The interiorized interiority devours and consumes itself when the totalized totality of the ideal object 'I' that folds a living intra-subjective iteration turns inside out into the possibility of its absence and death. Idealism unravels from within the moment interiority gathers itself, but this unravelling has to be positively understood following the protocols of the thing, with its ineluctable indeterminacy and vacillation between 'who' and 'what' – in this case, between the I *who* hears its own speech and the *what* or the ideal objectivity of the 'I' heard, spoken, and consumed in it.

The strongest point of Hegelian idealism is, likewise, the movement of interiorization, and likewise it proves to be its weakest spot that marks the lines of fire for what I call 'the inner front.' Discussing Hegel's philosophical appropriation of Christianity, Derrida writes in *Glas*:

But the spirituality of the Christian Last Supper consum(mat)es its signs, does not let them fall outside, loves without remain(s) ... Love – remains interior ... Consum(mat)ed without remain(s), the mystical object becomes subjective again ... The thing becomes thing again because consum(mat)ed – the thing is essentially consum(mat)ed, the process of consum(mat)ing constitutes it as thing rather than breaching/broaching it as such [*La chose redevient chose parce que consommée – la chose est essentielle-ment consommée, le procès de consommation la constitue en chose plutôt qu'il ne l'entame comme telle*]. (G 71/84, left)

Indeed, spiritualism 'loves without remain(s)' because it transubstantiates and incorporates, relieves and re-elevates, everything into the interiority of Spirit, preventing the beloved thing and even the object of love from breathing on their own. The pneumatology of spiritualism is here tantamount to the thing's assisted respiration in the speculative involution, the turning inward of life. The communal consumption of the body and blood of Christ in the Last Supper uses and discards the thing as a 'vanishing mediator' instrumental to the inter-subjective grounding of subjectivity. And yet the thing's incorporation is only provisional, in so far as its presumed success betrays the consummation of the subjective love as the *passage*, the inspired escape route for the thing itself. Spiritually consumed, the thing 'essentially' comes into its own (as the other) because 'the process of con-sum(mat)ing constitutes it as thing rather than breaching/broaching it as such,' that is, because in this process it does not deviate from its ownmost fugitive and animated pattern of barely remaining, being ruined, becoming other. Thus, the thing follows the rule of the hymen – 'the consummation of differends' (D 212) – whose polysemy includes both virginal intactness and the breach of the 'protective membrane' in marital consummation.[27]

Of course, we cannot afford to omit a major difference between idealism and Derridian deconstruction. In contrast to idealism that ruins the thing and endeavours to ruin its ruins, deconstruction lets the thing ruin itself and mourns the remains of this 'auto-analysis.'[28] Within the constellation of *Glas*, *Memoirs of the Blind*, and *Cinders*, the name of this receptive work of mourning is 'love': 'A narcissistic melancholy, a memory – in mourning of love itself. How to love anything other than the possibility of ruin?' (MB 68). That love, which remains interior, posits an ideal of absolute transparency according to which it knows its object and knows itself in loving this object. Conversely, both psychoanalysis and deconstruction subscribe to the opacity of that toward which love directs itself along with the inflection in this conscious directedness. The love of ruins leaves a certain modality of knowing, the subjectivized love of objects, and philosophy itself, as the love of wisdom (*sophia*), in ruins.

The whatness of the *thing* X, the substantiality of its synthetic self-binding and 'auto-analysis,' escapes theoretical investigations:

> This thing [the cinder] of which one knows nothing, knows neither what past is still carried in these gray dusty words, nor what substance came to consume itself there before extinguishing itself there ... Will one still say of such a thing that it even preserves the identity of a cinder? [*une telle chose, dira-t-on encore qu'elle garde même une identité de cendre?*]. (CIN 41–3)

This elusive and impossible thing does not preserve its identity, because it is no longer repeated in objective ideality by the subject who hears himself speak. Even if it hauntingly comes back to us after extinguishing itself, its return will not depend on a wilful subjective repetition. Instead, it will lead the afterlife of consummation and of the consummation of consummation that evinces the passing away of substance.[29]

The return of the repressed in the guise of the thing is the repressed possibility of Husserlian idealism that mobilizes stasis, puts it in motion by running on the treadmill of sameness and re-tracing the ideal object, all the while reductively discarding the debris of the non-ideal thing, under the illusion that the object's edification is the business of the living psyche ('the living present') alone. It is also the repressed possibility of Hegelian idealism that, time and again, consumes and consummates, constitutes and de-constitutes, the thing, makes it fall to the tomb (G 22) and re-elevates or monumentalizes it in the interiority of Spirit. The resistant, unappropriated and unappropriable, thingly remainder instigates and frustrates the two idealisms, while the 'modest' task around which deconstruction and psychoanalysis busy themselves consists in the acknowledgment of this disavowed drive and the registration of the frustration it sublimates *in the aftermath of the idealist/ psychologist reduction of the thing*.[30]

Deconstructive and psychoanalytic not-knowing is not a defect, but the highest degree of fidelity to the extended psychic thing. Analytic not-knowing is neither ignorance, nor a piece of Socratic wisdom that renders the axiom 'I know that I do not know' fundamental to the Delphic desideratum, 'Know thyself.' In excess of representation, it does not coil back to the pure absence of the unmediated noumena but welcomes 'an apparition in the sense of a visitation, of the "thing in itself" as the supplement of its "own" supplement [*de la 'chose même' en supplément de son 'propre' supplément*]' (PC 270/288). In other words, the unknown thing is not unknown 'in itself,' but as the spectral supplement of the 'originary' fetishistic supplement that has prosthetically replaced the theoretical fiction of the absent thing. (The phrase 'as the supplement of its "own" supplement,' therefore, fictionalizes the property and the propriety of the thing, making it secondary to the fetishistic prosthesis and suspending its 'own' absence between quotation marks.)

An address destined to the unknown – to one's reader, for example – is not impossible, even though, within deconstructive and psychoanalytic contexts, it will not obey the 'criteria of self-conscious knowledge.' As Derrida intimates, 'The "things" that I throw, eject, project, or cast (*lance*) in your direction ... fall, often and well enough, upon you, at least upon certain of those among you' (MC 3). The throw is a recognizably Heideggerian gesture alluding to the *Geworfenheit* side of the structure of care, whereas the 'fall' harkens back to the factical being-in-the world of Dasein as *Verfallen*. In the Derridian rendition, these terms acquire a tinge of materiality and come to resist idealism, given that the repeated and repeatable (hence, potentially idealizable) gesture of throwing 'things' often leads to unpredictable and singular outcomes, haphazard falls, disseminated effects. If the throw of the thing is the throw of a dice, then taking chances with it will unavoidably produce those remains that do not fall in the place for which the thing was intended, that do not arrive at all or arrive with an indeterminate delay, that elude the all-consuming interiority of the subject.

Exempt from the order of self-consciousness knowledge, the throw of the thing that resists idealism entails a ground-shift, favouring the unconscious, into which things sometimes fall. Where, to follow a geological/agricultural metaphor, the psychic substrate divides itself, seismically multiplying the furrows and creases in which consciousness will grow, there the ground will be the most fertile not only for the 'fallen' things, but also for the inversion of this fall's effects. 'The limit between the conscious and unconscious, that is, between the unconscious "I" and the other of consciousness, is perhaps this possibility of my fortune [*mes chances*] to be misfortune [*malchance*] and for my misfortune to be in truth fortunate [*une chance*]' (MC 21). The intrinsic divisibility of the unconscious formalized in the fracture 'between the unconscious "I" and the other of consciousness' is the extended psychic thing receptive to things in their non-identity and reversibility: to one thing as the other, to the fortunate as the misfortunate, and vice versa.

More precisely, it is receptive to the reversibility of the effects of these things – their 'chances' – deprived of causality[31] and, therefore, rendered indeterminate with reference to their randomness and necessity.[32]

In a move akin to the experimental inclusion of the 'I' under the rubric of Husserlian ideal objectivity, Derrida analyses psychoanalysis, as an artefact of the extended psychic thing, in terms of the 'necessity' built into its quotidian procedure of meaning-making:

> What happens to an interpretive science when its object is psychic and when it thus implicates in some respect the subject itself of that science? ... And when an analytic attitude itself becomes a symptom? When there is a tendency to interpret the incidents or accidents that befall us – opportunely or not – by means of the reintroduction of determinism, necessity, or signification, does this signify in turn an abnormal or pathological relation to the real? (MC 20)

Slightly reformulated, these questions inquire into the legitimacy of the subtraction of the psychic thing from the order of the real via Freud's cunning solution that espouses external 'objective' chance at the expense of internal psychical necessity (MC 23). The 'pathological relation to the real,' qua *res*, betokens the undue circumscription of 'reality' to non-psychic phenomena, to the things or events that fall on and befall no one in particular. But since psychoanalysis itself partakes, at once, of the real/scientific development *and* of the psychic self-relatedness, it disturbs the circumscription it has effectuated, as well as the neat division it institutes between necessity and chance. At this critical juncture, analysis and the analytic attitude compelled to fall back on itself are transfigured into resistances to analysis; the thing 'psychoanalysis' ruins itself, burns itself with its own desire; the symptom is no longer an effect of a repressed cause or *chose*, but of the analytic effect that wishes to turn it into a gold mine of meaning.[33]

Unlike the idealist approaches to the psyche, psychoanalysis does not unravel in the face of the test to which deconstruction submits it. What keeps it safe, what immunizes it to the fate of idealism? First and foremost, the fact that it pre-emptively *unravels itself* to the extent that it generally does not exhibit the same essential and exclusive insistence on interiority as idealism, but comes to terms with the irreducibility of the remains, resistance and the tension Freud terms 'the drive': 'Every resistance supposes a tension, above all, an internal tension. Since a purely internal tension is impossible, it is a matter of an absolute inheritance of the other or the outside at the heart of the internal and auto-affective tension' (RP 26). Because the non-analysable, futural remains inhabit the core of psychoanalysis, which is mindful of its hopeless fight against them, the analytic thing inherently tied to resistance is simultaneously bound and unbound, related and unrelated to this 'internal exteriority.' The throw *of* psychoanalysis triggered by deconstruction falls back on itself in its non-analytic alterity.

With this throw, the thing 'psychoanalysis' ruins itself and, therefore, induces deconstructive love. To understand if not the deconstructive lover herself, then her mode of loving things, we should, perhaps, contrast it to the Spinozan proposition that 'one who loves necessarily strives to have present and preserve the thing he loves; and ... one who hates strives to remove and destroy the thing he hates.'[34] Complicating this formula, deconstruction does not merely opt for a destructive, hateful treatment of the thing in the name of love. Instead, it lovingly and mournfully preserves (*conservare*) the thing in its 'own' falling apart, auto-destructiveness, and self-dissemination. The analytic thing falls apart thanks to the very '*philolytic* principle of analysis' (RP 33) it hypostatizes, that is, thanks to the unmeasured and immeasurable love of spacing, differentiation, and divisibility. Once unleashed, this principle will not spare the 'cause' of its formalization, but will bind it to the inner divisibility of psychoanalysis. Thus, deconstruction loves psychoanalysis analytically, the way psychoanalysis loves the psyche, the way, auto-erotically, psychoanalysis will have loved itself.

3.2. The thing at work: On commodity fetishism, or the phenomenology of value

The thinghood of the thing is contingent upon the work of its self-iteration and self-dissemination, and so we ought to search for the workability, or operationality, of work in a repetitive, non-ideal departure of the thing from itself and from the productive subject. In the current historical conjuncture, however, capitalism in general and commodity fetishism in particular seek to appropriate each element of the thingly work. In this section, I outline the appropriative commodity-economic transformation that interacts with the phenomenology of the thing and its work. While value brings the sociality of the thing into the light of phenomena, monetarism valorizes its detachment and non-relationality, and globalization (*mondialisation*) privileges the uncertain bond that perseveres after the withdrawal of the world-giving thing.

3.2.1. The enframing (of) value

The unbound bonds of the remains interlace and interconnect the psychoanalytic fetish and 'commodity fetishism.' More concretely, the cut umbilical cord returns in the image of the unlaced, abandoned, useless shoes that Derrida borrows from Heidegger, who, in turn, borrows them from Van Gogh. These coveted shoes are the main subject of *The Truth in Painting*, which erects an overarching, albeit porous, frame of the frame, enclosing the aesthetic and the economic, the biological as well as the philosophical. *The Truth in Painting* elaborates on the thickness, non-transparency, and non-coincidence of the inner and outer limits of the frame, folding into itself all the blocked passages and impossible traversals between and beyond these limits. In this regard, the commodity-economic framework of value is not an exception: its inner limit touches on use-value, the outer limit corresponds to exchange-value, and it is from the uneven overlapping of the two that the economic subtractions and additions, reductions and 'surpluses,' take their cues.[35] Let us observe, then, how the framework of value puts the frames of the thing to work.

In the first subtraction, what interests Heidegger is 'not the denuding of the foot, for example, but the denuding of the shoes that have become naked things again, without usefulness, stripped of their use-value' (TP 300).[36] On the one hand, the elimination of the inner frame denudes the things themselves in their truth as useless, or removes the phenomenological structure of being-intended-for superimposed on them. The shoes exit, walk out as though of their own accord, from the total context of signification and, in being unworkable – no longer ready to hand – come into their own. Their almost theatrical exit implies, for late Heidegger, the ultimate truth of the thing devoid of signification and liberated from the exigencies of use.

On the other hand – Derrida's hand raised in protest to Heidegger – the deframing of use-value's inner frame merely displaces the thing to the outer limits of exchange-value. The irreducible duality of the frame implies that it is not enough to subtract the thing from the category of use-value, since, in such a subtraction, it would immediately enter a different regime of usefulness, namely, exchange-value's im-material intentionality exploited throughout the pulsion of capital.[37] The spectre of Marx's inverted walking table reappears in the image of the auto-propelled shoes. Even if it is considered on its own terms, the Heideggerian displacement of utility loses its radicality because the shoes are paired (which means, prepared for the resumption of use) and because their pairing stays un-questioned: Heidegger 'bound them [the shoes] together in order to bind them to the law of normal usage' (TP 333). Above all, it is impossible to abstract something like 'truth' from signification and to arrive at the im-mediacy of a world without a frame, or a world without the *thickness* of the frame, which amounts to one and the same thing. Pure uselessness would merely resurrect another version of the transcendental signified predicated on absence and lack.[38]

The act of stripping the thing itself is the hallmark of phenomeno-logical reduction, which elliptically signals a reduction of the frame, or of the layers of sense enframing things. A by-product of the 'striptease of the thing' in the commodity-economic domain is the occlusion of the denuded foot (which is a sign not only for the peasant 'proximity to the earth' Heidegger tends to romanticize, but also for the abjection of poverty) by the nudity of the shoe-thing. The paradox of the opacity that persists where there is nothing else to hide is in line with the logic of commodity fetishism, whereby a human bearer (*Träger*) of the com-modity recedes behind the thingly and representative relations of value. The thing untethered from its user and from the category of equipment is not automatically released from all bonds; rather, at the fork of the event, it is equally handed over to the artistic disclosure of its truth and to its quantified integration into the circuits of capital. Or, according to the Derridian anagram, the thing is never naked (*nu*) and *its effect is not one* (*un*).

Second, the thickness of the frame requires an exclusion of that which is outside its inner and outer parts. The 'outside of the outside' is structurally indeterminate because it calls both for the overcoming of the use- and exchange-value in a recuperated, non-teleological view of Nature, and for the intensification of what is presumably overcome in the machinations of surplus value – value above value. Derrida reads *'plus-value'* (which translates the German *Mehrwert*) on the model of other expressions that include the untranslatable *'plus de,'* meaning, si-multaneously, 'more than' and 'no more.' Surplus value aporetically conjoins the two meanings – more than value and no more value – and forms a remainder that 'overflows (itself), into inadequation, excess, the supplement' (TP 298).

For Marx, the excess of the actual labour time over labour time that 'will keep the worker alive'[39] is an indicator of the inadequation and in-justice that, in not being restituted, drives the growth of capital. But how do the abandoned shoes enter the picture here? In their uselessness, the shoes have fallen; they neither support (by being-underneath, *hypokeimenon*) nor bear the working subject (TP 285).[40] There are two possible explanations for this lack of support: either 1) the worker has stopped working and is resting in a certain fullness of the accomplishment (*désoeuvrement*), or 2) she is still working without being supported or restituted for the expenditure of her labour power, above and beyond the minimum needed for subsistence. Although the two options grow from the same root, we most easily recognize the apparatus of surplus value in the second. Outside the process of production and circulation, surplus value picks up, gathers together, and elevates the fallen shoes into the prosthetic support for capital. The thing continues to work, but not 'for us'; 'surplus value is unleashed by the annulment of their [the shoes'] use-value' (TP 258).

Third, a subtraction of the outer frame (exchange-value) portends certain problems of its own. At the extreme, it results in the fetishization of use-value, which is the concept Marx has vacated for interminable analysis. The denaturalization of the denaturalized commodity structure fabricates an illusion of unmediated presence, for which Derrida chastises both Heidegger and his critic, Schapiro. The latter is chided for looking at the painting without a frame, for disregarding its materiality, and for mistaking the painted shoes for the 'real' shoes. The recession of the painting leaves behind the shoes – the things 'present' in front of us – as well as their disputed possession (TP 272). Eliminating the actual frame of the painting and that which it enframes, Schapiro denies the shoes their represented, representative, and exemplary status, their capacity, time and again, to stand in for the thing in general, to relate to other things from the depth of their unrelatedness and abandon, to put themselves in the shoes of other things, in a word, to socialize.

Heidegger commits the same hermeneutical fallacy but produces a diametrically opposed effect. He fetishizes the painting and extorts from the painted shoes their self-generated discourse of truth: 'Once they are painted, these shoes talk, this thing produced and detached from its subject begins to talk (about it)' (TP 323). The painted thing serves as an exemplary channel for the disclosure of truth when its detachment from use separates it from us, unseals the space from which discourse may arise and seals the unbound thinghood in its quasi-sacredness. But neither Schapiro nor Heidegger lives up to the task. Delivering a fetishized fetish, they usefully employ and profit from uselessness[41] by insisting on the originary truth of the thing, whether painted or produced otherwise, the truth it tells and the one told about it, be it the exact determination of its rightful proprietor or of its 'thinghood.' And, conversely, Marx's theorization of use-value as the supplement of the supplement methodologically anteceded by exchange-value in *Capital* clears the scene for a de-fetishized fetish.

The frame harbours yet another potentiality, which makes up its thickness in the very moment when it turns inside out, interiorizes its outside, but also exteriorizes its inside. Derrida's word for this reversal is 'invagination' which does not signify a total incorporation of the remainder inside something that is no longer a thing, but 'the inward refolding of *la gaine* [the sheath, girdle], the inverted reapplication of the outer edge to the inside of a form where the outside then opens a pocket' (LO 97). Putting dialectical jargon aside, we might note that invagination governs the spiralling circuits of capital in a calculated play of overlapping and unhinging commodity frames. The realization of value, its fleeting transformation into a thing (*res*), depends on its 'inward refolding' into use-value, which it must immediately leave behind or unfold, becoming de-realized. In keeping with this, the crises of capital should be understood in terms of the inflexibility and the subsequent disjointure of these frames, when value remains de-realized, *or* when it is held over by the thing too long. Thus, the vitality of capital is defined by the ease with which it moves into and out of things.

Still, the realization without realization of value is, to some extent, independent of use-value. Born of the comparison, interaction, and sociality of things, value stands for the abstracted principle of thinghood, for the becoming-thing of the thing, where 'the always other or the other-thing ... makes of the thing a thing, the thingness, shall we say, of the thing [*la chose autre ou l'autre chose ... fait de la chose une chose, la choséité, allons-y, de la chose*]' (SI 92/3). Through the relatedness of things to one another, from which their 'thingness' and value spring forth, the becoming-thing of the thing shines with the utmost lucidity, even if the same phenomenological shining occludes the relations between the human 'bearers' of the commodities. The problem, however, is that, to the extent that it wrests the valuable or the symbolic and discards the materiality of the 'shell' wherein the trace is built right into the substrate, the lucidity of this abstraction is complicit with all attempts to master and to dominate the thing that do not let it breathe and do not respect its *self*-remarking signification.

The repetitive substitution and invagination that ground value exploit the internal instability of the thing, capitalize on its unrest, re-present it as such, but forego the difficulty of replacing the irreplaceable. Although any process of production involves 'idealization, autonomization and automation, dematerialization and spectral incorporation, mourning work coextensive with all work, and so forth' (SM 166), the specifically capitalist production obsessed with the self-valorization of value releases, autonomizes, and incorporates the thing into the kind of idealized, dematerialized, living-dead intentionality that does not leave any breathing space for its virtual singularity. Its presumed independence from the human producer extends into the worst of slaveries, once the alien intentionality of capital binds to and overwrites the self-remarking, self-remarked itinerary of the thing. And finally, the work of mourning instigated by the injustice of surplus value overlaps with and intensifies the work of mourning driven by the dissemination of the product that now exists 'without me.'

An aspect of the same movement, the exteriorization of the inner frame hurls use-value outward. This projection of use-value does not aim to return the shoes to their rightful owner (either the peasant or the painter or, for that matter, anyone else), but to discharge the debt incurred to the thing itself, that is to say, to the things (the shoes) themselves.[42] This aim reaches the threshold of the impossible, given that the demand of the thing is silent, given that 'demanding everything and *nothing*, the thing puts the debtor (the one who would wish to say properly *my thing*) in a situation of absolute heteronomy' (SI 48). Nonetheless, the impossible claim corroborates the event whereby, instead of being appropriated and expropriated, the thing itself, like the singularly universal sponge in *Signsponge*, immemorially and receptively conditions, absorbs, and 'propriates' everything, whether proper or not.

The event of thingly propriation is the restitution of time, including the labour time expended on its 'production' and the ecstatic temporality of its self-remarking, to the thing itself in what will have been another vision, another dream of the re-appropriation of surplus value. The shoe at rest, then, not only temporalizes by delaying its being-worn-out beyond repair, but also messianically awaits, 'without the horizon of expectation,' the turning of time, or the return of the time that elapsed in use: 'Moved by a mysterious force, the thing itself demands gift *and* restitution, it requires therefore "time", "term", "delay", "interval" of temporalization' (GT 40). To repay a debt to the thing itself it is not enough to render it useless or to discard the material substratum in which the traces of use abide. Rather, this repayment should stimulate the reversal of usage and its consequences, the ghostly *revenance* of the thing's devalued, worn-out value, and finally, the supplemental replacement of the irreplaceable.

Overwriting the back-and-forth invaginations, subtractions, and projections I have described is the question, What does the frame enframe? The obvious answer brings up the thing, but also the work – the thing whose thinghood works, and the animated work whose workability bethings, becomes another thing in the supplemental series of displacements and substitutions. The *'three things of the thing* [trois choses de la chose]' Derrida enumerates in *Specters of Marx* (9/29) inevitably refer themselves back to work in a move that deconstructs the distinction Heidegger solidifies in 'The Origin of the Work of Art.' From the work of mourning (*le travail du deuil*), through the iterative generativity of ghostly generations, to its transformative self-elaboration ('the thing *works*, whether it transforms or transforms itself, poses or decomposes itself [*la chose* travaille, *qu'elle transforme ou se transforme, qu'elle pose ou se décompose*]'), the thing is a self-disruptive, disseminative process that retraces itself as other (SM 9/30). This notion of thinghood will explain the enigmatic syntagma 'the three things of the thing,' which accentuates the multiplicity dwelling in each thing, that is to say, the difference of forces constitutive of the things 'in' the thing, of three (the number is not just double, simply divided against itself, but triple) others in the same. Although this thingly composition coincides with its decomposition, the genitive form of the syntagma harbours the propriative event of restitution, releasing the thing into its own, abandoning, and loving it in its creative self-ruination.

Before the instant of restitution arrives, parergonal capital binds itself to the inner workings of the thing. In a 'phenomenological "conjuring trick,"' the inapparent is made to appear in the disembodied body of the commodity as 'a "thing" without phenomenon, a thing in flight that surpasses the senses [*une 'chose' sans phénomène, une chose en fuite qui passé les sens*]' (SM 150). The non-phenomenal difference of forces residing in the thing, the very destabilizing difference that is responsible for the perpetual slippage of the thing itself from the phenomenological grasp and for its flight that steers away from the precalculated trajectory of the throw, undergoes quantification in the process of exchange. The thing that poses and decomposes itself in the realm refractory to the light of phenomenology is ex-posed and betrayed (in the double meaning of 'being betrayed'), thematized and lost in its exposition, which relies *only* on numerical values. Thus, violating the law of the thing that operates 'without an exchange and

without the transaction' (SI 14), the conjuring trick levels and objectifies the traces of thingly work.

These traces epitomizing the amount of the socially necessary labour
time that has gone into the production of a commodity-thing are
parted, unjustly shared, and subsequently obscured in their phenomenality. If commodity fetishism has a core around which it revolves, it is
the trick of making the inapparent appear qua inapparent, of making
surplus value, the outside of the outside, withdraw as soon as it approaches us (or as soon as we approach it practically or theoretically),
and of turning the effects of this withdrawal into profit. The producer
receives back only a part of the thing's work, even as the capitalist
capitalizes on, renders futural, reinvests, forces the remainder to work
further in the form of the remains – in the form of the temporal-
temporalizing thing that it is.

In the most fetishistic, abbreviated, '"incomplete" circle M=M' (money
yielding more money), capital hallucinates its utopia of a parergon without the ergon, a frame without the enframed, a pure 'supplement with
nothing to supplement' (TP 302), not even replacing another replacement. This empty frame with a reduced thickness defies all geometrical
linearity when it contracts the circle to a point exempt from the work's
duration, giving expression to circulation time tending to zero and
dreaming up this *Augenblick* in the evanescence of purely financial transactions carried out in the global communication networks. The detachment and formalization of the frame fetishistically transpose the myth of
the self-sufficient thing onto the prosthesis of consciousness that capital
furnishes in the capacity of an 'automatic subject'.[43] But since there is no
selective inheritance, since there are no brakes on the event, which, futurally, comes to us from the past, the parergon must become an heir to the
self-interruptive iteration, work, ergon of the thing. Its detachment and
formalization spell out the loss of the frame's flexibility and the ablation
of the differential of forces on which capital relies. Hence, the double bind
par excellence: binding itself to the thing that disseminates itself and falls
into pieces, capital ruins itself, but unbinding itself from the ruinous
thing, it loses its borrowed energy and comes undone. The enframed
'working thing' or 'thinging work' de-borders the enframing (of) value.
Setting the thing to work is unhinging the frame.

3.2.2. Money, credit, and other 'counterfeit things'

In keeping with the standard Marxist interpretation, the qualitative
materiality of the thing dissolves in the indifference of monetary

quantification. Money is the great 'leveler' and 'cynic,' for when 'everything becomes saleable and purchasable ... every qualitative difference between commodities is extinguished.'[44] This diagnosis is certainly not wrong, since it takes seriously *'the question of the thing ...* insofar as it would include the substantial power, the intrinsic value of the gift and the call for the countergift' that undermines the 'logic of relation and exchange' (GT 74). But it appears to be lopsided, because anything that claims the power and the right to disband or to cut right through the knot of the thing only further entangles this knot.

What this formally correct diagnosis misses is that the thing is its own double and that it possesses a substantial 'social' dimension of its own, to the extent that it relates to itself as other in the course of self-remarking forays (the emergence of 'intrinsic value' in self-relatedness) and to the extent that it mutely addresses itself to its debtor ('calls for the countergift' of signification). A singular universal losing and disseminating itself in defiance of the law of exchange, it indifferently conditions and absorbs, like the exemplary sponge, everything in its path (SI 102). The singularity of the thing is inseparable from its 'work,' which capital abusively re-channels into the axiomatics of the general equivalent.[45]

Although the thing has a certain absorbent indifference in common with monetary equalization, its modus operandi is receptive to material difference. In contrast, money comes across as an abstract general equivalent in the interactions between commodities that 'would permit translation, metaphorization, metonymization, exchange within an ultimately homogeneous semantic circle ... [of] ... the transcendental signifier or signified' (GT 51–2). In each case, its objective would be the same: to give a foretaste of 'what the Thing given is' (GT 53), to formulate the conditions of possibility for knowing the thing given and received in exchange, and to secure its identity on the two sides of the equation. But the principle of pure translatability keeps nothing save for the name of the thing capitalized in its counterfeit synthetic propriety, transcendental unity, and subordination to the ontological question of being. Here, the thing 'itself' escapes more swiftly than ever because, transcendental appearances notwithstanding, it does not keep its self-identity across the acts of giving and receiving, across its infinite self-giving as other and the absorbent, spongy receptivity that lets the remains fall down and out of the equalizing transaction. The interposition of money in the role of a transitory, temporary representative of the given thing – a representative that overwrites the self-giving of the thing – permits us to recognize and, by means of such recognition, 'suffices to annul' the thing itself, whose materiality it symbolically supplants (GT 13).

This annulment does not imply that money is not a thing, or else that it does not perversely borrow certain features of thinghood. How does the force of monetary quantification, 'this obscure thing, disconcerting and perhaps immaterial, that is called *money*,' borrow, convert, and pervert – borrow *as* intrinsically pervertible, convertible, and, therefore, 'extrinsic' – the thing? In other words, how does the conversion of a thing into 'true' money counterfeit the principle of thinghood? And by virtue of what does counterfeit money approximate the paradigm of the thing?

If money signifies anything, it betokens the final separation of the worker from his product that anticipates the sale before its materialization in the process of production. This surplus separation gambles on the independence of the thing, whose breathing space 'without me' is transmogrified into money that cuts the work-thing from the productive subject, acting as the figure of detachment, analysis, and cutting (*coupure*).[46] Set apart from the subject, the 'converted,' monetarized work-thing is, in the same blow, isolated from need (*incipit* freedom!), spilling over into the sphere of *chrematistics*, where the 'infiniteness of accumulation and desire has been introduced into the finite circle of the *oikos*.'[47] On the other side of the same coin, such conversion valorizes the cut at the expense of the bond – the very ligature of obligation – and turns the detachment of the thing into profitability. 'Money is the *pharmakon* of freedom,' or so the post-Derridian lesson of *Capital* resounds in a confirmation of the indeterminacy of the event open even to the possibility of its own closure.

Glas personalizes the *pharmakon* 'money' that harnesses the very thing it sets free in the character of the miser: 'He is above his work: his work, by being able in this way to cut itself off and to fall from him, is not equal to him [*Il est au-dessus de son oeuvre: celle-ci, à pouvoir ainsi se couper et tomber de lui, ne lui est pas égale*]. He raises himself above the remain(s). The most consistent miser: he carries on him only liquid cash and whatever (a passport) helps identify his *seing*' (G 206/231, right). This is neither the first nor the most fateful incident in which the great equalizer and leveller has encouraged inequality by placing someone or something above someone or something else. Within the limits of the capitalist production process, in the course of what I've termed 'surplus-separation,' the worker has been separated from the product even before calling it forth into being. Indeed, this divorcement, which ultimately leads to injustice, is a preparatory step toward capitalism, and money as a representative of circulation is only the most superficial, symptomatic layer of this injustice. Yet, having taken these objections into account, it is worth attending to its *en-ergia*, to the fashion in which money is made to work, supervening upon the thing's trajectory.

The *coupure*, or the banknote cut, enables the miser to raise himself above the remains without any expenditure of effort, thanks to the 'cuttability/culpability' of the work that falls, falls apart, and disseminates itself in the thingly remains. The *'sans* of the pure cut' of money merely detaches the cut of the thing from its bond, consummates and epitomizes its ownmost self-ruining, purifies its absolution from all ties left behind or carried away by the effortless osmotic flow of 'liquid cash.' But, as a *pharmakon*, monetarism can afford a strategy that stands for the exact opposite of consummating the remainder in letting it fall; it can also incorporate or consume the remains in the artifice of non-subjective interiority. '*Monnaie*, money, change: in French, at least, it is the same word (and the word is a coin, a piece of change). The word says at once the monetary thing in general and the remainder of a monetary operation [*la chose monétaire en général et le reste d'une opération monétaire*]' (GT 103/133).[48] The word says at once the thing and the trace of its work, since the monetary thing is conceptualized as *a trace at work*. It is also an expression of the commodity's value and a remainder of the past financial transactions that labours to erase, to cross out, and to forget all signs of 'qualitative difference,' including the difference between the price and the remaining change. Whatever the price, the purchased thing will be priceless, both exorbitantly expensive and 'free,' since in the end one will need to subtract its cost from the total sum of money (the principal amount) identical with the dispensed change.

It is no secret that the ideality of the money-form issues from the spiritual consumption of the thing and of money itself in the Hegelian schema, where a part exchanges itself for and contains the whole. But – another double bind – this consumption preserves and even mimics the features of the consumed thing. To say, for instance, that the monetary sign is 'spectropoetic,' that it engenders ghosts and thus describes 'some spectral "thing," which is to say "someone" [*décrire quelque 'chose' de spectral, c'est-à-dire 'quelqu'un'*]' (SM 45/80), is to confirm that it occupies an indeterminate position between the 'who' and the 'what.'[49] Similarly, to convert the price into a remainder that disseminates itself in the indifference to quantity, where there is absolute parity (typical of the general economy and immeasurable in numerical terms) between 'too much' and 'too little,' is to exploit the trait of the thing's absorbent indifference. In both cases, the thing's resistance to idealization is idealized, counterfeited. And, conversely, the locus of non-idealized resistance in the economic domain migrates to counterfeit money, that is, to the subversive counterfeiting of the counterfeit and the self-annulment of quantity.[50]

While counterfeit currency is a sign gone awry, the self-iteration of the thing is the quasi-transcendental condition of possibility *and* impossibility for signification. All signs desperately strive to catch up with, replicate, and remark the self-remarking procedures of the thing, but something fails to arrive – eventfully – across the untraversable divide between the thingly archi-writing and the object of writing.[51] One corollary of this gap is the divergence between the 'word' and the 'thing' it names, but nowhere is this divergence as blatant as in the case of counterfeit money: 'Recall that the thing – as counterfeit money – is not a thing like any other [*n'est pas une chose comme une autre*]; it is a sign and an incorrectly titled sign, a sign without value, if not without meaning' (GT 85/113). Counterfeit money 'is not a thing like any other' not because all other things signify or give themselves faithfully and meaningfully, but because it comes close to the very thinghood of the thing seducing and disorienting the movement of signification, when it – groundlessly, as it were – gives itself for true money and is taken as such without corresponding or being equivalent to anything at all.[52] Thus, the absolved relationality of the thing untranslatable into objective, empirical signification and the relational absolution of the empty sign of the sign, untranslatable into the order of 'real' value, converge in their effect of shuttering the transcendental delusion that one could secure meaning once and for all.

Counterfeit money gives itself out as what it is not and 'is what it is only by not giving itself *as such* and by not appearing *as such*, by not exhibiting its titles' (GT 98). Passing as the 'true' money, concealing its identity, which is its non-identity with anything it may signify, the dangerous counterfeit supplement precedes the thing supplemented and, therefore, represents a possibility of fictitiousness that hides in all monetary assignations. It bears the marks of a generalized, defetishized fetish that lends it the chance of substitution (counterfeit money stands for the currency that is not counterfeit *and* for everything it can buy) but withholds from it the opposition between the fetish and the thing. As a result, this surreptitious supplement resists and indefinitely postpones the presentation of something like 'true money.' In an analogy to the thing whose self-remarking iterations deviate from the objectifying repetition that generates the ideal and self-identical entity 'as such,' counterfeit money unequal to itself disturbs the relations of equivalence in which it participates.

This inherent, insidious, parasitical fictitiousness breaches the 'security' of financial transactions and thereby foregrounds the issue of credit in the sense of trust, credulity, credibility, but also in the sense of the payment's deferral and a special fund from which one can borrow. Credit is the prosthesis intended to support and fortify the frailty of the monetary thesis. It compensates for the infirmity of liquid cash, which at any moment may liquidate itself in counterfeit signs without value, and for the instability of knowledge no longer able to rely on the surety of transcendental translation substantiated by the traditional belief in 'the distinction between the real and the unreal' (SM 11). Ultimately, however, the supplement of fiduciary trust only displaces the problem when I defer the monetary deferral and 'give my word' instead of handing over either the 'thing itself' or its abstract equivalent. The payment is still to come, but, symbolically, it has been already accounted for, and thus I am prevented from paying by the credited payment itself that remains pending.[53]

What does credit have to do with the thing we have abandoned in the purity of its detachment intensified by the monetary cut? In a mix of Weberianism and Kantianism, Derrida associates the appeal to trust with one of the sources of religion 'at the limits of reason alone' and with that which undercuts all capitalist rationality. Broadly conceived, religion entails the affirmative re-linking (*re-legere/re-ligare*) that 'links up with itself in order to link up with the other' (AR 55). It would not be difficult to recognize in this re-assemblage the work of the thing that remarks itself as other, that repeatedly separates from itself so as to bind to itself (as) the other.[54] What credit, which always alludes to religion, restores is not trust per se, but rather the thingly bond of the bound and the unbound that has been upset by the pure cut of money. The sociality of the social reasserts itself in this 'extension' of the tie incommensurate with any other extension or spatiality (AR 80).

The extension of credit, understood as the spacing of sociality and as the virtualized and virtually inflated means of payment, prefigures the auto-immunization of the monetary system and of the social bond alike. As a *pharmakon*, it counters the unsettling effects of counterfeit money with a much more serious likelihood, of the perjury that haunts all witnessing, testimonies, and oaths.[55] To be sure, this counter-action entrusted with time futurizes, defers, encourages an increase in consumption, allots more time to make a payment, but all the same withholds a guarantee that the laborious detours would not be interrupted by various contestations of the given oath, announcements of bankruptcy, and the resistant non-arrival of the thing itself. Where there is no universal gold standard, and even where a certain 'we' endeavours to set up a transcendental guarantor old or new – for instance, in proclaiming, 'In God we trust!' – there credit supplants knowledge and announces, as though a priori, the prospects of discrediting itself. Ostensibly hyper-idealizing, it adds ligature and obligation to the thingly detachment distilled into money. Shying from the bright light of phenomena, it demonstrates that a 'certain interruptive unraveling is the condition of the "social bond", the very respiration of all "community"' (AR 99) where the common thing, res publica, respires, breathes again in self-disseminated and spongy receptivity to alterity.

3.2.3. Becoming-thing of the thing, becoming-world of the world

Evincing the abstract principle of sociality and purifying the cut of non-relationality, the commodity follows the course of the becoming-thing of the thing as such. The ideality of the 'as such' wrought from the substantiality of the thing fully deserves the title of fetishism. But, in addition to reconfiguring commodity fetishism, Derrida facilitates the thinking of what may be termed 'world fetishism': the inflation of discourses, processes, theories, and practices of globalization, *mondialisation*, the becoming-world of the world (N 375). Not only do the two phenomena, or better, the two phenomenalizations, of the thing and of the world, dovetail, thanks to the idealization they precipitate, but they are also deeply imbricated with each other, with 'religion,' and with the economic rationality that propels them.

Like the process of commodification, *mondialisation* denotes the *essentially* social time-space of the relentless being-with.[56] The sociality of the world mediated through the infinite variety of media and telecommunication systems translates into a kind of contiguity, in which any given point on the nascent homogenized plane instantaneously finds itself in the closest proximity to every other point. Increasingly, the 're-linked' world ('religion,' in the broad sense, is the place where this re-linking accomplishes itself)[57] comes to affect itself both as a referential totality of things signifying their usefulness and as the *wherein* of this totality.[58] Its ideal, contradicting the monetary cut on which it nonetheless depends, is a sociality without respite and without respiration, a purified relationality of the absolute bond that defies all unravelling, and a complete consumption/consummation of the différantial spacing on the smooth surface of the globe.

Such an ideal is, certainly, impossible. Auto-affection cannot operate outside the hetero-affective fold,[59] and so the 'new world order' turns inside out and into a 'new world disorder,' the disjointure or disadjustment of the world that wears itself out 'in expansion, in growth itself, which is to say, in the becoming worldwide of the world [*cette usure dans l'expansion, dans la croissance même, c'est-à-dire dans la mondialisation du monde*]' (SM 78/130). Formally, this wear and tear is redolent of the Heideggerian unhandy, broken, unworkable thing that drops out of the total context of referentiality and constitutes a breach in this totality. But what if, to return to Derrida, the disarticulated articulation of the world that auto-affectively comes into its own is a higher-level reflection of the 'normal' self-ruination of the thing that falls apart in remarking itself as other? The event of *mondialisation* projects the commodity-thing writ large onto the inflated body of the *socium* and, in doing so, telegraphically transmits all the contradictions of the commodity-economic logic from the so-called uneven development (the non-coincidence of the world, the globe, the earth, etc.) to the aporetic coexistence of the pure cut of money and the pure contiguity of the world. Thus, the event of *mondialisation* reluctantly confirms the irreducibility of the thing's detached relationality.

Negatively and obliquely, the worlding world conjures up the thing via the exclusion of work: 'Let us say or make as if the world began where work ended, as if the globalization of the world has both as its horizon and its origin the disappearance of what we call *work*, this old word, painfully charged with so much meaning and history' (N 377). The palaeonymization of work is an outcome of 1) the ambiguous vacillation between *désoeuvrement* and the unrecognized or conceptually unrecognizable labour converted into surplus value, 2) the non-affirmative 'end' of the mournful 'working-through' in a melancholic identification that 'acts out,' and 3) the parergonal frame that has disencumbered itself from the ergon it enframes. The thing slips away along with 'this old word' to which it is bound, but this time its recession is fostered not by the ideality of the 'as such,' but by the virtuality of the 'as if' ('as if the world began where work ended'), which is to say, by the avowed theoretical fiction that lays bare the grounds of its own incredible credibility. This virtual withdrawal writes the fable where the 'end of work' – its culmination: its goal and cessation – produces a very particular product – the world – that, in the course of *mondialisation*, scratches out from its surface the label 'Made in ...' or, simply, 'Made!' and that, consequently, represents itself as a sui generis simple unity busy with affecting itself. In other words, the theoretical fiction of a world beyond work is a part of the metaphysical myth of the origin, which is so powerful in the psychic domain and which labours to suppress the other of origin and the other origins (e.g., archiwriting, as well as the self-remarking, self-disseminating work of the thing), clinically presenting meta-symptoms of the most stubborn resistance to analysis.

The withdrawal of work from the beginning of the world takes us back to *Of Spirit*, where Derrida examines Heidegger's definition of the thing as 'worldless' and uncovers a certain taken-for-granted yet unarticulated syllogism: 1) the philosopher's paradigmatic thing – the stone – is 'without world [*weltlos*]' (OS 48); 2) the world is always spiritual (OS 47); and 3) '*Geist* thus forms part of the series of non-things, of what in general one claims to oppose to the thing. It is what in no way allows itself to be thingified [Geist *fait donc alors partie de la série des non-choses, de ce qu'on prétend en général opposer à la chose. C'est ce qui ne se laisse d'aucune façon chosifier*]' (OS 16/35). The worldly spirituality that Dasein dispenses to itself requires, at minimum, the ability discursively to relate to oneself as other (to place and to hear a call from oneself to oneself), to lag behind and to run ahead of oneself, and, in this daily ecstasis, to relate to the being of beings. The ecstatic relationality of Dasein is denied to the worldless, breathless, inanimate thing determined in its mute 'whatness': this is the most traditional element of Heidegger's ontology. Nonetheless, one of the constant unorthodox threads running through Heidegger's work and isolated in *Of Spirit* is the *avoidance* of spirit[60] that, positively understood, veers on the side of the thing in an attempt to bring us close to its breathlessness, its exemption from the spirit of humanism. To steer clear of *Geist*, for Heidegger, would be to avoid 'what in no way allows itself to be thingified,' what 'claims to oppose the thing' but is inevitably included 'in' the *différantial* receptacle it opposes, and to embrace, analytically, more than the *human* Dasein in its everydayness.

Despite this cautionary avoidance, the becoming-world of the world revolves around the forgetting of its birth or emanation – tantamount to the forgetting of 'becoming' itself – from the thing's sociality before and beyond commerce and other activities of Dasein. It is on account of such interested, invested forgetting that the thing haunts, if to haunt is to cause a dehiscence, to have and to form the world, to cleave open a spacing without dwelling in it:

> The animated work becomes that thing, the Thing that, like an elusive specter, *engineers* a habitation without proper inhabiting, call it a *haunting* of both memory and translation [*L'oeuvre animée devient cette chose, la Chose qui s'ingénie à habiter sans proprement habiter, soit à* hanter, *tel un insaisissable spectre, et la mémoire et la traduction*] ... The Thing haunts, for example, it causes, it inhabits without residing [*La Chose hante, par exemple, elle* cause, *elle habite sans y résider*]. (SM 18/42)

Let us try to keep abreast of this passage's blistering locution. The animated work, '*l'oeuvre animée*,' is part and parcel of spirit (*anima* in Latin can mean 'spirit,' 'breath,' or 'soul') that breathes without me as soon as I dissolve my living bond with it. Part and parcel of spirit, it parts and parcels spiritual unity into spectral dissemination ('like an elusive specter'). In turn, the becoming-animated of work – its spectrality – is nothing else than the thing immediately capitalized ('that thing, the Thing') in order to emphasize the hesitation between its 'whatness' and its 'whoness.' While the state of being animated is also animating, in the transition from the passive to the active voice, the Thing assumes the properties of a 'who' and '*engineers* [s'ingénie] a habitation.' The 'engineering' of habitation is meaningful in the context of the etymology on which Derrida elaborates elsewhere[61] and which draws together such words as 'genius,' 'genesis,' 'genealogy,' and 'genre.' In the light of this juxtaposition, the animated-animating work-thing stands at the 'genesis' of habitation, but it does not inhabit that which it generates ('without proper inhabiting'), or, in other words, it absents itself from the spacing it yields. Termed 'haunting,' the movement of the giving withdrawal, whose objects are not confined to memory and translation, affects the indwelling of *any* interiority, the world inhabited by something or someone other than the Thing that haunts and does not abide ('*sans y résider*'). It does not abide in the 'there' it engineers or causes (note, again, the ambiguity of the Latin *causa*: thing or cause), but the mere acknowledgment of its ingenuous generativity suffices to dispute and displace all designations of 'worldlessness.' Thus, hauntology is the operationality of the thing that works and that 'worlds,' disseminating and diffracting, in an ironic twist on the ontico-ontological difference, the spiritual unity of the world into a multiplicity of spectres.

It is no accident that the becoming-world of the world is forgetful of its own genealogy: the thing causes forgetting when, instead of inhabiting, it haunts memory and gives the world only to retract itself from it by forcing everything to begin 'before it begins' (SM 161). The phenomenalization of the world attempts to erase what is already under erasure by way of hypostatizing the withdrawal proper to the thing, foregoing its quasi-transcendental, world-giving 'function,' and reducing it to a worldless entity within the world. Structurally, the hypostatized withdrawal is compatible with the monetary purification of the thingly detachment. That is to say, the itinerary of the world at the end of work leads to money, to the always-spiritual currency[62] that puts one above one's work, disengages one from it, turns one into a general miser. Both the fall of the remainder concurrent with the purification of the thingly cut and its incorporation in *monnaie* are the preconditions for the auto-affection of the world that exchanges itself for itself and for the ostensibly non-relational non-world of the thing from which it is born in the networks of unequal exchange. Pure exchangeability, the becoming-world of the world expresses itself in the institution of the world market, in 'a front among fronts, a confrontation' of commodities (SM 155). But the 'real' confrontation, lacking either a front or a frontier, the confrontation on the 'front without front' of the event (PTT 91), transpires between the market and the work of the thing that underwrites and interrupts it, engineers and haunts it, because the world is always the world *of* things.

4 On the Thing
That Deconstructs Aesthetics

Ayant à mettre en scène, il est mis en scène, il se met en scène. Le récit dès lors s'adresse au corps du lecteur qui est mis par les choses en scène, elle-même.

La Dissémination

The *transcendental retrait* or *withdrawal* at once calls for and forbids the self-portrait. Not that of the author and presumed signatory, but that of the 'source-point' of drawing, the eye and the finger, if you will.

Memoirs of the Blind

4.1. Style, the signature of the thing

With Derrida, we shall envisage the thing as a 'deconstructor' of the work of art, and the artwork as a way of setting free the alterity of things. Both tasks are executed in style, by means of style that punctures and rends apart the fabrics of identity and recognition. In brief, whereas the thing divides the artistic signature in two, depriving it of its identity and absorbing the idiomaticity of style, the artwork functions as a playground for the confusion of the subjective signature and the thingly countersignature that, in remarking and dissimulating itself, points the subject out.

4.1.1. The point of style

When it comes to style, Derrida goes right to the point, to its pointed and sharp 'end.' Whether transforming *peinture* (or painting) into *pointure* (or pointing) in the 'Restitutions' section of *The Truth in Paint-ing*, or adumbrating Nietzsche's aesthetization of distance in *Spurs*, he deposits this sharp end, this pointed thing right at the core of style: 'In the question of style there is always the weight or *examen* of some pointed object [*le pesant d'un objet pointu*]. At times this object might be only a quill or a stylus. But it could just as easily be a stiletto, or even a rapier [*un stylet, voire d'un poignard*]' (S 36/37). Precisely where it is im-possible to point out the 'thing itself,' the thing itself intentionally points, poignantly touches the artist and the spectator, prickles as though with a stiletto, or retreats and defends itself with a rapier (*poi-gnard*). Like a fencer, it gives (a blow) and briskly withdraws itself in and from the act of giving. In turn, the artist and the 'workly' side of an artwork form a network of passageways and media for the event of the aesthetic thing, which may or may not arrive in stylistic pointing and wounding, whose economy overturns the ontological procedures of pointing out, identification, and indicative signification (*pace* Husserl).[1]

What are the reasons for this overturning? First, the unsustainable point is an *Augenblick* that, however fine, breaks into two, detaches from itself, and – split against itself – becomes contrapunctal. The point is no point, *ne … point*, no-thing, that is the double of the thing 'in' the thing. Or, as Derrida writes, in a eulogy for Roland Barthes: 'It is in-deed necessary … to recognize, and this is not a concession, that the *punctum* is not what it is' (WM 57). At the point of style, the thing loses all self-identity and escapes recognition, but this escape is what needs to be recognized in and through aesthetic practices. The stylistic sharp-ness of pointure is a sign that the thing has immemorially cut itself loose from 'us' and from itself in the absolute alterity that overflows the opposition of the other to the same.[2] Thus absolved, it eludes iden-tification and sets an orbit for all the subjective quests and examina-tions that only 'turn round the point … never getting down to it' (WM 58). The virtual core of style is, therefore, simultaneously empty and full; the thing synonymous with the stylistic *punctum* that rends[3] ev-erything and – above all – itself is something and nothing for us. It is the untouchable possibility of touching, the absolute sharpness of that which touches us but cannot, itself, be touched.

Second, although the subject is no longer able to point out the thing in the aftermath of the inversion of intentionality, the thing is 'that which "points" me, or "points" (to) what I am awkwardly trying to say [*ce qui me 'point' ou 'point' ici ce que j'essaie maladroitement de dire*]' (WM 57/86).[4] The thing itself always expresses its point better than 'I' ever could because all my attempts to understand it bring it too close and, losing sight of its proper detachment, betray it.

The protocols of de-distancing always go too far in bringing the thing close to us, but this predicament of expression need not be a paralysing impasse. Positively put, the thing is a pointed pointer, a middle voice suspended between the 'who' and the 'what,' the active and the passive. As such, it offers me certain pointers – the kind of guidance and directionality that are the markers of style – and, prior to this offering, directs itself toward me, aims at me from the unbridgeable distance of the point to itself, and points me out. The thingly pointers, then, act as the non-subjective schemata or paths for action and thought, for the 'creation' of an artwork and for the 'judgment' passed on it, only when they withdraw themselves from these paths and, consequently, leave every saying and doing awkward, non-direct, *maladroit*.

A model for the schematism I am referring to is the archi-trace built into the thingly substratum itself, for instance, a vein that runs through the stone and imposes a certain material necessity on the potential form of a future sculpture, a necessity with which the sculptor cannot not contend. The consequences of this imposition are both fleeting and long lasting, given that the completed sculpture will indirectly express the course of the initial vein it has erased, ruined, but also commemorated and monumentalized.

It is possible to graft the *ontological* inversion of pointing onto the stylistic signatures of the thing.[5] Often enough, when the artist and the author sign under the sway of an idealist illusion, they ignore the thing's separation and bind the artwork to themselves, authenticating, in addition to their works, their proper names and the right of appropriation enshrined in the legality of 'copyright.' Besides this literal inscription of the name in the work, 'the set of idiomatic marks that a signer might leave by accident or intention in his product' furnishes what 'we sometimes call … the style' (SI 54). Thus, style is a kind of signature that, similarly, connotes truncation and cutting. Yet neither the literal nor the metaphorical sense exhausts Derrida's articulation of the 'signature,' because the thing or the substratum into which the name and the stylistic idiom of the artist are etched countersigns, dividing the signature against itself and rendering it what it is not. More literal than the literal and more metaphorical than the metaphorical, the thing's countersignature is not the opposite of signature, but its 'own' material underside.

In the course a bewildering exchange with the materials on which he works, the artist or the interpreter of a text has 'to make the thing sign and to change the thing into his (or its) signature [*faire signer la chose et transformer la chose en sa signature*]' (SI 126/127). But this transformation is not seamless. It is unclear, for instance, if the personal pronoun '*sa*' designates the artist or the thing, that is, if the artist changes the thing into his signature, or creatively permits the thing to sign for itself, to impress its own signature, intensifying the preceding '*faire signer la chose*,' or, indeed, if both alternatives apply at once. This uncertainty characterizes the event of the thing.

Another complication arising from this exchange is that the countersignature of the thing appears (qua inapparent) the moment when its materiality asserts itself, when the point of the brush or of the stiletto meets the texture, the grain, the pressure, and the resistance of paper or stone that guide and derail, empower and limit the kinesics of the artist's hand. In other words, the tenacious materiality of the countersignature directs the artist as much as it takes all guidance away from him and afflicts his practice with undecidability.[6]

We can summarize the contradiction of guiding-derailing as follows: on the one hand, to make the thing sign is to deliver 'a shattering blow, a quasi-arbitrary affirmation of mastery by means of the exercise of style, the egotistic impression of a form [*un coup de force, d'une affirmation quasi arbitraire de maîtrise à travers l'exercice du style, l'impression égotiste d'une forme*]' (MP 295/351). To make the thing sign is to dominate it through one's signature, but, on the other hand, it is to externalize the 'egotistic impression' of one's name and other idiosyncrasies into style that immediately becomes foreign to the artist and consigns him to a life in the midst of this foreignness: 'If my style marks itself, it is only on the surface which remains invisible and illegible for me. [*Si mon style se marque, c'est seulement sur une face qui me reste invisible, illisible.*] *Point of speculum*: here I am blind to my style, deaf to what is most spontaneous in my voice' (MP 296/352). Mastery and loss of mastery go hand in hand where one accepts and puts to work the signature's divisibility, its eccentricity, its exteriority to itself that facilitate its absorption, appropriation, elaboration (and castration) by the thing in which it is carved. The atomic fission of the point, which, like the signature, is never one and simple, explodes into the work of art that dispenses to the thing the proper and the improper, its own and the artist's signature, such that the former both confirms and denies the latter. This aporetic combination of the counter-signatory confirmation

and denial of mastery over the stylistic signature weaves the infrastructure for the event of art.

4.1.2. *Spongy stones, stony sponges, and the countersignature of the thing*

In the tricky process of negotiation between the thing and the work of
art, the artist's style and stylus toil to remark and retrace the thing's
self-remarking itinerary, which haunts, if not some version of aesthetic
spontaneity and freedom of imagination, then the unity and unicity of
the artistic idiom. To a certain extent this endeavour is successful owing to the iterability of the 'first' signature (as a supplement, the countersignature of the thing comes before that which it supplements), that
is, the iterability of a singularity that generalizes itself in repetition
(L 21). But, in the end, the failure of appropriative retracing may be attributed to the fact that it is oblivious to the detachment of the thing
from itself and from us and to the resistance of a split, deranged point
to everything that would incorporate it into the flow of linearity. Whatever limited success this retracing enjoys is based on dismissing the ir-
retrievable departure of style from the creative subject, of the thing
from itself, and of both from intentional directionality.

The divergence of the signature from the countersignature, which
diverges from itself, opens the spacing of *différance* that temporalizes
the spatial punctuality of style and converts it into a divided instant
standing outside itself.[7] Despite the confusion of signatures between
the artist and the thing on which she works, despite the impositions of
mastery and form on 'mute matter,' the resistant and errant spacing of
the archi-trace has nothing in common with the extension that proliferates from it. From the lacuna of this extension without extension, the
archi-trace of the countersignature gives time that indefinitely defers
the pure presentation of artistic expressivity, interiority, and spontaneity in the exteriority of the thing itself. If I am to come to myself, I must
come, anachronistically, from the time of the other, through the indefinite deferral and suspension of 'my' time.

In the *différance* of my time and my style, of the thing and the other, of
the thing as the other who/that returns as long as there is art to haunt my
signature, 'what is called poetry or literature, art itself ... in other words,
a certain experience of language, of the mark or of the trait *as such* – is
perhaps only an intense familiarity with the ineluctable originarity of the
specter' (SQ 53). The experience of the mark *as such* is the experience not
of an idealized abstraction, but of the thing's self-remarking forays, of its

iterable turns and returns to itself as other before and after all interference on behalf of the active subject. From the standpoint of its detached indifference and pointed cut, the thing haunts, absorbs, de- or ex-propriates the signatory-artist, spirits away the prosthesis of her presence.

What are the 'workings' of this expropriation? How does it come to pass? The answer lies right on the surface – on the strange surface formed by the exteriority of the thing internalizing everything in the manner of a sponge, which embodies what it is not when it imbibes the proper and the improper alike (SI 72). Its exchange with the artist takes place in a liquid, self-liquidating field where the operations of spongy absorption invaginate the thing and the work by turning the exteriority of the thing into a container, a crypt, a differential receptacle for the subject's own interiority, and by translating the work's depth into a 'quasi-arbitrary,' superficial impression of form.[8] The artistic interiority encrypts itself in the exteriority of the thing precisely because the spectral thing haunts, provides a habitation and a world without residing in or inhabiting it. In Derridian aesthetics, even the stone and paper are spongy; they are brimming with receptivity that takes over the propriative mechanisms of signing one's name.

An infinite chain of invaginations produces the sheer exposure of that which encloses and interiorizes until 'at the limit, of the text, of the world, there would remain nothing more than an enormous signature, big with everything it will have engulfed in advance but pregnant with itself alone [*un énorme signature, gross de tout ce qu'elle aura d'avance englouti mas d'elle seule enceinte*]' (G 39/48, left). Alluding to the de-fetishized fetish of the phantom-mother, the signature of the thing engulfs everything a priori, virtually, and 'in advance,' yet without sharing the ground with anything that may flourish from it (note that it is 'pregnant with itself alone'). The archi-trace of the thing presages, 'at the limit,' at the point of 'no point,' on the brink of the world it does not inhabit, the artistic styles and stylizing blows it will have received. Still, the actualization of these blows, their empirical coming into being, is not predetermined by this first quasi-transcendental signature full of its own emptiness. The a priori inflation of the virtual – neither potential nor actual – thingly signature, which does and does not set itself to work as a condition of possibility for the artistic signature, makes possible the event of art.

The event of art belongs to the structure of the signature that falls (to the tomb) – *la signature/tombe* (S 127). According to the logic of *Glas* and *Signsponge*, the signature's fall into the text results in its fallout with the text, since 'by inserting it [the signature] into the body of the text, you monumentalize, institute, and erect it into a thing or a stony object [*l'érige en chose ou objet pierreux*] ... The erection-tomb falls. Step, and stop, of man [*L'érection-tombe. Pas d'homme*]' (SI 56/57). It turns out that not only is every stone a sponge, but every sponge is a stone, a head-stone and a monument for the thingified name. With an eye to Hegel's *Aufhebung*, Derrida deconstructs the difference between the fall and the re-elevating erection of the signatory's remains.[9] What falls (to the tomb) is monumentalized, and, vice versa, what is externalized or monumentalized falls into the interiority of the tomb; what is com-memorated is erased, and, conversely, the erased is commemorated in analogy to a fragile albeit resistant stony vein the sculptor both retraces and ruins. In a whirlpool of indeterminate attributions, a signed name may refer to the name of the name, the person, or the thing. Be this as it may, in the capacity of a signature, it has fallen and has been picked up, borne, supported, countersigned by the stone or paper in which it is stylistically inscribed.

In the bodies of the text and the artwork, the signature evinces the 'reified' remains of the one who signs. For this reason, even the most punctual man is never on time; he is never present to himself in the in-stant of confronting his signature. A certain end of man (and of naive humanism) follows the absorption of the artist's proper, identifiable id-iom in the signature of the thing, marking the expropriation of his sin-gularity and, therefore, the instant of his death. But, given that the idiomatic signature already supplants the living presence of the absent author, this expropriation comes to signify the death of death, which, to repeat, is not quite a renaissance or a resurrection, but a survival (living on, over and above 'pure living') of the encrypted subjective in-teriority in the thing that absorbs it. That is why Derrida plays on the ambiguity of '*pas d'homme*,' which denotes, in a dancelike sequence of approaching and distancing, the deadly 'not' of man – replaced by his signature replaced by the thingly countersignature – and the 'step' of man in the direction of spectral life, of coming to terms with his fini-tude and the irreducibility of death.[10] So, the event of the thing partici-pates in the deconstruction of humanism.

Does the expropriation of artistic subjectivity by the thing open a leeway for an auto-immunizing machination, a 'feigned castration,' or a safekeeping of the absent ipseity? Regarding his own signature, sign-ing his name twice with the already-familiar encryptions '*déjà*' (*D*errida, *J*acques) and '*derrière*' (*Derri*da), Derrida writes: 'I am already [*déjà*] (dead) signifies that I am behind [*derrière*] … At the same time, by cutting myself off, by entrenching myself, by withdrawing my presence, by dying, I escape the blows in advance' (G 84, right). The act of signing one's name twice or an indefinite number of times (for instance, in the conclusion of 'Signature Event Context') is not the same as taking over and mastering the thing's countersignature. The question, rather, is, Do I still recognize myself in the encryption of the signatory that/who abides by the rules of thingly expropriation and experiences the withdrawal of the withdrawal? This is where style recoils into an invisible and illegible surface for inscription, which does not spare my ipseity but leaves me deaf and blind to all 'mineness.'

On the eve of the signature's fall, on the edge of the thing and of the work, the one who signs signals that the work has been finished, truncated, cut short,[11] sealed[12] – *c'est fini*. This termination unfurls the term, the time, the life, or the after-life of the thing, the artefact of art that starts to breathe and sets itself to work without me.[13] The continuous discontinuity of survival, interrupted by the end of work, reproduces the framework of the thing absolved from the subject and from itself, remarking and disseminating itself. But, a blow for a blow, the thing, too, countersigns, cuts and intensifies the initial cut from within. Derrida's reading of Kant construes this freeing up of the cut from itself and of the work from its end in terms of 'vague beauty,' for *vaga* 'is the indefinite thing [*la chose indéfinie*], without determination and without destination (*Bestimmung*), without end (*fin*), without *bout*, without limit' (TP 92/105).[14] Countersignature de-limits the signature's limitation, cutting short the signature's initial cut. Beyond the sharp end of style that signs for the artist, and beyond the thing's bifold negation of the end (*in-dé-finie*), one will have glimpsed the beautiful in all its extravagance: in all its 'wandering,' non-identifiable vagueness.

4.1.3. *Painting with an auto-affective eye (double vision)*

A case in point for the operations of the stylistic signature is the genre of self-portraiture under the subheading of painting. For several reasons, Derrida deems painting to be more than an art among the arts.[15] Why is it accorded a special status? First, its protocols gravitate toward the procedures for outlining the trace as such, that is, toward the supplementarity of reproduction that precedes and disturbs all aspirations to *poiesis* and dreams of pure presence.[16] Drawing is spacing and tracing; therefore, it is a kind of writing. Second, the graphics of drawing bear upon the contestation of the very 'truth of truth' (TP 282) – not upon those limited attempts to establish a precise and adequate corre-lation between a representation and what it represents, but upon the appearing of what appears (or appears to appear) to us in the refrac-tory effects of frames, parerga, and so on. Third, all painting is a point-ing, an exhibitionistic showing with nothing in sight except for the material means of painting, hence an 'obscure self-showing,'[17] portray-ing itself as the 'thing itself' (US 89). Thus, in different ways, the three explanations say that the privilege of painting rests on its quasi-transcendental style.

Self-portraiture, in particular, arrests Derrida's attention because of the permanent fissures and intrusions of alterity in the apparently auto-affective exercise of depicting oneself. Let us methodically go through the list of these fissures that situate hetero-affection at the heart of auto-affection and isolate the countersignature of the thing in drawing. If I am now drawing myself, how many are we in this scene? 'I am drawing myself' echoes Husserl's 'I hear myself speak'; in both cases, the spatio-temporal delay between my departure from and arrival at myself makes us at least two. The draughtsman, the 'who,' is at the same time the model, the 'what.' While he turns himself into a representing-represented thing, it receives and absorbs his likeness. Finally, the medi-ator in this exchange is sense, itself divided in 'double vision.'

Double vision occasions the double bind of blindness in a condensed version of the aporia that energizes the overall argument of *Memoirs of the Blind*. On the one hand, the artist who sees himself seeing sees noth-ing *visible* save for the condition of possibility for visually registering things in the world. Prior to seeing the entities in the world, such tran-scendental vision gives something to be seen. Its ageless act of pure looking escapes the confines of empirical recognition, 'sees itself blind,' sees itself disappear (MB 57).[18] On the other hand, the artist who sees his eye ready to be drawn transfigures it into a thing, into something seen and, therefore, something unseeing, something blind: 'Your eyes are not only seeing but also visible. And since they are *visi-ble* (things or objects in the world [*choses ou objets dans la monde*]) as much as *seeing* (at the origin of the world [*à l'origin du monde*]), I could precisely touch them' (OT 3/ 13). Touching or touching up his own eye with the brush-strokes on a canvas, the draughtsman shuttles between a thing in the world and the origin of the world (in the thing itself). He practises the aesthetic version of phenomenological reduction and strips the layers of functional signification from the eye-thing, which, unworkable and unadorned, appears in its mereness.[19] Consequently, transcendental blindness surpasses the traditionally negative scope within which the empirical phenomenon of vision's absence falls. Serving as the impossible condition of possibility for seeing and for the appearing of the thing, it stands for vision's double, for the contrapunctal vision of the thing: sight from the standpoint of the thing.

The splitting of the eye, the division that occurs in the 'thing' of sight, has been a long-standing theme in Derrida's work, a theme that goes as far back as *Speech and Phenomena*, where the 'punctuality of the instant [*ponctualité de l'instant*],' the unsustainable 'source point' of the living present irretrievably loses itself in the blink of an eye (SP 62/68). It is here that the source point enucleates or gouges out the ocular origin of vision and sees itself reflected in the well of tears that, in their very purity, occlude it. Requiring a constant repetition of the living present, this point necessitates, by the same token, spacing and death, so that by the time the artist signs his self-portrait, death is looking him in the eye from his own indifferent, absolved, thingified gaze that emanates from the other (thing).

In self-portraiture, which according to the full title of *Memoirs of the Blind* is a ruin, death arrives 'as soon as the draftsman considers himself, fascinated, fixed on the image, yet disappearing before his own eyes into the abyss' because 'the movement by which he tries desperately to recapture himself is already, in its very present, an act of memory' (MB 68). As though responding to Bergson, Derrida implies that it is a mistake to speak of pure perception onto which individual accidents of memory 'are merely grafted.'[20] Memory is at work in the present, in that it permeates perception with the temporal flow of retention-protention and causes vision to lag behind itself. This time lag and this temporalization become especially blatant when I shift my gaze away from one thing to another, from the 'model' to the canvas, from my whoness to my whatness, in order to reproduce – belatedly, 'by heart' – the one on the other.

There is, nonetheless, a limit to the mad rush of memorialized perception and to the substitution of things with other things. Concomitantly with conditioning the perceptual time lag, the thing itself draws this limit as it enters its fugitive mode:

> Just as I was about to draw, I no longer *saw* the thing [*au moment de dessiner, je ne* voyais *plus la chose*]. For it immediately flees [*s'évade*], drops out of sight, and almost nothing of it remains; it disappears before my eyes,

which, in truth, no longer perceive anything but the mocking arrogance of this disappearing apparition [*apparition disparaissante*]. As long as it remains in front of me, the thing defies me [*Pour autant qu'elle reste devant moi, la chose me défie*]. (MB 36/43)

Before it conjures up Bergson, Derrida's virtual response addresses Kant, in particular the 'first two moments of the transcendental synthesis': the apprehension of an object in intuition and its reproduction in imagination. The intuitive apprehension of that which 'remains' (Derrida is careful not to use the copula) in front of me is displaced and endlessly deferred by imaginative reproduction[21] that, in vain, strives to restitute the present of perception and, with it, the thing and truth themselves.[22] Admittedly, the fugitive spectrality of the thing imbricated with its material resistance ('the thing defies me'), or else the 'heterogeneity between the thing drawn and the drawing *trait*' (MB 45), is a quandary for all genres of painting. That having been said, self-portraiture remains unique because what it remembers and reproduces is the portraitist's own blind interiority stylistically pointed out, supported by and exposed to exteriority, the artist's self entrusted to the thing, and the singularity of the idiomatic stylistic marks assimilated in the experience of the mark 'as such.' The disappearance of the thing between its two modalities absorbs and countersigns the disappearance of the artist, who cannot recapture, re-gather, or intuitively apprehend herself in the present of her life. From the hither side of life, the artist's self-styling signature falls on the canvas, monumentalizes her eye, and, in so doing, ruins it as a seeing and weeping organ. A tragic sight, self-portrait weeps for the loss of life never lived and for the eye's capacity to see and to weep.

Despite the inherence of death in self-portraiture, the thing's countersignature promises survival by virtue of its looking at us (as well as at the draughtsman and at him in us), by virtue of its ordering, ordaining, and assigning 'a place to the spectator, to the visitor, to the one whose seeing blinds' (MB 62). What kind of an uncanny place is it, if not the place of displacement and substitution? When the draughtsman binds his signature to the countersignature of the thing, it works as a mirror for his face, but for us, the spectators facing it, it reflects the other (the draughtsman) who interposes himself in our place through the medium of his portrait. His spectral *pas* – step/not – takes him behind the thingly painted uncanny mirror with the excess of tain on both sides. In line with the structure of invagination, the mirror will expropriate, absorb, and encrypt the artist's singularity, only to reflect and project it with marked indifference, regardless of the subject who stands in front of it. At the price of abandoning mastery and becoming foreign to herself in the abysses of memory and on the surface of style, at the expense of becoming blind to herself, the self-portraitist keeps a trace of herself in the other, be it the thing, or the spectator who re-finds himself in the other's self-portrait.

In addition to the outright descent into blindness, double vision carries the connotations of being vague or blurred, for instance, when tears veil the gaze that 'neither sees nor does not see: it is indifferent to its blurred vision [*Il ne voit ni ne voit pas, il est indifférent à la vue brouillée*]' (MB 127/128). Such blurring alone corresponds to the vague beauty of the indefinite thing liberated from serving an end, just as a tearing or a visible eye uncoupled from the purpose of seeing attains its thingly mereness. Thus, the meaning of the truth in painting, which makes light of the correspondence theory of truth, entails the adequation of two 'inadequacies': the deficient (because over-rich, excessive) sight, and the indefinite thing lacking either a limit or a strict determination. Vaguely formulated, this adequation postulates that we continually receive things that receive us and welcome us in the world. We are blind to this infinite receptivity that points us out without being pointed out or restituted, but our blindness can be appreciated and sublated in the aesthetic experience: 'What guides the graphic point, the quill, pencil, or scalpel is the respectful *observance* of a commandment, the acknowledgement before knowledge, the gratitude of the receiving before seeing, the blessing before the knowing' (MB 29–30). What guides these instruments of style that threaten to pierce the eye in the very instant they give it a sharper sense of vision is what wounds itself in wounding the other, withdraws itself and withdraws its guidance as soon as seeing and knowing reassert their primacy and, mutatis mutandis, the priority of identity, identification, and recognition.

On a more literal register, double vision ensues when two distinct monocular or cyclopic visions are not synthesized into one and do not yield a unified viewpoint. Derrida's emphasis on ocular un-pairing, the detachment of one eye from another and from its socket substantiates the point he makes in *The Truth in Painting* on the subject of the paired shoes (abandoned but still available for the resumption of 'normal' use). It highlights the sublime 'obscenity' of aesthetic experience, in which the thing frees itself from use and from itself by way of its extraction from synthetic bonds.

Commenting on an episode from Homer's *Odyssey*, Derrida writes: 'The eye of a cyclops gives rise to heterogeneous representations ... An eye, the one-and-only-eye, the monocle, is never an object [*Un oeil, l'oeil-un, le monocle, n'est jamais un objet*]. Sometimes it appears open like a wound whose fleshy lips are still bleeding: the obscenity of a scar, the impossible suture of a slit, frontal genitality' (MB 89–92/94). The intricacy of the visual cleft is that, even though it analyses synthetic binocular vision into two monocles, the monocle itself is not one. In the eye of a cyclops, the synthetic one becomes the unpaired two it has always been underneath the ruses of contrived self-identity. Instead of propagating a thesis and an antithesis, unpairing generates an antinomy, 'gives rise to heterogeneous representations,' two independent points of view, sources, perspectives, hypotheses constantly competing with each other. The dehiscence of the two lids of one eye (the paradigm of hetero-affection in auto-affection) is an effect of the virtual spacing that provides habitation without abiding, without enclosing itself in either of the contested perspectives. The assertion that this eye is 'never an object' is another way of saying that it is a non-objectifiable thing, whose withdrawal from the realm of representation occasions the emergence and registration of recognizable objects, or better, allows them to take shape between the eyelids, in the void of the pupil. And, inversely, were it able, momentarily, to suture and to cover itself with 'the obscenity of a scar,' recalling the immemorial experience of castration ('frontal genitality'), the eye would have to blink, to bring together the eyelids, to veil itself, to lapse back into the non-presence and non-coincidence of the instant.

4.2. Subjectile, the 'epoch' of the thing

The subjectile[23] is the aesthetic means or the 'how' capable of disengaging and liberating the thing's alterity. The argument of this section outlines three stages of this disengagement: 1) the process, through which the subjectile infiltrates aesthetic practices, reducing the subject-object correlation to a self-remarking and disseminated thing, 2) the meaning of the thing's thrownness exacerbated by the thrownness of the artist, and 3) the subsequent itinerary of a purposeless thing that remains free and disengaged since it does not arrive at a pre-given destination but renders representation (and itself) abyssal. It is on the verge of this abyss that the event of the thing in art looms before and after all empirical happenings, fads and fashions, installations, and exhibitions.

4.2.1. Reductio ad rem: *In the memory of ...*

In the footsteps of Heidegger, who emphasizes the role of the work and the thing in art, Derrida redraws the boundaries of aesthetic experience and reshuffles its component parts. What is remarkable is that he does so by means of a superfluous supplement that forgoes the addition of anything strictly speaking new to the traditional (Kantian) subject-object edifice. Calling this supplement 'the subjectile' and locating it between and below the ossified structures of aesthetic discourse, Derrida pays particular attention to its dynamism and force, or rather to the differential of forces that energizes these structures without being reducible to them. Indeed, the subjectile metonymically stands in for art as such and is the reductive force – superfluous, or even 'wasted' – capable of releasing the instability of the thing from the constraints of representation and from the strictures of subjective and objective forms that grow in multifarious sedimentations above it. In the non-representational epoch of the thing, a transfigured practice of *epoché* grounded in the exercise of phenomenological reduction thus aligns itself with the non-identity of the thing split at the point of style.[24]

The non-identical thing is beside itself, stands outside itself, is exterior both to itself and to the interiority of the subject it absorbs. Radical exteriority is deranged: mad, maddening, beyond its own range or limit. The interiorization of subjective interiority in the ecstatic thingly exteriority requires a rethinking of the relation between the inside and the outside, the surface and the depth, and the Derridian rendition of Artaud's 'subjectile' offers a springboard for this task. As the immemorial and doubly passive 'thrown throwing' that underlies 'thrown projection', that deconstructs the oppositionality of subjects/objects, movement/stasis, means/ends, and that reconfigures the spatiality of being-in-the-world, the subjectile 'is nothing, however, nothing but a solidified interval *between* above and below, visible and invisible, before and behind, this side and that' (US 78). In other words, the subjectile is a heteronym of invagination that incessantly unfolds, turns interiority inside out only to carefully fold or carelessly crumple it and create a pocket on the inside before dissolving it again, back into the outside surface of the textile. Its thrust is also that of Husserlian reduction, which is oriented toward and aims at the exteriority of the 'things themselves,' stripping the layers of subjective belief and historical sedimentations of imposed meanings in order to reach if not some inner kernel of the thing's originary essence, then at least a certain exteriority of sense that is more interior still than all interiority we include under the heading of the 'subject.'

But, in contrast to phenomenological bracketing, the particular reduction of the subjectile does not culminate in the institution either of a transcendental ego or of a self-same ideal object. While 'To Unsense the Subjectile' reinterprets the sub-ject as that which is thrown below and the ob-ject as that against which the subject is thrown, the subjectile brackets the spatial prefixes 'sub-' and 'ob-' that belong to the two terms. In so doing, it isolates the moment of hurling, or ' –jection,' before its interiorization in 'introjection' and its exteriorization in 'projection'; what remains is the throwing gesture of a send-off indifferent to who or what is being thrown and 'interposed between the –ject of the object and the –ject of the subject' (US 80). Besides exploring the dynamic basis for Heidegger's thrown projection, this remainder 'intrinsically' opens interiority to exteriority[25] and, hence, reduces, 'epochalizes,' and temporalizes spatiality in the interval of différance ('between above and below') that does not fit inside the spatial order it summons into being.

It follows that the subjectile sets to work or operationalizes the thing with its vacillation between the 'who' and the 'what,' its exceptionality in and non-belonging to the very space it spaces (temporalizes), and its vacillation between absorbent indifference and the exteriorization of the interior. Like the thing, 'a subjectile is never identified with the subject or the object even when it occupies their place and being [*occupant parfois leur place et en tenant lieu, un subjectile ne s'identifie jamais au sujet ou à l'objet*]' (US 72/60). But in what way is this non-identity of the supplementing and the supplemented relevant to art? At what point does the subjectile-thing bring aesthetic experience into the fray of hurling gestures devoid of subjects and objects?

The establishment of a triangular nexus linking the subjectile, the thing, and art passes through the detour of memory. In the course of reading Paul de Man's interpretation of Hegel's 'provocative declaration' that art is 'a thing of the past,' Derrida notes:

If art is a thing of the past, this comes from its link, through writing, the sign, *tekhnè*, with that thinking memory, that memory without memory, with that power of *Gedächtnis* without *Erinnerung*. This power, we now know, is *pre-occupied* by a past which has never been present and will never allow itself to be reanimated in the interiority of consciousness. (MPD 65)

First of all, the Hegelian declaration defines art as a thing. In and of it-self, this will transport aesthetic practice into the realm beyond creative interiority where 'expressivity' no longer signifies the exterior-ization of the subject's private pathos. But art is not a thing in the ab-stract. The determination proper to it is the 'thing of the past,' the thing endowed with a memory of the past that has 'never been present,' or differently put, in terms that are decidedly Levinasian, a trace that has never been internal to consciousness.[26] Derrida calls this memory *of* ex-teriority a 'pre-occupation with the past' in the sense of 1) a nagging obsession or fascination with something that has never been present and that, consequently, cannot be represented, brought into the pres-ent's midst, without being lost as such, and 2) a prior occupation (marked by the prefix *pre-*), a spacing before space, a self-effacing and withdrawing welcome extended to subjective memory (*Erinnerung*) and to interiority.

In the manner of the subjectile, the thing pre-occupies subjects and objects. It sanctions their appearing only by irrecoverably disappear-ing, by absenting itself from the present (whether purely 'living,' or inscribed in the retention-protention continuum), intuition, and sym-bolic representation. In opposition to this series of terms, Derrida and de Man identify art with a certain delay, for which 'writing, the sign, *tekhnè*' are responsible. In the Kantian spirit, the pre-occupation with and of the thing becomes accessible only a posteriori, thanks to *Gedächtnis*, the memory devoid of recollection that does not gather the subject's interiority and is, therefore, unable to 'recover this past' (MPD 66).[27] The irrecoverable past of the first throw, the unchosen 'thrown throwing' that bars the 'throwing off' of projection, announces itself in the glowing half-light of radical passivity only in retrospect, in a 'rear-view mirror,' by virtue of a reduction affecting meaningful pro-jection, masterful resoluteness, and sovereign decision-making.

The memory of the subjectile is a memory of receptivity and impas-sive suffering that transpires on the obverse of the thing's 'material schematism,' the cleaving open of the 'real' of archi-writing. Whereas the proto-trace of the thing lodged in its material substratum has im-posed a certain inexorable necessity on the form of the artwork, the subjectile has 'suffered everything that as a support it had to with-stand, and to withstand passively under all the blows' but without re-vealing anything 'of what it is feeling, suffering, bearing' (US 122, 137). That's why Derrida can say that the mute passivity of the thing as the absolute other, inassimilable to the interiority of the subject, gives a formal injunction (the law), both stern and indifferent: 'The thing remains an other whose law demands the impossible [*La chose reste un autre dont la loi demande l'impossible*]' (SI 14/15). The trace of the thing and the blows left on the 'body' of the subjectile disseminate and erase themselves in giving form, providing support, or giving in to that which violently retraces them.[28] So understood, form names nothing but the scar tissue constantly forming and growing in the memory and in the place of the thingly cut.

But Artaud's examples of the thingly suffering – the crumpled and soiled paper, *either* botched, spoiled, and wasted, *or* preserved in its very botching, *or*, again, 'successfully' subjected to the weight and pointed blows of the pencil and of the hand – pale in comparison with the reduction and retreat of paper itself in the virtualization of aesthetic and typographical media.[29] The most severe blow does not even leave a mark; it withdraws the withdrawal and reduces the reduction of the subjectile, not in the sense of negating them but in the sense of bringing to light, making apparent, making phenomenal the thing's non-expressive, non-revelatory suffering by causing that which bears it to disappear in toto. Although the reduction of the materiality of paper is nothing new, although it is always included in the (self-)giving of paper, it mirrors the 'vulgarity of circumcision' because it, too, seeks to present and represent the self-remarked itinerary of the thing *as such*, even if this presentation no longer occurs tangibly, in flesh and blood, but virtually and reductively.

Despite all its figurative and virtual manifestations, the subjectile cannot be separated from the body proper[30] that survives, the 'real' body that dies away from death, promised and given in the experience of reduction. In her turn, the survivor undergoes a reductive de-distancing from that language, which is separated from the body whose literality transcends the opposition of the exterior letter and the interior spirit of the text. Neither meaningful nor meaningless, the reduction heralded by the subjectile suspends a relation to meaning in the becoming-literal and becoming-material of language that 'no longer sublimate[s] itself or make[s] itself subtle toward some sense or some object [*se sublimer ou se subtiliser en direction d'un sens ou d'un objet*]' (US 118/88).[31]

With this refusal to be tamed and, literally, to underlie, to put itself under some object, the subjectile's inordinate –*jection* approximates the inexpressively expressive, non-revelatory language of the thing that marks itself off or undergoes a senseless mishandling before being remarked by the subject and sublimated into an object of sense. It repeats the story of *shibboleth*, the password that works only if one pronounces it correctly, the password in which the 'relation to the meaning or the thing was suspended, neutralized, bracketed: the opposite, one might say, of a phenomenological *epochē*, which preserves, above all, the meaning' (SQ 22). Bypassing meaning and subjective memory, the subjectile relates to the thing from the depths of non-relationality, by way of deepening the cut and exacerbating the self-dissociation of the thing. This relation without relation is more than justifiable in view of the thing's absolution from itself, its exteriority to itself that does not admit any straightforward recognition and identification, nor any subtlety 'toward some sense or some object.'[32] Un-sensed, foreign to sense, the subjectile reduces the otherwise irreducible phenomenological pre-occupations with pure consciousness and ideal objectivity and faithfully shadows the alterity of the thing.

4.2.2. Thrown together: The artist and the thing

The subjectile reduces the subject and the object to the force of the *–ject* or *–jection* that underpins these congealed forms, but the 'product' of this reduction leads a life of its own in what Derrida refers to as the 'jetty' – a word derived from the French verb *jeter*, 'to throw.'[33] Both stabilizing and destabilizing, the jetty plays on the indeterminacy of the throw's meaning and trajectory. Something thrown in a particular direction will be preserved upon arrival (or so one hopes), but before this hope has a chance to arise on one's practical and theoretical horizons, the act of throwing invokes something expendable and worth throwing *out*. Of course, the two senses of the throw – delivery and expendability – are intertwined. The ejected missive or missile, which may or may not arrive at its destination, is disseminated, thus potentially wasted, sent for nothing. But only the wasted residue remains, is commemorated, monumentalized, and delivered in its 'proper' ruination and erasure. The work of the thing's self-remarking dissemination is already evident in this duality of the jetty.

Nourished by several sources, from Heidegger to Freud and beyond, the throw has entered a number of Derrida's works that belong to the 'middle period,' such as *Glas* and *The Postcard*. The latter book, for instance, conceives of the throw as one of the moments of the *fort/da* play with the spool 'thrown in front of or beneath oneself.' In this case, the thrown thing is safely attached to the child by a string that bespeaks an attempted reparation of its prior detachment and separation, as well as the constancy of the rhythm, whereby the send-offs follow the returns: 'To speculate: it would be never to throw the thing (but does the child ever throw it without its being attached to a string?), that is to keep it at a distance continuously, but always at the same distance' (PC 315). The narcissistic great speculator, be it the child or his grandfather, throws the thing without throwing it, consigning it to chance or letting it go, rhythmically replaces all displacements, recollects himself around the thing's fictitious departure, and sutures the cut tie.

Even in the otherwise risky infrastructure of *Glas*, the throw does not dare to proceed without the safety nets (however contrived) called upon to capture the remains, the 'cut morsels,' the ostensibly absolved things that fall into the recomposed text: 'The morsels, which I cut [*coupe*] and sew [*couds*] in the text ... must neither destroy its form ... nor recompose or recapture [*ressaisir*] its integrity in one of those nets – formal or semantic – that we have feigned to throw and rethrow without counting' (G 169, right). The throw is feigned, and the feigning – infinitely repeated ('without counting'). The formal and semantic nets multiply and enmesh the strings of the spool securing the subject (whether it is a singular 'I' or a plural 'we'), who, despite its scission between the two columns of the text, cuts, sews, and cares for the integrity of the inevitably mutilated form at the expense of the force released in the suspension and ejection of the morsels. It appears, therefore, that in the texts of the middle period, the throw is still too formal and, as a result of this formality, is excessively manipulated by the thrower, who only pretends to let the thing go and who remains immune to the experience of being thrown, abandoned, wasted along with the emancipated thing.

A drastic change of strategy becomes evident in Derrida's engagement with Artaud's non-representational aesthetic practice, where the artist and the thing of art co-participate in the gesture of hurling constituting the artwork:

All the heterogeneous categories of 'means' are deliberately associated in the same series, and they are means of 'pure painting': the thing to represent, the sky and the plain just as much as the body of the artist and the material, that is the place from which painting spurts forth (the tubes) but also these two supports or receptacles of the spurt projected forth, the 'canvases' and this support of the support which is an easel (US 97).

The purity of 'pure painting' is the effect of its reduction to the subjectile's indifferent force that throws a sketch on the canvas; that squirts,
destines, and wastes the paint; that inheres in the stroke of the brush,
in the blow of the hand that delivers it, or in the artist's (e.g., Jackson
Pollock's) treading on the canvas. Pure painting is pure movement, a
plastic art of pointing. In it, the means are not only on a par with one
another ('associated in the same series'), but they are also the only
ends, the only conceivable targets and delimitations of praxis. If the
body of the artist is thrown alongside all the other things that spurt
forth into the artwork, then, like any subjectile, it must impassively
suffer its 'supporting role' as pure means and come to terms with the
possibility that, in throwing itself, it may be throwing itself out. Thus,
Derrida would agree with Heidegger that Dasein is in the world not
quite in the same way the water is in a glass, but he would rethink the
existential spatiality and thrownness of Dasein under the rubric of
throwing out and wasting. We are aborted into the world like a by-
product of being – wasted, yet kept and preserved in our ownmost
being-wasted with others and alongside things.[34] The name for this
preservation of the existential waste is art.

How to understand the togetherness of this throw, the alliance,
which the work of the subjectile signs and seals, between the artist and
the art-thing? And what about the release, the freeing up of the thing?
How do I let it fall and permit it to breathe without me at the end of my
work, if I throw myself with it? It is undeniable that, being thrown
along with the thing, the artist no longer accompanies it or binds himself to it from the standpoint of presence and of the present. Since the
thingly –*jection* is a futural and uncertain throw of a dice, he takes a
chance, gives himself the chance, and turns himself into the chance of
the thing. To say that he disseminates and wastes himself together with
the thing is to confirm that the artist joins its ownmost disjointure and
falling apart.[35] Such disseminated togetherness is inaugurated by the
repeatable (potentially idealizable) gesture of a throwing that does not
anticipate the trajectory of the actual repeated throw, does not pre-
scribe what materials are to be thrown, and does not predict the time-
place of their fall. Therefore, the heterogeneity of the means in pure
painting, including the artist herself, may be 'associated in the same series' without becoming immediately levelled and homogenized.

Glas summarizes the counterpoint to this joint ejection particularly
well: in a reciprocal retreat, the artist withdraws, while the work
does not remain present to the artist, but 'fall[s] from him like a thing

truncated in space [*tomber de lui comme une chose tronque dans l'espace*], like some wonderful excrement on top of which the master sits enthroned while forgetting himself' (G 258/286, left). A truncated thing is a signed and cut thing that survives thanks to the sublimational self-forgetting of the artist,[36] which the memory of exteriority (*Gedächtnis*) keeps. But a beautiful thing countersigns the artistic signature with its own vagueness and indefiniteness; it signs against signing and cuts in order not to be cut. So, what if, in being thrown together with the thing, the artist borrows this countersignature and cunningly signs by way of countersigning? The outcome of this resistance to the cut conforms to the extravagant aesthetics of *The Truth in Painting*, which leaves vague and indefinite both the artist herself and the aesthetic thing without a destination, a purpose, or an end.

At this precise moment, two figures of freedom collide in the confrontation between the artist's excremental release *of* the thing and his release *with* the thing. The thing's absolution takes another turn toward the non-identical by dividing itself in two: freedom of self-determination and freedom from any determination whatsoever.[37] Whereas the former substantiates the thing's self-remarking iteration prior to the emergence of a formalized system of signification, the latter concerns the dissemination of its effects, or their non-arrival at a predetermined destination. The impossible but necessary task, then, is to maintain the two non-synthetically, in the midst of an aporia that prescribes, at the same time, a falling away from and a falling with the thing.

Thrown together with the thing on the 'working' side of the work of art, the artist feels everything inflicted on it immediately inflicted on her, right on the surface of her own skin. 'Forcing the thing a little [*forçant un peu la chose*]' (US 139/101), she forces herself a little; cutting, scraping, filing, sewing, unsewing, shredding, stitching it, she cuts, scrapes, and so on, herself (US 140–2). On the empirical level, there is certainly a difference between the impassive, mute suffering of the thing and the passionate suffering of a living body in the throes of agonizing pain phenomenally enacted by contemporary performance artists, such as Stellarc. But, on the quasi-transcendental level of the subjectile, on the plane of a reduced 'pure' painting that aporetically incorporates into itself a whole series of heterogeneous means, this difference is transcribed into a much more 'indifferent' differential of forces partaking of the dynamics of the throw. In phenomenological terms, the subjectile is the residue of reduction, a de-individualized *act* that materially aims at the ideality of sense.[38] Although, in its subjectilian per-version, this act is no longer purely mental, and although it lacks a final destination (sense) toward which it may have been oriented, it retains the kind of difference that distinguishes, for instance, the look or the gaze from the act of looking.

Does artistic passion imitate the suffering of the thing? If the concept of mimesis still made sense in the non-representational realm of the subjectile, then it would have undergone a profound and irreversible transformation to account for the jointure of thrownness.[39] As Derrida warns the reader in 'The Double Session,' which doubles Plato with Mallarmé, one should not hurry to translate mimesis as imitation; rather, it either 'signifies the presentation of the thing itself [*la présentation de la chose même*]' or 'sets up a relation of *homoiōsis* or *adaequatio* between two (terms)' (D 193/219). And indeed, while the first option would not be applicable to the artist who takes a chance, who throws herself or is thrown with the thing, refusing to bind herself to its presence or representation, the second option is not far off the mark, except that the relation set up between the two is the adequation of non-adequation, treason, and betrayal of truth (US 107) whereby the artist joins the thing's disjointure and takes part in its dissemination. The 'presentation of the thing itself' would negate it as a thing that is never present to itself: this is a dead end skirted by the effort of setting up a relation 'in flight' (that is to say, in the interminable negotiation between the artist and the art-thing), in flux, in the 'gushing forth' of the subjectile that 'does not come from an originating being' but is born in and borne by the throw itself (US 96).[40]

Even if we were careless enough to translate mimesis as imitation, who or what will have been a mime and who or what will have been imitated, given that there are no layers of reality independent of artistic 'representation' after 'the thing to represent' – including 'the sky and the plain' – has been associated in the same series with the means of pure painting? Before being one, before being signified, before 'being,' the subjectile thing is already internally ruptured, miming and remarking itself. But so is *phusis* internally affected with *tekhnè* in Derrida's interpretation of Kant's and Aristotle's aesthetics. The mimetic function of the subjectile is the transference, shuttling, or translation of effects that traverse the series of heterogeneous means without a cause hypostatized in the thing itself, in the imitated referent, in the final instance of truth. In this, it is similar to the Kantian idea of aesthetic beauty, which does not copy this or that thing but reproduces the productivity of productive nature.[41]

Kant understands this productivity in terms of its originary character and takes the aesthetic reproduction to be derivative or secondary. Nevertheless, even for him, it is not an empirical referent, but something that reaches back to the time (if we may still call it 'time') before nature's 'critical dissociation,' and therefore, we might add, before the time of the transcendental aesthetic.[42] Pre-occupied by the immemorial past of nature that has not yet split against itself, art, which is a thing of the past, is the evidence of this split and the aspiration to obliterate this very evidence. Non-natural, artificial beauty is natural production differed and deferred, but this difference and this deferral embody mimesis in the beautiful thing itself that mimes and remarks, gives and erases itself. Thus, 'the thing is *mimesis* [*La chose, c'est la mimésis*]' (SI 138/139).

The togetherness or the doubling of the throw, binding the artist to the thing, is a permutation of mimesis minus the self-sufficient end (e.g., truthful representation or production), which the movement of the subjectile brackets. 'The referent is lifted, but reference remains: what is left is only the writing of dreams, a fiction that is not imaginary, *mimicry without imitation*, without verisimilitude, without truth or falsity ...' (D 211). The accounting for 'what is left' describes deconstructive hyper-mimesis, the subjectile suspended – both hovering in mid-air and bracketed, such that its 'epochalized' motion is no longer opposed to stasis – in the togetherness of the artist's and the art-thing's throw.

4.2.3. Instead of arriving: 'The bottom without bottom of things'

The artist and the thing are thrown together, but their falls are infinitely deferred. The suspension of the subjectile does not allow them to hit the ground unless we call by that dubious name a certain 'ground without ground,' an abyss. Admittedly, the abyss of representation has been already made palpable in the confusion *within* the heterogeneous means and the confusion *between* the means and ends of pure painting, as much as in memory's preoccupation with the immemorial, indefinite past that has never been present. And yet there is another, deeper stratum to the abyss. This stratum, which is absent from the relation binding the thing to whatever aims at it, is buried in the thing itself, whether one defines it as 'beautiful,' that is, as necessarily vague, vagabond, and extravagant, or whether its silence, its 'obstinacy of not showing' the suffering of the subjectile, means 'that at bottom, at the bottom without bottom of things [*qu'au fond, au fond sans fond des choses*] ... it has nothing to complain about' (US 138/99).

The thing's self-remarking dissemination is excessive and abyssal not merely because it gives and withdraws the ground from underneath our bare feet and feetless shoes, but also because it flees from itself and positively 'de-fines' or ruins (*abîmer*) itself throughout its fugal movement.

There are, then, two abysses – that of representation and that of the thing itself – and each of the two has a double bottom that constitutes it as an abyss: 'The present presents itself as the simplicity of a bottom or ground ... As soon as there is a double bottom, there is no bottom or ground at all in the process of formation' (D 308). So if 'bottom' or 'ground' refers to the simplicity and fundamentality of the present, then its originary repetition in representation (in other words, the infinite reflection of the two)[43] introduces a second bottom that, instead of reinforcing the first, leaves the present groundless. Representation itself falls into the abyss of the unrepresentable. In traditional aesthetics, this abyss, this immense, immeasurable, and incommensurable dimension that overwhelms the subject and her imagination, is classified under the heading of 'the sublime.' But the other abyss, the beautiful 'bottom without bottom of things,' is not sublime, because it places no demand, however negative and impossible, on our knowledge and judgment, but belongs exclusively to the thing that remarks and withdraws itself in the face of all attempts at its objectification. Still, Derrida seems to confine this second level of the abyss to a Kantian architectonics with a tinge of Platonism: 'Surreptitiously, a place where everything appears, itself it disappears under the phenomena, it's the thing in itself [*la chose en soi*] or again the transcendental object = X taking the relay of the *khōra*' (US 143/102).

Derrida's thing in itself is neither a limit to human knowledge, with which it shares no horizon, nor a prosthetic device recruited by various epistemological programs in order to support them from a position of relative exteriority. For Derrida, the thing in itself is a hauntological entity *and* an impossible condition of possibility that, like the signature, is big with everything in advance, but full of or sated with itself alone, satisfied with the iteration of its own indefinite vagueness and emptiness: with the thing in the thing in the thing in the thing ... The thing's radical and absolute exteriority interiorizes everything, including itself, ad infinitum, even as it disappears with every unique apparition of the phenomena effectively born from its abyssal repetitions, and even as, thanks to its bottomlessness, it does not hold (read, does not hold together or synthesize) anything inside itself.

What could be seen as the philosophical revival of Hegel's 'bad infinity' is the aporetic conjoining, hinging and unhinging, of the thing's plentitude on the abyss. It is in this faint light that I want to read the opening line of the 'Parergon' section of *The Truth in Painting* –' It's enough to say: abyss and satire of the abyss [*c'est assez dire: abîme et satire de l'abîme*]' (TP 17/21) – the line that is, itself, abyssal, and that puts an abyss in the abyss because the 'smallest circle' of satisfaction, of 'it's enough,' addressed to a particular instance of excess, already inscribes in itself the figure of the largest circle: *sati*, the 'Enough!' of Homeric laughter mocking all existence, satire.[44] The satire of satire is that it is satisfied with the bottomless bottom of the abyss, of the presumed negativity of the thing's absolution, which, amid patient suffering, directs itself to us and bears things in silence. 'It's enough to say' this cryptic expression once and anew each time, acknowledging, with the same nod, the bad infinity of the thing's invagination and its permanent interruption with the decisive 'Enough!' Suffice it to say that this will be an event of saying: repeatable, yet non-idealizable, unobjected, touching the abyss, relevant to the thing called 'abyss' and the abyss of the thing. That is why the first line of 'Parergon' hangs on the outer edge of the text's first internal frame, immodestly enclosing the empty space drawn from the abyss.

'Enough!' may also betoken the incapacity to endure pain and suffer any longer, a protest or simply a cry of pain that marks the instant when the two trajectories of the throw diverge, when the throes of a living body's agony put an end to reduction (bracketing or diminution), when I fall out with the thing and can accompany it no more. The impatience of suffering botches, uncouples, unhinges the throw, which, as such, sends off something botched, ready to be wasted. This 'something' is the pathos of artistic suffering and the 'subjectilian Thing': 'That the Thing – which is above all not a thing for hypostasis – *should betray* [*Que la Chose – qui n'est surtout pas une chose à hypostasier –* trahisse], that it should be, in its very "botching," what he [Artaud] must "give life and existence" to, that is what was clearly shown' (US 137/99). Below, I develop, as though from the deconstructive 'negatives,' two snapshots of this artistic 'gift of life and existence' handed over to the botched thing across the abyss.

The first snapshot portrays a flower. In the last sentences of 'White Mythology,' Derrida writes,

There is always, absent from every garden, a dried flower in a book; and by virtue of the repetition in which it endlessly puts itself into *abîme*, no

language can reduce itself into the structure of an anthology [*Il y a toujours, absente de tout jardin, une fleur séchée dans un livre; et en raison de la ré-
pétition où elle s'abîme sans fin, aucun langage ne peut réduire en soi la structure
d'une anthologie*]. (MP 271/358)

The dried flower (of rhetoric) in a book is dead, immemorially up-
rooted, ungrounded, picked with the '*sans* of a pure cut,' removed
from the natural domain, and preserved as a bookmark.[45] Its death
does not go unnoticed in the garden, from which it is always absent. A
metonymy for nature, the garden undergoes a critical dissociation
thanks to the loss of the flower, which stands in for consciousness and
subjectivity. But the flower leads a strange and sublime after-life of the
remains, repeatedly putting itself in the abyss of representation, revel-
ling in its cut, and keeping itself by keeping that which deflowers it.
Endlessly, the dried flower reiterates and, thus, delays or postpones its
own end by putting itself *en abîme*.

Conversely, the role of art in this parable is to force the abyss of representation to reflect its double (the abyss of the thing), to throw and to
throw away, extravagantly, the thing 'flower' along with the book in
which it is kept, along with the work. Language cannot be antholo-
gized: the bookmark is irretrievably misplaced, the labour of notation
botched and betrayed, though this botching betrayal, which art encourages, gives a different life and existence to the dry flower that now
emancipates itself from its artificial function and, with this, tries to recuperate the time before its cut, prior to the garden's self-dissociation.
As a consequence, the flower will be neither absolutely present in nor
absolutely absent from the garden, but will memorialize a non-
representable past (mere life itself) and will satisfy its own purpose-
lessness and disengaged, free, vague emptiness reflected in the thing in
the thing in the thing ... Remarking and disseminating itself, the
thrown dry flower gives place to everything else that happens in its
place, in the garden, in the after-life of survival, where 'everything will
flower at the edge of a deconsecrated tomb' (TP 81-2).[46]

The second snapshot of the artistic gift of life and existence depicts the
'biodegradable.' At once a degradation of life (death as the degradability
of *biōs* and as the life-death *gradations within life*) and its re-composition
into compost, something biodegradable is 'hardly a thing since it remains a thing that does not remain, an essentially decomposable thing
destined to pass away, to lose its identity as a thing and to become again
a non-thing' (B 813). Instead of a dry flower, in 'Biodegradables' we are

dealing with a leaf of paper (perhaps a page from the book in which the flower was kept) – a thing that is decidedly not 'natural,' a subjectile support of the signifier that, in ruining itself, decomposes the unity of work into culture. Only in wasting itself, in not keeping itself and its spongy identity, does a biodegradable thing survive. And the aesthetic practice assists it in this, embracing the decomposable, self-disseminated thing wasted without a purpose, without an end.

This release of artifice from its function by means of art establishes the abyssal and 'enigmatic kinship between waste and the "masterpiece"' that promises to the biodegradable a chance to 'return to organic nature while losing there its artificial identity' (B 828, 845). That, in such a return, the prior unity of organic nature is restored is as absurd a proposition as the claim that the recycling of paper regenerates the very cut tree from which it was produced. The detour of memory is indispensable to something other than redemption; what, in an indelible metaphoric displacement, Derrida terms 'the organic nature' is, in fact, the very culture into which the thing and the work decompose themselves. But neither is culture a new figure of the simple ground there, where beyond a slew of agricultural metaphors, biodegradability indicates 'the worst but also the best that one could wish for a piece of writing' (B 824). Were 'the worst' and 'the best' reducible to a ground, they would have immediately rendered it double, that is to say, non-simple and abyssal.

The double – the worst and the best – bottom of the abyss abounding in unpredictable effects makes the biodegradable thing a suitable candidate for the coming of the event exuding a sense of possibility and betrayal, arrival and non-arrival. But what or who arrives? A self-referential, performative gesture that finally says, 'Enough!,' the gesture of satisfaction with the bottomless bottom of the thing in the thing, and so on, attaches to the paper (i.e., to the material support of writing and to the article itself written for the journal) the following postscript: 'This paper is biodegradable ... For example, what can be the future destiny of a document that would now give one to read, like right here, this sole phrase: "Forget it, drop it, *all of this is biodegradable*"?' (B 873). With these commanding words, it is the thing itself that arrives in precluding the possibility of its reception and, indeed, of its arrival.

4.3. Parergon, the thing alongside the work

Parergon is arguably the best-known element of Derrida's aesthetic theory, the element that migrated into this theory from the margins of the Kantian text. Ensconced right on the border between the thing and the work (*ergon*), as the superfluous supplement to the latter, parergon holds up *ergon* from the outside like Wittgenstein's ladder, effacing itself and withdrawing from its prosthetic position. But what exactly is it (if the question 'What is …?' is still appropriate here)? With the subjectile, parergon shares a certain ephemeral superfluity, given that, in Kant's view, it captures not an 'intrinsic constituent' of the object, but an 'adjunct,' non-formal adornment, which, like a gilded frame, does not contribute to the viewer's disinterested pleasure, but distracts her attention from the work.[47] Stylistically, it discloses the persistence of artistic idiosyncrasy, the artist's inability to eliminate the residue of her signature from the thing that, in return for this residue, countersigns the presumed purity of the work. It epitomizes a detached attachment, a fetishized thing and a thingified fetish, seductive yet disavowed.

Neither a work nor a non-work, parergon is the becoming-work of the work, the operationalization of *opera* from an unworkable position in the thing itself, for instance, after the work has been already done, accomplished: 'A parergon comes against, beside, and in addition to the *ergon*, the work done [*fait*], the fact [*le fait*], the work, but it does not fall to one side [*il ne tombe pas à côté*], it touches and cooperates within the operation from a certain outside' (TP 54/63). This specification encapsulates the whole economimetic structure of the thing 'parergon' (and of Derrida's book). But the problem is that this abstract definition cannot do justice to that which it defines, since, formalizing and operationalizing parergonal operationalization, it drags it into the interiority of work. To compensate for this failure, one might be tempted to give a series of empirical, singular examples of parerga in order to determine the sense of this phenomenon. Nevertheless, the exclusive attention to singularity will also fail, because parergonality draws on but is not simply equivalent to these examples and their 'exemplarity.'[48]

If parergon is an impossible condition of possibility for a particular work, be it the work of an artist or of a philosopher, that is because it comes after that which it conditions, after the 'labour time' that has elapsed, after the work that has been done (*fait*) and turned into a fact (*le fait*). As we've come to realize, after the work is cut short and signed, the thing frees itself from productive subjectivity and begins to breathe on its own: to animate, to inspire, and perhaps even to work at transforming the very meaning of 'work,' decomposing, disseminating, and reiterating itself. But the logic of parergonality adds an important detail to this narrative: the work of the thing a posteriori enables the work of the work that takes place a priori, thus casting the freedom of the thing in an altogether different light.

It is not by the grace of an arbitrary, fait accompli decision to terminate subjective activity that the thing has been freed, but thanks to the quasi-transcendental anachronism that puts the first second, and renders the second first. The name of this anachronism is supplementarity, and 'parergon' is but a heteronym that casts into sharper relief the labour of supplementation and the Kantian synthetic a priori. The coming 'against' or 'beside' of the parergon does not pinpoint an objective ontological region bordering on the territory of work, but expresses the thingly spacing of spatiality that does not have a frontier and is not commensurate with any extension. Hence, in addition to being 'first of all' on the border and on board with the ergon – 'It is, first of all, the on (the) bo(a)rd(er) [*Il est d'abord l'à-bord*]' (TP 54) – the thingly parergon de-borders or overflows the work, falls overboard.

What causes the overflowing of parergon is not some transcendental plentitude exceeding the empirical, nor the empirical-sensory 'richness' filling and fulfilling the bareness of transcendental schematism and intentionality. The Derridian parergon is excluded as indigestible, indeed, vomited from the theoretical delineation of the transcendental and the empirical, as 'what, proceeding from this exclusion, gives it form, limit, and contour' (E 21). Instantiating a 'single "thing" [that] is unassimilable,' it 'will therefore form the transcendental of the transcendental, the non-transcendentalisable, the non-idealizable, and that is *disgusting*' (E 22).

This 'superfluous' reading of Kant on the superfluous, which indulges in the parergonal treatment of the parergon,[49] holds in store at least five consequences for the role of the thing in aesthetics. First, the parergon standing alongside the work elliptically signifies 'the thing alongside the work.' In fact, parerga form a subterranean economy with ellipses, with their analogous presumption of redundancy that bestows meaning in exchange for silencing the superfluous part of the statement. Second, this 'thing' is singular and unassimilable, that is, detached or absolved from the aesthetic constitution it accompanies as unrepresentable. Derrida puts the singular, non-identical, non-identifiable, non-empirical 'thing' between quotation marks, though it is not difficult to recognize in it the dethroned Kantian thing in itself.

Third, the parergonal thing, reserved or put aside, makes possible the very constitution it eludes (and, in truth, de-constitutes or deconstructs) when it works to give what it constitutes 'form, limit, and contour.' The parergon is as determinately indeterminate as the horizon, but its detachment warns us against using this phenomenological term. In turn, no horizon is absolute, because there is, in addition to it, a horizon of the horizon, 'the transcendental of the transcendental,' which is the thing at the limit of the limit of the transcendental schema. This consequence itself has two corollaries: 1) the doubling of the limit and of the transcendental yields the thickness of the parergonal frame that boasts an inner and an outer edge, and 2) the thing in itself introduces into the transcendental constitution its own abyssal, empty plentitude and acts as a catalyst in the return of Hegel's 'bad infinity,' of the multiplication and proliferation of the frame within the frame ...

Fourth, the parergonal limit is the possibility of possibility, such that the first possibility conditions the second and appears as impossible and unworkable within the conditioned field. That is to say, the question of the quasi-transcendental shelters the possible and the impossible *within* possibility itself, when, for instance, the thing enables the work, which empirically disables the thing. And fifth, the four consequences I have enumerated here are not static, but move in a descending spiral where the unassimilable parergonal thing provokes disgust and, as disgusting, becomes ever more unassimilable, disengaged, and detached. Finally, the disgusting detachment of the 'single "thing"' on the hither side of the concept – as blurry and vague as the beautiful *and* as immensely unrepresentable as the sublime – circumscribes the form and the limit of the system that vomits it out.

Excluded, non-assimilated, vomited, the parergonal frame 'stands out [*se détache*] against two grounds [*fonds*], but with respect to each of those two grounds, it merges [*se fond*] into the other' (TP 61). The 'two grounds' comprised of the work and of the wall allude to the abyssal, double bottom without bottom of things. The duality of the ground facilitates the unmistakable thingly detached attachment of parergonality: whenever the frame stands out in relation to the work it enframes, it merges with the wall, and whenever it stands out in relation to the wall, it merges with the work. In the act of giving itself and what it enframes, it withdraws or erases itself. (Curiously enough, Derrida often methodically adopts the aesthetics of parergonality in his own writings. Besides the parergonal approach to Kant on the parergon, the best example of this is the enframing of Levinas, whose work stands out against two backgrounds named, in a shorthand, 'Husserl' and 'Heidegger.' In 'Violence and Metaphysics,' Derrida shows that as soon as Levinas emerges against one background, he immediately merges with the other. For instance, when he criticizes Husserl's theoreticism and 'the primacy of light,' he does so in the name of the historicity and facticity of man (WD 87ff), and when he rails against Heidegger's 'ontological violence,' he accepts the Husserlian understanding of being that levels the ontico-ontological difference and presents the ontological as the neutral 'nonreality of the ideal' that '*is* – as object or as thought-being' (WD 134). Derrida chides Levinas for his insufficiently immanent critique of the two and highlights the non-simplicity of the same – internally divided, abyssal, parergonal – inheritance that quivers in the confines of its outer and inner frames.)

Whether it concerns a work of art, or a text (which, like Kant's Third *Critique*, may itself be a beautiful object),[50] the thickness of the non-idealizable parergonal frame depends on the becoming-other of the work in the thing and on the becoming-other of the thing in the work. The logic of parergonality ignores the demand to 'economize on the abyss,' to 'save oneself from falling into the bottomless depths by weaving and folding back the cloth to infinity' (TP 37). The thing and the work fall into each other. In keeping with Heidegger's 'The Origin of the Work of Art,' the former is put to work in aesthetic theory when various oppositions, such as matter/form, are superimposed on it, or 'fall violently on the thing [*tombent violemment sur la chose*]' (TP 64). In this context, Derrida is taking liberties with Heidegger's word *Überfall*, which may be translated as 'assault' or 'attack' but means, literally, 'fall over.' The work assaults the thing, but it equally (better, equiprimordially) falls into the thing the moment it becomes external to the 'worker,' departs from all ideational auto-production that brackets embodiment and materiality, and 'is produced in the presentation of a singular thing – the exemplar' (TP 110). The fall from the idea of beauty into the exemplary, unassimilable, singularly universal beautiful thing sets the limit to the free play of imagination, which the countersignature of the material archi-trace cuts short.

The interminable simultaneity of the two 'free falls' prevents the parergon from falling to one side, *either* of the work *or* of the thing. Further, because spatiality is not yet determined in this spacing before space, we cannot presuppose the existence of any fixed dimensions 'above' and 'below,' 'left' and 'right,' to orient the fall. Parergonal redoubling of the thing and the work in sublime elevation, beyond the continuum of measurable heights, forever disturbs the clear directionality or the dimensionality of their falls: 'Very high, absolutely high, higher than any comparable height, more than comparative, a size not measurable in height, the sublime is *superelevation* beyond itself [sur-élévation *au delà d'elle-même*]' (TP 122/141). The colossal erection of the 'absolutely high' capitalizes on 'the most high,' which is Levinas's manner of designating, in one pen-stroke, the face of the other and a secularized version of an attribute of the Hebrew God (*el' elyon*). But superelevation, elevation above elevation, is not the modality of an excellent existent, since what is above elevation is not above or below all things measurable and commensurable in space.[51] The 'being-below' of the sublime and of sublation coincides with the 'being-above' of elevation; the fall to the tomb is monumentalized, erected, re-elevated in its 'colossal' falling and relief.

In spite of their simultaneity, in spite of falling alongside each other, the two falls fall out with one another and are asymmetrical. The parergonal becoming-thing of the work is its becoming-other, for the work loses itself qua work on the border, 'at the limit between work and absence of work' (TP 64). The thing, too, loses itself in becoming a work, but this loss is an integral part of the thing that becomes other to itself when it remarks and disseminates itself. The becoming-work of the thing, the becoming-other of the thing, is the becoming-thing of the thing. The logic of the parergon is conducive to this becoming, which preserves thinghood by refusing to keep any thing safe and sound, while art is the place of the 'contract' between the thing and the other thing, between the thing and itself: '*A link is re-contracted in art* between the thing and the other thing, *between the familiar thing and the thing as other, as the other thing* [lien est recontracté dans l'art, *entre la chose et l'autre chose*, entre la chose familière et la chose comme autre, comme autre chose]' (JDP 13).

Conclusion:
Post-Deconstructive Realism:
Of What Remains

... la pensée de l'événement ... comme discours *de* la chose.
La Chose: Heidegger/Blanchot

In *On Touching*, Derrida argues that 'for Nancy, touch remains the motif of an absolute, irredentist, and post-deconstructive realism
[*réalisme ... post-déconstructif*] ... an absolute realism, but irreducible to
any of the tradition's realisms' (OT 46/60). The ambition of *The Event of
the Thing* has been to situate what Derrida terms 'post-deconstructive
realism' within deconstruction itself and to indicate how the deconstructive event comes to pass in the thing that no longer warrants the
stability of the onto-metaphysical project, in the non-identical thing
whose escape from us eventuates the worldhood of the phenomenological world. It is undeniable that the 'post-deconstructive within deconstruction' is an anachronism, a disordering of the temporality of
'before,' 'during,' and 'after,' but it is an anachronistic disorder that the
thing itself orders and commands before *and* after objectification.
Above all, the question that ripens in this syntagma is, What does it
mean to go through, to experience, or to suffer deconstruction, and
what remains of these goings-through, experiences, or sufferings?
    Derrida's own deconstructive or post-deconstructive realism is, cer-
tainly, not the same as 'any of the tradition's realisms,' be they empirical or transcendental, since at its core is found the split thing, the
indwelling of *différance*, the concrete figure without figure undermining and invalidating the logical principle of identity. The thing is not
the same thing as what or who it is. Its non-identity with itself renders
it interchangeable with any other thing and with the other of the thing

(the athing); its absolute alterity does not allow the new realism to os-
sify in a determinate encyclopaedic definition ready to be catalogued
in the annals of philosophy, but necessitates its unfolding as a series of
discontinuous beginnings and interim, provisional conjunctures. One
could object that these assertions are not new, that, in Derrida, we en-
counter another version of empirical realism[1] or, indeed, of hyper-em-
piricism dependent upon the thing's utter singularity and resistance to
conceptualization. But this is only a half-truth. For Derrida never fails
to pair the thing's singularity with its 'empty' universality or virtual
generality, thanks to which it sheds all vestiges of monadism and nurtures a sort of intrinsic sociality despite its detachment from us. The
unfulfillable demand of supplementation – to replace the irreplaceable
– moderates hyper-empiricist singularity.

The symmetrically opposed objection that post-deconstructive realism is a mask for transcendental idealism is also untenable. For several
reasons, the way in which the deconstructive thing conditions the
event (double affirmative, double perhaps) has nothing in common
with transcendental causality: first, in contrast to the latter, the thing is
not a wholly transcendental principle but the spacing fissure or the
concrete opening of the world *in* the world; second, as a condition of
possibility, it is, simultaneously, unconditionally impossible; third, its
apriority is indistinguishable from the aposteriority of the irreducible
remainder that survives the process of idealist objectification; and
fourth, its formalism is not empty and abstract, but virtual and full,
even overfull (e.g., the formal *sans* of the pure cut that renders the
thing free of the content projected onto it by consciousness, or the formal repetition of the thing's self-remarking activity independent of all
such projections). In other words, Derrida's brand of realism would
have been bland and traditional had it not inherited the indeterminacy,
non-identity, and fugal character from the thing 'itself.'

That is why, in the inner dialogue he transcribes in *Veils*, it is difficult
for Derrida to recognize *himself* in the advocate of realism, however
novel or deconstructively custom-made it may have been:

> When you refer thus to the irreducible reality of an event (outside dis-
> course but not outside text), I am really worried. It looks so unlike you,
> you look so unlike yourself, it looks so unlike the image of you that circu-
> lates in these regions. It's as though you were talking about the scenario
> for a soap in which (as happens) you have to change a character because
> the actor died or broke his contract. (V 79)

Derrida, something or someone in Derrida, cannot recognize himself in the advocate of the 'reality of an event' for a good reason, because, as soon as one binds one's thought to the unbound thing, the identity of this thought unravels and its identifiable image undergoes a disfiguration. In what follows, my purpose is not to help Derrida recognize himself in the post-deconstructive realist he is or has become, but to intensify this fruitful misrecognition and the tensions it entails.

Post-deconstructive realism is a realism of the remains, which is to say, of resistance to idealization on the 'inner front' of idealism. It does not begin with the evidence of the given thing itself, which, in fact, withholds itself from everything it gives, but compels us to recast what is irreducible in terms other than the immunity of the Husserlian pure ego to various reductions. In Derrida's texts, the remains denote 1) something that cannot be incorporated, consumed, or consummated in the interiority proper to idealism, and hence something vomited by the system; 2) the process of self-consummation; 3) the fragments, morsels, waste, and debris of textuality, which the virtual receptacle of the thing obstinately keeps (sense-less) or only provisionally accommodates, analysing, re-synthesizing, and projecting them into new units of sense; 4) the testimonial evidence to the past of violence and destruction given by the decomposition of the body *proper*; 5) survival, the living death of a phantom in and as the thing; 6) the material trace of writing, signature and countersignature; 7) the wounds that do not heal, or heal only to leave scar tissue behind, the immemorial event of birth, the memory of the double cut, memory as such; 8) the disruption of the trajectory and intentionality of the throw; 9) what falls down and is not recuperated or re-elevated; 10) dissemination of the work in the thing; 11) X without X (relation without relation, bottom without bottom, thing without thing, etc.), where, as in the case of –*ject*, which preserves nothing of subjects and objects save for the gesture of throwing, reduction stumbles upon something irreducible.

As every item in this open list will confirm, the remains with which post-deconstructive realism concerns itself do not partake of the extra-temporal permanence of substance, of the non-event that is said to underlie all empirical accidents in the world and endures as self-same. The only way to engage this palaeonymy is to say that the remains are the 'modifications without substance,' the hetero-affections of auto-affection that do not leave anything unaffected, un-constituted, or simple, or, again, the cinders in which substance has consumed itself before being extinguished. These modifications, then, are the modalities of the thing in which the 'who' and the 'what,' the cogitative and the extended, the living and the dead commune beyond the exigencies of monism or dualism, of the Spinozan unity or the Cartesian duality of substance.

With the subtraction of unchanging substance and retention of modifications, the keywords of deconstruction – trace, gift, archi-writing, and the rest – do not become ethereal or evanescent. Instead, on the model of the thing, their actual reality is fungible with the virtual reality-effects lacking an underlying primal cause. Thus de-substantialized, the thingly remains are intimately connected with time that announces itself in memory, survival, or dissemination, though one should keep in mind that they are both temporal and extra-temporal (temporalizing). Consistent with the logic of the event, they signal to us the rushing of the past from the future, where the 'always already' merges with the 'not yet,' for instance in the spacing and delay that constitute the events of birth, the regeneration of the text, or the strike of the countersignature and de-constitute the certainty of their arrival.

In addition to soliciting deconstructive concern, the remains permit 'post-deconstructive realism' anachronistically to inhabit deconstruction. In the notion of the thing, deconstruction's future comes to it from its past in the shape of an appeal to the oldest, most fundamental layer of the metaphysics of presence. It is only fitting that deconstruction tackles the groundwork or the ground-thing of metaphysics last, after contending with the higher strata it predicates and haunts: the 'political animal' that is the human and the 'living thing' that is the animal. These strata, whose deconstruction awaits and, as it were, prepares the ground for post-deconstructive realism, are thoroughly deconstructable. *Conversely, for Derrida, the thing is what remains after the deconstruction of the human, the animal, and the metaphysical belief in the thing itself, in its oneness and self-identity. The thing understood as the remains stands on the side of what has been called 'the undeconstructable' within deconstruction itself, of what both animates and outlives the deconstructive goings-through, experiences, or sufferings.* One cannot afford to 'go through' deconstruction and avoid paying close attention to the threshold, which, at the last stage for the closure of metaphysics, the thing guards and leaves open, guards in leaving open. Deepening the closure, the realism of the other thing, or of the thing as other, is the event of deconstruction that always already happens in every one of its 'works' *and* is yet to come at the (immanent, non-teleological) ends of deconstruction in the undeconstructable.

That one will never cross the threshold of the event's textual mediation and that one always crosses it is an axiom from which deconstructive temporality follows. But no axiom can exclude a counter-axiomatic tension. Excusing himself with the experience of fatigue, with the feeling of being tired induced by the task of weaving an endless textual cloth, Derrida confesses to a temptation to cross the threshold once and for all:

> Ah, how tired we are, how I would like finally to touch 'veil,' the word and the thing thus named, the thing itself and the vocable! I would like not only to see them, toward them or through them, the word and the thing, but maintain a discourse about them that would, finally, touch, in short a 'relevant' discourse that would say them properly, even if it no longer gives anything to be seen. (V 23-4)

To touch the thing itself: to traverse the distance and to maintain it in spite of, or thanks to, this traversal that echoes Heidegger's de-severance (*Ent-fernung*): to remark the thing's self-remark immanently, without dominating it and without losing oneself as the tempted-desiring I. These are the three daring quasi-phenomenological aspirations of post-deconstructive realism, which strives, at once, toward 'the thing itself and the vocable,' toward the thing and the other of the thing that, in conjunction, form the non-principle of thinghood. Nonetheless, because the thing in question is not any thing whatsoever but veil (*voile*), which is to say 'every thing,' because of this obscure singular universality, the supplement of blind discourse, the only proper and relevant discourse capable of touching the thing after rending phenomenology and severing *phenomena* from *logos*, is indispensable. The undeconstructable remains are the outcome of this rupture that, paradoxically, touches 'the thing itself and the vocable' despite the disintegration of the phenomenological unity of seeing and saying. Below the unity of the word, the thing and the vocable, the one and the other, the one as the other call forth the event.

Derrida is well aware of the risks inherent in the fatigued, impatient desire that, in a vulgar fashion, motivates and undermines all traditional realisms with their claims of extra-discursivity or extra-textuality: 'Such a ["realist"] political history or philosophy would deck itself out in "realism" just in time to fall short of the thing – and to repeat, repeat and repeat again, with neither consciousness nor memory of its compulsive droning [*Elles s'affubleraient de 'réalisme' au moment de tourner court devant la chose – et de répéter, répéter, répéter sans même la conscience ou la mémoire du ressassement*]' (PF 81/99). The reason for the divergence between the 'realist' disguises of political history or

philosophy and the thing they miss is that they bet on the unproblem-
atic crossing of the textual threshold and, therefore, refuse to operate
within the temporal fold of the 'always already' (*Ereignis* in abyss, the
immemorial event of thingly ex-propriation) and the 'not yet' (temporalizing delay in the thing itself, the coming of the horizon-less event,
in which the thing's self-remark would agree with the systems of signification 'founded' on it). This refusal causes realism to lose sight of the
remains and to lapse into a pure repetition, or rather the repetition of
repetition – 'to repeat, repeat and repeat again' – that puts it on the side
of hyper-idealism.

In the purely instrumental sense, post-deconstructive realism man-
dates a detour through deconstruction so that we could hold on to the
temporal fold of which traditional realisms fall short, and so that we
could reimagine each one of the terms in the 'not negative im-possible'
which is Derrida's shorthand for the 'real': 'the real as a coming or the
event of the other, where it resists all re-appropriation, even ana-
onto-phenomenological appropriation. The real is this not negative
im-possible, this im-possible coming or invention of the event ... In
this sense, nothing is more "realist" than deconstruction' (PM 96). On
the one hand, the resistance of the real to all re-appropriation is contingent upon the 'always already' of the thing's immemorial expropriation that puts *Ereignis* in abyss. The thing itself imposes a restriction
(hence, something negative) on all subsequent attempts at its re-appropriation, even as it positively enables the ana-onto-phenomenological
apparatus that undertakes these attempts. To put it differently, the
non-negative facet of the real refers to the retreat, the withdrawal, the
escape of the thing itself that leaves the world in its trail. The memory
or the trace of this withdrawal is the double negation – 'not negative' –
that makes up the positivity of the deconstructive real, the post-
critical, post-reductive positivity of the remains. On the other hand,
the im-possible coming of the event invokes the time of the 'not yet,'
the delay of the 'perhaps' within every possible thing that happens
without being recognized as such, without reaching the limit of its
identity, and without giving itself at once, in flesh and blood. The positively im-possible event remains to come, renders futural the remains
of the past and thus, remains the event of the thing.

Is there anything beyond the pure instrumentality, more instrumental still than any technicity or technique, of post-deconstructive realism? Can it dodge the need and even the desire to become a channel, a
medium, or a conduit for the thing's relation to itself as other, like the

syringe in 'Circumfession' that is introduced in the vein 'only to allow the passage and to disappear as instrument' (CI 7)? Is it able to survive in a form other than a superfluous, supplementary interpolation and self-erasure of the 'thought of the event' in the place or in the vein of the 'discourse *of* the thing,' the discourse from, about, and proper to the thing: '*la pensée de l'événement ... comme discours* de *la chose*' (JDP 13/12)?

Notes

1. The Event of the Thing

1 Further references to the texts of Jacques Derrida will be made parenthetically, with the abbreviated title followed by the page number in English. The number after a slash indicates the page in the French version of the text. For the full titles and bibliographic information, please consult the list of abbreviations.

2 Is it by accident that the titles of Derrida's most influential engagement with these thinkers reference 'spectres' in the case of Marx and 'spirit' in the case of Heidegger? If the difference between the spectre and the spirit is the hallmark of difference as such, is the Marx-Heidegger (spectre-spirit) dyad the sine qua non of the hauntological? A concrete symptom of this is the prominence of the table as the exemplary thing in Marx's *Capital* and in Heidegger's *What Is a Thing?* As Derrida would note, in both cases it is with reference to the table (which is supposed to underlie, to be placed underneath in a supporting manner proper to a *hypokeimenon* or substance) that the process of dematerialization occurs, situating the thing at the juncture of the material and the immaterial, the spectral and the spiritual, the practical and the theoretical, and so on.

3 Martin Heidegger, *What Is a Thing?* trans. W.B. Barton and Vera Deutsch (Chicago: Henry Regnery, 1967), p. 71. Alain Badiou misses the point, therefore, when in the opening of *Being and Event* (trans. Oliver Feltham [New York: Continuum, 2005]) he contends that Heidegger's ontology absolutely eschews a mathematical grounding (pp. 9ff). Rather, it is the impoverished modern perspective on mathematics that furnishes the object of Heidegger's critique.

4 Heidegger, *What Is a Thing?* p. 13. Heidegger's problematic is an offshoot of Husserlian phenomenology. Cf. especially §40, '"Primary" and "Secondary"

Qualities. The Physical Thing Given "In Person" a "Mere Appearance" of the "True Physical Thing" Determined in Physics,' in Edmund Husserl, *Ideas Pertaining to Pure Phenomenology and to Phenomenological Philosophy*, First Book, trans. F. Kersten (Dordrecht, Boston, London: Kluwer, 1998), pp. 84–5 (cited hereafter as '*Ideas I*').

5 'Marx is wondering how to describe the sudden looming up of the mystical character of the commodity, the mystification of the thing itself [*la mystification de la chose même*]' (SM 149/237). In keeping with the mystique of this genitive, the event of the thing pertains both to the self-mystification of the thing and to the mystification of the thing overwritten with the commodity-economic structure. The surprising 'looming up of the mystical character of the commodity' cannot be explained solely in terms of the historical process of commodification, but needs to be supplemented with the self-virtualizing, self-disseminating work of the thing itself.

6 Cf. SI 106 and Alan Bass's *Interpretation and Difference: The Strangeness of Care* (Stanford: Stanford University Press, 2006), especially the chapter titled 'Derrida: Spectral, Binding Interpretation.'

7 This infinitization of the virtual stands in a sharp contrast to Slavoj Žižek's quasi-Deleuzian slippage between the virtual and the symbolic, where the symbolic excess of the virtual automatically yields the real equated with the actual: '*Actuality constitutes itself when a VIRTUAL (symbolic) supplement is added to the pre-ontological real*'; '*Actual reality is the real filtered through the virtual*'; '*The Excess of the virtual … sustains actualization*' (Slavoj Žižek, *Organs without Bodies: Deleuze and Consequences* [New York and London: Routledge, 2004], pp. 84–5).

8 A case in point is Plato's *Symposium*, where, according to Diotima's words conveyed by Socrates, the preservation of every living entity is accomplished by its replacement (therefore in the light of a certain difference of the same from itself), and where mortal beings partake of immortality by engendering what emanates from them: 'Every mortal thing is preserved in this way; not by keeping it exactly the same forever, like the divine, but by replacing what goes off or is antiquated with something other [*heteron*], in the semblance of the original. Through this device, Socrates, a mortal thing partakes of [*metexei*] immortality' (208a–b).

9 *Glas* represents the leap from Kant's *Moralität* to Hegel's *Sittlichkeit* in terms of a shift from the immoral moral consciousness that 'remains formal and virtual' to the actual presence of the 'Idea of freedom' (G 11, left). Moreover, this shift comes to govern the actualization of that difference – spotted by means of a perceptual act – which Hegel (*Phenomenology of Spirit*, trans. A.V. Miller (Oxford and New York: Oxford University Press), p. 75) locates

in the *presence* of the thing itself in its comportment toward other things: 'Each is thereby determined as being itself a *different* Thing, and it has its essential difference in its own self ... As a matter of fact, since differentness is present in it [in the Thing], it is of course necessarily present as an *actual* difference manifoldly constituted.' It goes without saying that one would need to deconstruct the actual presence of difference in the thing available for perception. But a more interesting material for deconstruction is contained in Hegel's supplementary interjections ('as a matter of fact,' 'of course'), which miss the event of the thing not because of 'sense certainty,' which will undergo sublation, but because of the unshakeable belief that the difference inherent in the thing simply and actually presents itself to us. The question that arises alongside this belief is whether Hegel succeeds in overcoming the *deceptiveness* and 'unreliability of Things' in a way that avoids the Kantian pitfalls he criticizes, or whether he, too, 'does not secure them *their* truth, but convinces *himself* of untruth' (p. 79). Finally, Derrida's objective may be construed in terms of a detour from Hegel back to Kant through virtualizing or de-actualizing the manifoldness of difference in the thing itself.

10 Here, I agree with Geoff Bennington's assessment that the spirit is 'always already' its own ghost, in 'Spirit's Spirit Spirits Spirit' (in David Wood, ed., *Of Derrida, Heidegger, and Spirit* [Evanston: Northwestern University Press, 1993], pp. 82–92).

11 In turn, the spectre is, *'first of all, something (some thing) between life and death, neither alive, nor dead* [Qu'est-ce que ça veut dire, specter? D'abord, c'est quelque chose entre la vie et la mort, ni vivant ni mort]' (MJ 23).

12 The breath of the thing corresponds to the Freudian 'stage' of *Animatismus* and the 'universal being-for-life' (*der algemeinen Belebtheit*), where life is extended to everything, including the 'so-called inorganic, dead matter (*hylē*) ... deprived of breath.' Derrida's own conclusion is that 'a quasi-originary *Belebtheit* ... must if not present itself, at least announce itself to some pre-empirical or pre-positive experience' (HC 112, 114).

13 The deconstruction of analytical distinctions positions *Being and Time* on the side of 'good common sense,' *bon sens naturel*, according to which the very definition of the thing is that *'a thing cannot be a subject, can neither speak nor say "I"* [une chose ne peut être un sujet, ne peut parler ni dire Je]' (JDP 13/1).

14 In *Interpretation and Difference*, Alan Bass recalls that Derrida cites Horatio's question 'Has this thing appeared again tonight?' 'in relation to the "thing-like" intermediate state between life and death, and in relation to coming back, *revenance*' (p. 133). He later adds, 'As a *thing* the fetish is not quite dead, but not quite alive either. It is virtually alive, and thus must be thought "hauntologically"' (p. 135).

15 'I cannot, I should not be able to, testify to my own death, to its *instance* as *deferred immanence*' (DE 46).

16 The endeavour of maintaining the delicate and fragile balance between idealism and realism is patently Husserlian in spirit. Cf. Paul Ricoeur, *Husserl: An Analysis of His Phenomenology* (Evanston: Northwestern University Press, 1967).

17 Derrida seems to be following the Levinasian analysis of the aporetics of dying and 'death agony' that demonstrates the infinite deferral of death from the standpoint of the dying subject: 'Dying is agony because in dying a being does not come to an end while coming to an end; he has no more time, that is, can no longer wend his way anywhere, but thus he goes where one cannot go, suffocates – how much longer' (Emmanuel Levinas, *Totality and Infinity*, trans. Alphonso Lingis [Pittsburgh: Duquesne University Press, 1961], p. 56).

18 The virtual time-place dwelling in the thing itself is the philosophical luggage transferred from Heidegger's notion of *Zeitraum*: 'The question "What is a thing?" included in itself the question "What is *Zeitraum* (time-span)?", the puzzling unity of space and time within which, as it seems, the basic character of things, to be only this one, is determined' (Heidegger, *What Is a Thing?* p. 17). While a lot more could be said regarding this conceptual assemblage, I will limit myself to two remarks: 1) Heidegger opposes the unity and the thisness of the thing, which, like the Greek temple, gathers together the exterior environing elements, to the Hegelian move that identifies the presence of actual difference in the things handed over to immediate perception, and 2) foreshadowing the auto-deconstruction of the categorial/existential barriers, Heidegger deduces virtual space-time before its differentiation into two categories from the thing itself. The manner in which Derrida will take over this deduction has to do with the conceptual translation of the unity of *Zeitraum* into the articulated disunity of *différance* as the movement of temporalizing space and spatializing time 'in' the thing itself.

19 'A certain reinterpretation of Plato's *Timaeus* had named *khōra* … a spacing from 'before' the world, the cosmos, or the globe, from "before" any "chronophenomenology" … *Khōra* would make or give *place*; it would give rise … to what is called the coming of the event' (R *xiv*). 'I try to reach a place *from* which this distinction between *who* and *what* comes to appear and become determined,' in other words, a place 'anterior to this distinction … Why call that a *place*, a placement, a spacing, an interval, a sort of *khōra*?' (PM 80).

20 At the disjunction between the actual and the virtual, between nothing and everything, '*khōra* involves a negativity that escapes both the positive and negative theological register' (Mark C. Taylor, 'nO nOt nO,' in Harold

Coward and Toby Foshay, eds, *Derrida and Negative Theology* [Albany: SUNY Press, 1992], p. 188).

21 'The "now," the "then," and the "on that former occasion" thus have a seemingly obvious relational structure which we call *"datability"* [Datierbarkeit] ... *Wherein is such datability grounded, and to what does it essentially belong? ... Datability* of the "now," the "then," and the "on that former occasion" is evidence that these, *stemming from temporality, are themselves time*. The interpretive expression of the "now," the "then," and the "on that former occasion" is the primordial way of *assigning a time'* (Martin Heidegger, *Being and Time*, trans. John Macquarrie and Edward Robinson [San Francisco: Harper and Row, 1962], pp. 407–8 [page numbers refer to German pagination]).

22 For Paola Marrati (*Genesis and Trace: Derrida Reading Husserl and Heidegger* [Stanford: Stanford University Press, 2005]), the *'virtual level* implies that writing accomplishes ideality by delivering it of any empirical subject' (p. 82). The outcome of such 'deliverance,' however, is nothing but an ideal object; the non-accidental confusion of the virtual and the ideal parallels the sleight of hand that replaces the thing with the object.

23 In 'Full Dorsal: Derrida's Politics of Friendship' (*Postmodern Culture* 15(3), May 2005, muse.jhn.edu/journals/pmc/v015/15.3wills.html), David Wills reads this welcome in the light of the trusting turning of one's back to the other motivated by the 'perhaps': 'Such a turning of the back would be the figure for a particular fiduciary relation in the world, the trust that it implies, its presumption of non-enmity, something functioning beyond an economics of appropriation, within the *an*economics and *ana*logic of the *"perhaps"* that is the opening to a hospitality of radical otherness promoted by Derrida throughout his discussion.'

24 Geoffrey Bennington, *Interrupting Derrida* (London and New York: Routledge, 2000), p. 121. At the other end of the spectrum is Rorty's nominalist interpretation of Derrida, which refuses to take seriously the quasi-transcendental infrastructures embedded in his work. Cf. Richard Rorty, 'Is Derrida a Transcendental Philosopher?' in David Wood, ed., *Derrida: A Critical Reader* (Cambridge, MA and Oxford, UK: Blackwell, 1992), pp. 235–46.

25 'Fictional idealities' is the name Derrida gives to the effects of 'as if,' yet it would be too short-sighted to reduce them to *mere* fictions by acting 'as if the "as if" had no *real* effect [*comme si le 'comme si' était sans effet* réel]' (HC 31, 111/97, emphasis added).

26 To the thing belongs what Bass calls 'nonobjective reality': 'Nonobjective reality is experienced as "unreal," perverse, "weird," because of its uncanny, tension-raising, oscillating structure' (Bass, *Difference and Interpretation*, p. 136). Such is the reality of the virtual and of the 'as if.'

27 Bennington is correct in noting that 'radicalizing this thought [of the *per-haps*] about events in general in the context of *decisions* leads to a reinscription of the concept of decision away from the concept of the subject to which it is traditionally bound' (*Interrupting Derrida*, p. 27). The vector leading 'away from the concept of the subject' points in the direction of the thing to which 'perhaps' is tied.

28 'Et s'il (ce 'comme si') se décline selon le mode verbal du conditionnel, c'est aussi pour annoncer l'inconditionnel, l'éventuel ou le possible événement de l'inconditionnel impossible, le tout autre – que nous devrions désormais … dissocier de l'idée théologique de souveraineté' (USC 76).

29 Heidegger, *What Is a Thing?* p. 9.

30 Negatively and rather unsympathetically understood by critics such as John McCumber (*Philosophy and Freedom: Derrida, Rorty, Habermas, Foucault* [Bloomington and Indianapolis: Indiana University Press, 2000]), Derridian '"liberation"can indeed be only a groping for the unintelligible. To say that liberation from metaphysics includes the sacrifice of intelligibility itself, moreover, amounts to saying that there is simply no way out of metaphysics: deconstruction's promise of liberation … must … be retracted' (p. 39). McCumber misses the point, however, when he 1) mixes up the closure of metaphysics with the liberation or extrication of thought from metaphysics, and 2) confuses the 'groping for the unintelligible,' which is a quasi-transcendental condition of possibility for intelligibility, with the 'sacrifice of intelligibility itself,' which is tantamount to a devaluing of intelligibility, and to which Derrida would not subscribe.

31 It could be said of the exactitude in Derrida's punctuation what he says of Cixous's: 'The art of punctuation, which will never stop amazing me, is also an art and an ethics of punctuality' (HC 85).

32 'Il n'y a pas de signature sans *oui* [*there is no signature without a* yes]' (DP 53). 'The use of *oui* is always implicated in the moment of a signature' (AL 157).

33 Emphasis added. See also *Aporias*: 'The affirmation … was therefore the necessity of *experience* itself' (A 19). Broaching the thematics of the experience of alterity, Plotnitsky inches closer to the view that the thing 'is' the other when he states that, following Derrida, 'one could attempt to define "reality" by way of, or precisely as, radical alterity' (Arkady Plotnitsky, 'Complementarity, Idealization, and the Limits of Classical Conceptions of Reality,' in Christopher Norris and David Roden, eds, *Jacques Derrida*, vol. 3 [London, Thousand Oaks, New Delhi: Sage, 2003], p. 19). More important, the welcoming receptivity of interiority and the first 'yes' extended to the other are the undeniable traces of Levinas in Derrida and of Descartes in Levinas: 'To approach the Other in conversation is to welcome his

expression, in which at each instant he overflows the idea a thought would carry away from it [Levinas here cites without citing one of the Cartesian proofs of God's existence outlined in the *Meditations* – M.M.]. It is therefore to *receive* from the Other beyond the capacity of the I.' Several pages later, Levinas equates this *kath auto* expression of the other with the 'thing in itself' (Levinas, *Totality and Infinity*, pp. 51, 67).

34 'Even though it must leave nothing behind it ... this *forgetting of the gift* cannot be a simple non-experience, a simple non-appearance [*cet oubli du don ne peut pas être une simple non-expérience, une simple inapparence*], a self-effacement that is carried off with what it effaces ... For there to be gift event (we say event and not act), some thing must happen or arrive [*Pour qu'il y ait événement (nous ne disons pas acte) de don, il faut que quelque chose arrive*], in an instant, in an instant that no doubt does not belong to the economy of time' (GT 17/30).

35 In so far as it is allied with time, affirmation is disseminative and 'anti-reductive.' Cf. Christina Howells, *Derrida: Deconstruction from Phenomenology to Ethics* (Oxford and Malden, MA: Polity, 1999), pp. 78–9.

36 In the second 'yes,' 'the signer will make the thing sign [*le signataire fera signer la chose*], will make it enter into a singular contract and transform the singular demand into law by means of the placement in abyss. The transgression that enfranchises and frees up will be the law of repetition in abyss' (SI 50/1).

37 Derrida makes a similar suggestion a few pages earlier in 'Nombre de oui' when he writes, '*Language without language, it* [*the 'yes'*] *belongs without belonging to everything it institutes and everything it opens* [Langage sans langage, il appartient sans appartenir à l'ensemble qu'il institue et qu'il ouvre]' (PSY 644). The logic of simultaneous belonging and non-belonging portends the quasi-transcendental structure of this 'yes' *and* of the thing.

38 As one of Derrida's precursors, Nietzsche has already exposed the metaphysical myth of 'identical things.' For instance, in an aphorism from *Human, All Too Human* (Cambridge and New York: Cambridge University Press, 1996) titled, as though in anticipation of Heidegger *avant la lettre*, 'Fundamental Questions of Metaphysics,' Nietzsche writes: 'To the plants all things are usually in repose, eternal, every thing identical with itself. It is from the period of the lower organisms that man has inherited the belief that there are *identical things*' (p. 21). By situating the belief in identical things and, therefore, the very foundations of metaphysics in the midst of what may be called 'a vegetative state of thinking,' Nietzsche not only historicizes metaphysical notions and transgresses their conceptual boundaries – for example, plant/animal ('lower organisms'); consciousness

('belief')/thing – but also brings to the boiling point of excessive literalness the *naturalized perspective* shielding this thinking.

39 And yet, in this process, phenomenology itself fails to escape the kind of reduction it advocates. This will be the position of Sean Gaston (*The Impossible Mourning of Jacques Derrida* [London and New York: Continuum, 2006]), who enunciates Derrida's 'attempt to mark the difference (the almost nothing) between the *incomplete* as the *infinite* (phenomenology as a virtual presence, as anticipation …) and the *incomplete* as the *indefinite* (as writing, as *différance*, as the possibility and the ruin of phenomenology)' (p. 55). This difference is housed 'in the thing itself,' where the distinction between 'who' and 'what' is still lacking, where time and space are still in the process of gestation, and where their infinite, indefinite deferral portends 'the possibility and the ruin of phenomenology.'

40 Leonard Lawlor (*Derrida and Husserl: The Basic Problem of Phenomenology* [Bloomington and Indianapolis: Indiana University Press, 2002]) aptly puts his finger on the genealogy of *différance*, dating back to Husserl. If, indeed, this non-concept is related to Husserl's intentionality thesis and, especially, to its noematic element, then it is neither fully real, actual, external, nor reducible to a moment of consciousness: 'Other than consciousness,' noema is 'also a non-real thing' (p. 231). The extra step required beyond this initial acknowledgment is, of course, a reflection on what 'a non-real thing' might be.

41 It is the possibility of such non-arrival, then, that constitutes the event of the thing. In other words, contrary to the Husserl of *Ideas I* (§52), Derrida implies that the self-remarking thing *not given in the flesh or in person* is 'a sign of itself.'

42 In this regard, note the subject of Peter Fenves's 'hypothesis': '*Everything* acts in secret, and by disclosing that everything acts in this way, philosophy discloses itself' ('Out of the Blue: Secrecy, Radical Evil, and the Crypt of Faith,' in Richard Rand, ed., *Futures of Jacques Derrida* [Stanford: Stanford University Press, 2001], p. 99, emphasis added).

43 This criticism is essentially Husserlian, since it brings to mind those mental acts that are '*directed to something transcendent*,' be it another ego or a thing. 'Such,' Husserl writes, 'are all acts directed to essences or to intentive mental processes belonging to other Egos with other streams of mental processes, and likewise all acts directed to physical things or to realities of whatever sort' (*Ideas I*, p. 79, and passim).

44 Silvia Benso reaches a similar insight in her attempt to supplement the Levinasian 'love without things' with the Heideggerian 'things without love.' See Silvia Benso, *The Face of Things: A Different Side of Ethics* (New York: SUNY Press, 2000).

45 This passage ought to be read not only with an eye to *Writing and Difference* but also alongside the beginning of *Glas* as a transit point between the two apparitions of the *a* of *différance*: 'The thing: magnificent and classed, at once raised above all taxonomy, all nomenclature, and already identifiable in an order. To give a name is always, like any birth (certificate), to sublimate a singularity, to inform against it' (G 7, right). Here, the ease and the impossibility of the taxonomic order as it applies to the thing hinges on a broken dialectic, that is to say, on the incomplete sublation of its singularity.

46 Eberhard Gruber ('Du tautologique qui nous ente,' in M.-L. Maller, ed., *L'Animal autobiographique: Autour de Jacques Derrida* [Paris: Galilée, 1999]) explicates the transition in Derrida's *Geschlecht* series from the auto-heterology of the event (*Ereignis*) to its hetero-tautology. Highlighting the ultimate impossibility of reaching the 'thing itself' indicated by the word *Geschlecht*, Gruber writes, apropos of the event, that Derrida accomplishes '*a problematization of Ereignis in its homogeneous form as … an "originary unity [ursprüngliche Einigkeit]" in spite of its intrinsic diversity* [la problématisation du *Ereignis* sous la forme homogène en tant que … "union originaire" (ursprüngliche Einigkeit) en dépit de sa diversité intrinsèque]' (p. 139). I would add that the same problematization should remain cognizant of the thing that 'incorporates' the auto-heterology and the hetero-tautology of the event (in a certain 'application' of *différance*) when it becomes phonically indistinguishable and graphically differentiated from its other. In his turn, Derrida pays careful attention to the untranslatability of *Geschlecht*, with its '*irreducible tie to the question of humanity (versus animality), of a humanity whose name, like the tie of the name to the "thing" … remains … problematic* [le lien irréductible à la question de l'humanité (versus l'animalité), et d'une humanité dont le nom, comme le lien du nom à la chose … reste … problématique]' (PSY 419).

47 In his early phenomenological works, Derrida breaks down the Husserlian object, *Gegenstand*, into *Gegen-stand*, 'standing-against.' (The same is true of *ob-jet* in French and of the Greek αντικείμενον). The oppositionality essential to the objectivity of the object disappears from the Derridian interchangeability of the thing and its other (cf. SP 75, and passim).

48 The difference between Hegelian and Derridian views on negation and contradiction has incited a long-standing debate. Formally, the truth of a statement such as the one I am about to cite is hardly in doubt: 'Whereas for Hegel, the thinking that acknowledged a contradiction found, in that acknowledgement, the means to negate and overcome that contradiction, Levinas, Blanchot, and Derrida, among others, are drawn to what is not negated and so to what needs must be described in terms of a faltering or

weakening of negation' (Paul Davies, 'This Contradiction,' in Richard
Rand, ed., *Futures of Jacques Derrida* [Stanford: Stanford University Press,
2001], p. 31). But what is irretrievably lost in this formal correctness is the
concrete aporetic quality of 'what is *not* negated' (for instance, in the thing
by the athing), which, in fact, strengthens negation in the midst of its 'faltering.' This aporetic quality may be said to characterize Hegel's 'determinate negation.'

49 Translation modified.

50 Jacques Derrida, 'Hostipitality,' *Angelaki* 5(3), December 2000, p. 10.

51 One such inappropriable and catastrophic event will have been a nuclear
catastrophe: '"Reality," let us say the encompassing institution of the nuclear age, is constructed by a fable, on the basis of an event that has never
happened (except in fantasy, and that is not nothing at all), an event of
which one can only speak, an event whose advent remains an invention by
men (in all senses of the word "invention") or which, rather, remains to be
invented' (Jacques Derrida, 'No Apocalypse, Not Now [Full Speed Ahead,
Seven Missiles, Seven Missives],' *Diacritics 14*, Summer 1984, pp. 23–4).

52 On originary technicity, see Bernard Stiegler's *Technics and Time 1: The Fault
of Epimetheus*, trans. Richard Beardsworth and George Collins (Stanford:
Stanford University Press, 1998).

53 'This arche-writing, although its concept is *invoked* by the themes of "the
arbitrariness of the sign" and of difference, cannot and can never be recognized as the *object of a science*. It is that very thing which cannot let itself be
reduced to the form of *presence*' (OG 57).

54 Martin Heidegger, *Contributions to Philosophy (From Enowning)*, trans. Parvis
Emad and Kenneth Maly (Bloomington and Indianapolis: Indiana University Press, 1999), p. 21.

55 This double gesture is one of the factors precipitating Marian Hobson's
(*Jacques Derrida: Opening Lines* [London and New York: Routledge, 1998])
brief analysis of thinghood in Derrida, in which she writes that '"la chose"
is both an unobtainable singular, and the possibility of common everyday
things' (p. 133).

56 Cf. Martin Heidegger, *History of the Concept of Time: Prolegomena*, trans.
Theodore Kisiel (Bloomington and Indianapolis: Indiana University
Press, 1985).

57 The escape of the thing is synonymous with its withdrawal (*retrait*), which,
at the same time, refers to a repetition and an act of re-tracing: 'We must insist on this double writing of the *retrait*, suspension and *overabundant remaining*' (C 131).

58 Like Heidegger's Being, the thing is here placed 'under erasure.'

59 That is why David Willard is wrong in suggesting that Derrida's 'linguistic idealism' is expressed in his allowing beings to gain presence through naming and predication that bestow identity and thinghood. *Au contraire*, withdrawing itself, the thing can only give a gift of non-identity to everything that supplants it. Cf. David Willard, 'Predication as Originary Violence: A Phenomenological Critique of Derrida's View of Intentionality,' in G. Madison, ed., *Working through Derrida* (Evanston: Northwestern University Press, 1993). In his retort, Timothy Mooney ('Derrida's Empirical Realism,' *Philosophy and Social Criticism* 25(5), pp. 33–56) corrects Willard by noting that since *différance* is not a classical concept, it cannot stand for 'productive or originary causality' (p. 43).

60 This is a clear case where 'language can … "normally" become its own "abnormal" object,' owing to 'the structural iterability of the mark' (L 82). One could also refer to Giorgio Agamben's essay 'The Thing Itself' (in *Potentialities: Collected Essays in Philosophy*, trans. Daniel Heller-Roazen [Stanford: Stanford University Press, 1999]), dedicated to Jacques Derrida. In this treatment of Plato's esoteric doctrine, Agamben writes, 'The thing itself therefore has its essential place in language, even if language is certainly not adequate to it, on account, Plato says, of what is weak in language' (p. 31). This strong weakness or weak strength is precisely the language's normal becoming its own abnormal object.

61 Derrida writes, 'A sign is never an event, if by event we mean an irreplaceable and irreversible empirical particular' (SP 50). By 'event' Derrida does not mean 'an irreplaceable and irreversible empirical particular,' but rather the difference inherent in every iteration, replacement, and reversal. Nonetheless, taking at face value this strategically schematized stand-off between the 'empirical particular' and 'ideal signification,' one could conclude that, thanks to its placement in the abyss of the thing, signification absolves itself of its ties to ideality, and, by implication, something like an event of the sign becomes plausible.

62 In other words, language gives us the world and, at the same time, expropriates signifying subjects. Along these lines, Sean Gaston (*Derrida and Disinterest* [London and New York: Continuum, 2005]) accentuates the fact that in Levinas's philosophy, dispossession (which is synonymous with expropriation) is a hallmark of the other-oriented discourse, which yields the 'elemental non-possessive origin of the subject's possession of itself and the world' (p. 26).

63 Emphasis added.

64 From a different angle, Derrida corroborates this conclusion when he refuses to reduce the unit of meaning to a word: 'A "word" means nothing;

only sentences mean something' (PM 101). This Austinian assertion itself, however, will come under scrutiny in *Memoires: For Paul de Man*, where the mechanism of forgetting interferes both with the dictum that the word has no meaning and with the totality of the assertion (pp. 112ff).

65 The indeterminacy of this unit's survival is indebted to what in *Schibboleth: Pour Paul Celan* (Noisy-le-Sec: La Marelle, 2000) Derrida calls 'la migration du mot partagé [*the migration of a parted or shared word*].' While 'migration' straddles the transition from one word to another and from a word to the thing, 'partage,' meaning 'division' *and* 'sharing,' encompasses both the analytic moment and post-deconstructive synthesis. Such indeterminacy accompanying, 'le retour aux choses mêmes [*the return to the things themselves*]' suggests that 'on n'a plus à choisir entre les mots et les choses [*it is no longer necessary to choose between the words and the things*]' (DP 29).

66 The heaviness of the material remainder within language needs to be juxtaposed with 'the thought of the trace': 'This thought has no weight. It is, in the play of the system, that very thing which never has weight' (OG 93). Overshadowed by the tension between the weightlessness of the thought of the trace, on the one hand, and the weightiness of the material remainder on the other, the fragile balance between idealism and realism is perpetually threatened.

67 One aspect of such metaphysical fiction is the postulation of meta-language, which Derrida vehemently rejects, for instance in *Sovereignties in Question*: 'The poetic force of a word remains incalculable, all the more so, surely, when the unity of a word … is that of an *invented* composition, the inauguration of a new body' (p. 69). In the absence of such language, the thing would lack all elevation and sublimity: 'La chose chez Ponge manquerait d'élévation, de sublime' (Nathalie Roelens, 'La Chose littéraire / La Chose plastique,' in Michel Lisse, ed., *Passions de la littérature: Avec Jacques Derrida* [Paris: Galilée, 1996], p. 356).

68 The letters *gl* do not produce a non-expressive sign, in the indicative sense of signification, but a non-sign, which may not be digested in the 'solitary discourse of the soul.' In so doing, they arrest the movement of reduction 'to solitary mental discourse, to purely expressive discourse … [as] … a bracketing of all worldly and empirical existence' (Marrati, *Genesis and Trace*, p. 65).

69 What I call 'post-deconstructive synthesis' does not invalidate Derrida's own criticism of the synthetic and, potentially, totalizing activity of thought. In one sense, it stands for a certain 'being-with' or co-positing (*syn-thesis*) of the 'whole' and the 'fragment' that maintains open the interstices of spacing within the former and permits the latter to persist in its singularity. In another sense, 'post-deconstructive synthesis' glimpses the self-binding of the thing outside a conglomeration of subjects and objects.

70 'While it [the poetic production of new meaning] works *upon* language, the total new word foreign to the language also *returns* to the language, recomposes with it according to new networks of differences, becomes divided up again, etc., in short, does not become a master-word with the finally guaranteed integrity of a meaning or truth' (D 256).

71 Timothy Clark (*Derrida, Heidegger, Blanchot: Sources of Derrida's Notion and Practice of Literature* [Cambridge and New York: Cambridge University Press, 1992]) expresses well one facet of this becoming: 'As the thing given up to language, the language-thing or emergent poem becomes partly aerial, porous, urged out of its alien intransigence' (p. 157). But, despite the proviso 'partly,' this statement smacks of the kind of linguistic idealism, that is alien to Derrida and that Derrida fights against. Differently put, what Clark forgoes is the opposite pull of 'gravity' that ties the 'language-thing' to its material substratum.

72 Jacques Derrida, *Zhak Derrida v Moskve: Dekonstruktsiia Puteshestviia* [Jacques Derrida in Moscow: Deconstruction of a Journey], ed. Valerii Podoroga (Moscow: RIK 'Kul'tura,' 1993), pp. 154–5. My translation. I would like to cite two reasons why the existence of something 'beyond the confines of language' neither contests nor compromises the famous and all-too-often misunderstood dictum '*Il n'y a pas de hors-texte* [There is no outside-text]' (OG 158, 163). First, textuality extends well beyond the confines of language, especially beyond the bounds of 'natural' languages. Indeed, Derrida proceeds to specify that which exceeds languages in terms of textuality, 'the matter of traces derived from various texts,' carrying something like reality-effects. General textuality of which this excess forms a part is also a condition of possibility for language, an unmarked mark of the architrace from which it derives. Second, even if language and text were interchangeable, there would remain an enormous difference between the 'there is,' *il y a*, and 'existence.' The former suggests a pre-existential neutrality, which in fact anticipates the latter. It is in this difference between textuality and language that the event of the thing comes about.

73 This differentiation and the assertion to the effect that there are only things but not the 'thing itself' parallel Derrida's way of raising the question of animality (cf. 'The Animal That, Therefore, I Am (More to Follow),' trans. David Wills, *Critical Inquiry 28*, Winter 2002, p. 393).

74 The implication vis-à-vis the loss of subjective mastery is double: 1) the renunciation of naming rebels against the tradition traceable to the Bible, where the one who names an entity symbolically re-confirms the legitimacy of his (most often, *his*) dominion over it, and 2) trauma, ever since Freud, signals the inassimilable nature of particular memories that are not recalled at will, but obsessively return and haunt 'of their own accord.'

75 In Blanchot's 'The Instant of My Death,' 'the verb "attested" is the only word that explicitly signals the testimonial dimension of the narrative' in the sentence 'Even the bloated horses, on the road, in the fields, attested to a war that had gone on' (D 80). This prompts Derrida to invoke, on the next page, what he calls the 'testimonial thing [*la chose testimoniale*].'

76 To complicate this schema somewhat, one may consult Derrida's 1970s seminars on the thing in Blanchot, where the thing itself could be considered as 'the name of all the names': 'La Chose n'a-t-elle donc pas de nom? Est-elle au-delà de tous le noms? Ou bien est-elle le nom de tous les noms? [*Does the thing not have a name? Is it beyond all the names? Or, rather, is it the name of all the names?*]' (JDP 13/12).

77 In 'Punctuations: The Time of a Thesis,' Derrida intimates that his first 'registered' thesis title was 'The Ideality of the Literary Object' (EU 115). This title does not overwrite or disavow the materiality of the literary *thing*, which hovers on the unassimilable threshold of the transcendental phenomenological logic.

78 Among others, Maurice Merleau-Ponty articulates the second sense of the 'experience of the thing.' In *Phenomenology of Perception* (trans. Colin Smith [London and New York: Routledge, 2004]), things not only 'display themselves' to me, but also 'see' and guarantee the permanence of those dimensions of other things that are hidden from my view (p. 79).

79 At the same time, in *Derrida, Heidegger, Blanchot*, Clark warns, 'One must not assume that the "things" of Ponge's texts are anthropomorphisms, projections of human affairs upon the blankness of "mere things"' (p. 156). On the worldlessness of the thing and the paucity of the animal 'having' of the world, see Martin Heidegger, *The Fundamental Concepts of Metaphysics*, trans. William McNeill and Nicholas Walker (Bloomington: Indiana University Press, 1995), pp. 197ff.

80 Walter Benjamin has broached the topic of the survival of literary things in his 'Task of the Translator' (in *Illuminations: Essays and Reflection* [New York: Schocken, 1968]), where he argues that, thanks to the effects of translation, a literary work achieves posthumous fame (p. 72).

81 On 'puncturing punctuality' in speech and writing, see 'Signs and the Blink of an Eye' (SP 60ff).

82 In *Glas*, this phenomenon goes by the technical term 'antonomasia,' the conflation of proper and common names. Concerning antonomasia, Derrida writes: 'This alienation, already [*déjà*], even before I return to myself, promenades my proper name in the street, *classes* it in the "natural" world, freezes the appellation in an exterior thing, in its name or in its form' (G 183, right). Thus, the moment of rendering-common, or rendering-descriptive, of the proper name seems to be a privileged one.

83 On the role of description in poetry that allows things to be in their 'mere-ness,' see Simon Critchley's *Things Merely Are: Philosophy in the Poetry of Wallace Stevens* (London and New York: Routledge, 2005). The third dimension, supplementing naming and description, is a prescription that emanates from the thing itself and its law: '*Signéponge* déplace la perspective de la description vers la prescription, ou plus exactement, vers l'injonction' (Daniel Giovannangeli, 'La Chose même,' in Michel Lisse, ed., *Passions de la littérature: Avec Jacques Derrida* [Paris: Galilée, 1996], p. 92).

84 Likewise, in the last note to *The Secret Art of Antonin Artaud*, Derrida asks: 'Will I have been forcing things? [*Aurai-je forcé les choses?*] Perhaps it will be thought that I have given too much weight to this word the *subjectile* ... But first of all no reading, no interpretation could ever prove its efficacy and its necessity without a certain forcing. *You have to force things*' (US 156 n80). Such 'forcing' of things is the indispensable underside of 'immanent criticism.'

85 Socially, Juliet's supplication defies and inverts the patriarchal, patronymic convention, whereby the wife had to adopt her husband's name. But, at the deepest level, it raises anew the Shakespearean question of the name ('What's in a name?'), of name-giving (naming) and of taking a name. Centuries later, in the conclusion to *The Nomos of the Earth in the International Law of the* Jus Publicum Europaeum (New York: Telos, 2003), Carl Schmitt will voice his scepticism as to whether or not we have even heard these questions: 'Has the power to name and give names disappeared? Has even what that means, what a name is, disappeared?' (p. 349). Derrida's method, in turn, reawakens (in Husserlian terms, 'reactivates') the meaning of the name by highlighting its ambiguous relation to the thing, and thus revitalizes the connection between the two.

86 There is a clear parallel between the impossibility of choosing between mastery and non-mastery over things and the impossibility of choosing between the two substitutions (one proper name for another, *or* a common name for the proper name).

87 Cf. Julia Kristeva, 'Adolescence, le syndrome d'idéalité,' in *La Haine et le pardon* (Paris: Fayard, 2005), pp. 393–410.

2. 'This Thing Regards Us'

1 The 'intentionality thesis' is, arguably, the crux of Husserl's phenomenology. First enunciated by Brentano and modified by Husserl in an attempt to eliminate all traces of empirical 'psychologism,' this thesis describes the very structure of consciousness as its directedness to an object. In this sense, every act of consciousness ought to be understood as an intentional relation aiming at that which is intended by it. Cf. Heidegger, *History of the*

Concept of Time, pp. 36ff. Husserl himself states that intentionality can 'designate ... the general theme of "Objectively" oriented phenomenology' (*Ideas I*, p. 199).

2 In *Genesis and Trace*, Paola Marratti accentuates one aspect of this critique, namely, the empirical contamination of the transcendental (pp. 123ff). However counterintuitive the inverse (the transcendental contamination of the empirical) might be, it is indispensable to the thorough understanding of Derrida's work. 'Violence and Metaphysics' features the clearest example of this trend in the context of Derrida's critical discussion of the notion of singularity in Levinas's 'radical empiricism,' which operates with the transcendental categories, such as 'metaphysical desire,' 'the relation to the other,' and so on.

3 'We can thus say that in Husserl's hylomorphic production of meaning the material of sense is forcefully stamped by formal conceptuality, or even that conceptual form forcefully stamps out differences of sense, so that a meaningful concept is produced' (John Protevi, *Political Physics: Deleuze, Derrida, and the Body Politic* [London and New York: Athlone, 2001], p. 38).

4 To be sure, this circumscription contradicts the letter of Husserl's text, since at the core of *Ideas I* is the assertion that everything empirical and reducible is transcendent, whereas pure consciousness possesses the 'absolute being' of something immanent (e.g., §44). Nonetheless, the spirit of Husserl's own struggle to harmonize the claims that realism and idealism place on phenomenology justifies this theoretical gesture.

5 The spectrality of *noema* hinges on its non-real status within consciousness: 'The radical possibility of all spectrality should be sought in the direction that Husserl identifies ... as an intentional but *non-real* component of the phenomenological lived experience, namely, the *noema* ... Is not such "irreality" [*irréellité*], *its dependence both* in relation to the world *and* in relation to the *real* stuff of egological subjectivity, the very place of apparition, the essential, general, non-regional possibility of the specter?' (SM 189/216 n6). On the structure of intentionality as the subject's self-transcendence, see Emmanuel Levinas, *The Theory of Intuition in Husserl's Phenomenology*, 2nd ed. (Evanston: Northwestern University Press, 1995), p. 41.

6 For a summary of the noematic and hyletic openness, which Derrida diagnoses in Husserl's oeuvre, see Lawlor, *Derrida and Husserl*, pp. 29ff.

7 'Husserl's starting point for the analysis of consciousness is the *waking* ego ... On the other hand, Husserl has a Fichtean conception of consciousness running up against something "other" or "alien", something that does not belong to consciousness and that "awakens" it. This "other" can be characterized in different ways, but frequently he describes it simply as

hyle, matter, stuff (*Stoff*)' (Dermot Moran, *Edmund Husserl: Founder of Phenomenology* [Cambridge, UK and Malden, MA: Polity, 2005], p. 144).

8 For example: 'It follows that if, and in the extent to which, *matter* in this general economy designates … radical alterity (I will specify: in relation to philosophical oppositions), then what I write can be considered "materialist"' (P 64). Subscribing to this non-traditional notion of materialism, Derrida seems to evoke matter prior to its opposition to form (not *within* but *in relation to* 'philosophical oppositions'), and even prior to its conjugation with form in an 'originary' correlation.

9 Levinas goes as far as to say that, in Husserlian phenomenology, 'those elements which are deprived of intentionality constitute a special material or *hyletic* level' (Levinas, *The Theory of Intuition in Husserl's Phenomenology*, p. 38).

10 Psychoanalytic philosophy, especially in some of its Lacanian variations, considers 'internalization without incorporation' of the Real to be a schema for the dynamics of a traumatic experience: 'What blurs this clear distinction between the empty symbolic form and its contingent positive content is precisely the *Real*: a stain which sutures the empty frame on to a part of its content, the "indivisible remainder" of some "pathological" contingent materiality' (Slavoj Žižek, *The Ticklish Subject: The Absent Centre of Political Ontology* [London and New York: Verso, 1999], p. 277]).

11 Rodolph Gasché (*Inventions of Difference: On Jacques Derrida* [Cambridge and London: Harvard University Press, 1998]) compares the remains Derrida has spoken of in *Glas* with the Adornean notion of the non-identical. He writes: 'Absolute identity must exclude … what resists it as remainder, residue, refuse, or rest … Rather than a rigorously identifiable and decidable residue like the Adornean non-identical, the remainder that deconstruction discerns *in* a speculative totality and identical whole is "a remainder that is both quasi-transcendental and supplementary"' (p. 223). Regardless of the question whether the charge Gasché levels against Adorno is fair, it becomes clear that, in the case of intentional animation, the remainder refers to the ideality of consciousness, which is re-claimed by the material 'opaqueness of the body.' The residue of intentionality that the thing itself 'recycles' is, therefore, a shorthand for Derrida's own method of weaving together Husserlian idealism and realism.

12 The supplementarity of the thing with regard to the object would be a daring implication of Husserl's conception of *hylē* as a 'sensuous residuum' of experience (Moran, *Edmund Husserl*, p. 154). At the same time, the inversion of the intentionality thesis explores the potential two-directionality of 'animation' in Husserl, who writes apropos of the sensuousness of pleasure,

pain, and so on, 'We find those sensuous moments overlaid by a stratum which, as it were, "animates", which *bestows sense* (or essentially involves a bestowing of sense) – a stratum by which precisely the concrete intentive mental process arises from the *sensuous, which has in itself nothing pertaining to intentionality*' (Husserl, *Ideas I*, p. 203). In question, then, is the 'in itself' of the sensuous that does not exhibit the structure of intentionality, yet gives rise to the 'concrete intentive mental process.' On the following page, Husserl proceeds to leave 'undecided' the sensuous, hyletic foundations of intentionality.

13 The ground-shift in the making of sense is responsible for the fact that 'there is a menace of something *unheimlich*, something sinister, some Thing (*Chose terrifiante*) in the space between Derrida's lines akin to the *horror vacui* and the fear of madness' (John Llewelyn, *Derrida on the Threshold of Sense* [London: Macmillan, 1986], p. 102). The uncanniness of the thing is a symptom not of its senselessness, but of a different regime of producing sense 'not for us.'

14 Admittedly, the inversion of intentionality hints at the 'poverty' of the classical phenomenological notion of the thing compared to the thing that aims at us, for instance, in Ponge's texts. Apropos of the gap between the two and the way in which it informs Derrida's analyses, Daniel Giovannangeli (*Le Retard de la conscience: Husserl, Sartre, Derrida* [Brussels: Ousia, 2001]) writes, 'La coïncidence est seulement partielle entre Ponge et le phénoménologue: la chose pongienne est en excès sur la chose du phénoménologue [*There is only a partial coincidence between Ponge and a phenomenologist: the Pongean thing is in excess over the thing of a phenomenologist*]' (p. 126). Nonetheless, the 'poverty' of the phenomenological thing produces a schema, in the Kantian sense, for the exuberant, exorbitant, and 'excessive' flourishing of its post-phenomenological counterpart.

15 Therefore, in this inversion, the intentionality thesis is not negated but re-confirmed in what Derrida calls its 'absolute privilege': 'The silence of prehistoric arcana and buried civilizations, the entombment of lost intentions and guarded secrets, and the illegibility of the lapidary inscription disclose the transcendental sense of death as what unites these things to the absolute privilege [rightfulness – M.M.] of intentionality in the very instance of its essential failure [*en ce qui l'unit à l'absolu du droit intentionnel dans l'instance même de son échec*]' (IOG 88).

16 'Inversion' belongs to the phase of 'overturning' with which all deconstruction must begin: 'We must traverse a phase of *overturning* ... To deconstruct the opposition, first of all, is to overturn the hierarchy at a given moment. To overlook this phase of overturning is to forget the conflictual and

subordinating structure of opposition' (P 41). The particular, hierarchized 'structure of opposition' that will be overturned encompasses consciousness (both the subject and its object) and the thing.

17 In the second moment of the critique of Hegel, Derrida comes very close to the Adorno of *Negative Dialectics*, whose chief concern is the insufficiently negative notion of dialectical negation. Yet, at the same time, Derrida insists on the convergence of the thing's pure negativity and its absolute positivity.

18 First, the emphasis on figuration and its paucity in relation to the appearance of the thing seems to be a fragment of Derrida's response to Merleau-Ponty, for whom 'consciousness is structured as a relation between figure, background and horizon' (Barry Stocker, *Routledge Philosophy Guidebook to Derrida on Deconstruction* [London and New York: Routledge, 2006], p. 87). In part, this response will displace consciousness by positing it on the horizon of a figure-less thing. Second, since the phantomatic thing is what Derrida designates as the 'sensuous non-sensuous' in *Specters of Marx*, it establishes a complex relation with the figure of the figure in Lyotard's *Discours, Figure* (Paris: Klincksieck, 1971). Placing the figure squarely on the side of the sense, Lyotard nonetheless diagnoses a split between the 'figure-form' and the 'figure-matrix' on the one hand, and the 'figure-image' on the other. The first two are the invisible conditions of possibility for the visibility of the 'figure-image,' just as the figure-less thing in Derrida is a precondition for dispensing subjects and objects to sight. 'Taking the side of the figural' thus involves an opposition not only between the figure and discourse but also between two figures of the figure.

19 'Dasein's everyday possibilities of Being are for the Others to dispose of as they please. These Others, moreover, are not *definite* Others. On the contrary, *any* Other can represent them' (Heidegger, *Being and Time*, p. 126). 'Publicness proximally controls every way in which the world and Dasein get interpreted, and it is always right – not because there is some distinctive and primary relationship-of-Being in which it is related to "Things" … but because it is insensitive to every difference of level and of genuineness' (ibid., p. 127). 'Idle talk is the possibility of understanding everything without previously making the thing one's own … Idle talk is something which anyone can rake up' (ibid., p. 169). Thus, while the Heideggerian event consists in the 'propriation' of indefinite generality, Derrida detects traces of the event in a certain indefiniteness preceding the movement of such propriation.

20 Between 1975 and 1978, Derrida taught a total of three seminars under the general title *La Chose*. In 1975–6 he offered *La Chose (Heidegger/Ponge)*; in 1976–7 he gave *La Chose (Heidegger/Blanchot)*; and in 1977–8, *La Chose (Heidegger and the 'Other' of Heidegger)*. All three seminars were given at the École

Normale Supérieure and at Yale. While these texts have not been published in their entirety, their fragments may be found in the 'Legs de Freud' chapter of *the Postcard*, throughout *Psyche*, and in *Signsponge* and *Parages*. The full seminar transcripts are stored in the Jacques Derrida Papers archive (Boxes 13 and 14) at the University of California, Irvine. The dates and titles of these seminars have at least two implications. First, the Derridian preoccupation with 'the thing' in the mid- and late seventies indicates that the topic might be the key to understanding his writings of the 'middle period,' although I would argue that it is equally significant for the interpretation of his early and late works. Second, the centrality of Heidegger, running as a common thread across the three titles, intimates that, more than any other thinker, this philosopher supplies the background against which Derrida shapes his notion of the thing.

21 In the last two sentences, Derrida playfully explores the consequences of an 'academic' definition of the thing. *Le Robert* dictionary defines it, in one sense, as 'that which one cannot or does not want to name [*Ce qu'on ne peut ou ne veut pas nommer*]' (Cf. 'Chose' III).

22 Giorgio Agamben (*The Coming Community*, trans. Michael Hardt [Minneapolis and London: University of Minnesota Press, 1993]) follows Derrida's lead in salvaging the scholastic category of *quodlibet ens* as the non-indifference of 'whatever,' which 'is not "being, it does not matter which," but rather "being such that it always matters" … The Whatever in question here relates to singularity not in its indifference with respect to a common property … but only in its being *such as it is*. Singularity is thus freed from the false dilemma that obliges knowledge to choose between the ineffability of the individual and the intelligibility of the universal' (p. 1). This inexhaustible singularity is the reason why we will always 'have the thing' for the thing.

23 In his writings on the animal – which, along with the thing and the human, is one of the basic elements comprising the Western metaphysical edifice – Derrida utilizes a strikingly similar locution that interweaves vision and concern in an inverted structure of intentionality: 'Since so long ago, can we say that the animal has been looking at us, has concerned us [*que l'animal nous regarde*]'(Derrida, 'The Animal That, Therefore, I Am (More to Follow),' p. 372). The ghostly thing is an animal, given that it animates itself with the intentionality of its own.

24 Recall Levinas's succinct definition in *Totality and Infinity*: 'Already *of itself* ethics is an "optics"' (p. 29).

25 In a draft entry on *capture* prepared for the project *Les Immatériaux*, Derrida equates capture both with regard and with fascination. The spectral dematerialization of capture, which 'does not make matter disappear [*ne fait*

pas disparaître la matière],' resonates with the inversion of intentionality. This resonance transpires through the medium of 'the sublime fetishism [*le fétichisme sublime*]' of something that presents itself as unpresentable (*se présente comme imprésentable*) (JDP 59/1–5), namely, the regard of the thing itself.

26 Or again, 'I interest the thing that regards and concerns me [*j'intéresse la chose qui me regarde*]' (SI 128/129). This interest turns out to be reciprocal: '*For the moment, the thing does not bore me; rather it excites me a lot* [La chose pour le moment ne m'ennuie pas, elle m'excite même beaucoup]' (JDP 13 1). The latter statement is a stab at Heidegger, who writes in *The Fundamental Concepts of Metaphysics: World, Finitude, Solitude* (Bloomington and Indianapolis: Indiana University Press, 1995), 'Boredom is not simply an inner spiritual experience, rather something about it, namely *that which bores* and which lets being bored arise, comes toward us precisely *from out of the things themselves*' (p. 83).

27 Derrida's example for this articulation of causality involves, precisely, a key and a lock: '[il] est engagé comme on engage une clé dans une serrure [*it is engaged as one engages a key in a lock*]' (DP 18). More broadly, the re-articulation of causality entails re-imagining the role of the preposition 'with' on the model of *Mitsein*. One of the directions for this rethinking offered by Derrida is a certain inherent sociality of what I call 'the things of the senses' already apparent in the expressions '*to hear* with *the ear, to see* with *the eye* [entendre *avec* l'oreille, voir *avec* l'oeil]' – the expressions that ought to be de-functionalized and reinterpreted on the basis of the Heideggerian 'being-with' (Jacques Derrida, 'L'Oreille de Heidegger: Philopolémologie (*Geschlecht* IV),' in *Politiques de l'amitié* [Paris: Galilée, 1994], p. 380).

28 As such, the limit between the public and the non-public is not static: 'Today, everything can be launched in the public sphere and considered, at least by some people, as publishable, and so having the classic value, the virtually universal and even holy value of a public thing' (PM 32). Or, even more explicitly, 'The dividing line between the political and the apolitical is no longer assumed as soon as the *unconditional* engagement (and therefore the apparently transcendental engagement with respect to the public thing [*et donc apparemment transcendant au regard de la chose publique*]) with the friend supposes a priori reason and virtue' (PF 184/211). In the Kantian spirit, which informs Derrida's analysis, reason and virtue are precisely those things that *cannot* be private (ibid.), and therefore all the private relationships and engagements they undersign are thrust into the public sphere.

29 'Obsession is irreducible to consciousness even if it overwhelms it ... Obsession traverses consciousness countercurrentwise' (Emmanuel Levinas,

'Substitution,' in Sean Hand, ed., *Levinas Reader* [Oxford and Cambridge, MA: Blackwell, 1989], p. 91). The 'countercurrent' of obsession that traverses consciousness is tantamount to the inversion of intentionality. In Levinas's later writings, the early emphasis on obsession is transformed into a non-indifferent attitude to the other that overwhelms one's desire to persevere in being. See Emmanuel Levinas, *Otherwise Than Being, or Beyond Essence*, trans. Alphonso Lingis (Pittsburgh, PA: Duquesne University Press, 1998), pp. 164ff.

30 Moran, *Husserl*, p. 120.

31 Cf. John Sallis, *Being and Logos: Reading the Platonic Dialogues*, 3rd ed., (Bloomington and Indianapolis: Indiana University Press, 1996).

32 Mutatis mutandis, Derrida offers a similar reading of Roland Barthes's *punctum*: 'The *punctum* aims at me at the instant and place I aim at it' (WM 39).

33 For more on the law of the thing, see SI, passim.

34 The silent density within the subject is not negative and prohibitive; rather, it contains the promise and the 'continuing potentiality' of what Simon Morgan Wortham ('Unheard of,' *Textual Practice 20*(1), 2006) calls 'counter-auditability' (p. 127).

35 In response to Derrida's admission 'I do not know what to do with my September letter that I have been dragging around with me, like a strange, mute, eloquent, thing [*comme une chose étrange, muette, éloquente*], with its moments of sleep, talkative sequences' (PC 124/136), Geoffrey Hartman writes: 'Mute letters are the discreet jewels of meaning. Their potential, their reserve, is eloquent ... yet they suggest a *chose* ... that cannot be named as such' (*Saving the Text: Literature/Derrida/ Philosophy* [Baltimore and London: Johns Hopkins University Press, 1981], p. 46). The silent discretion of a mute letter that is 'like a ... thing' is not purely negative or privative; it withdraws from our senses and keeps a promise of meaning, like a jewel in the rough that conceals the futural sparkling of a precious stone. Its 'potential' is held in reserve precisely in the potentially infinite interval between its inscription and its decoding.

36 My translation.

37 The 'voice that keeps the silence' is aphonic and blank, a descendant of the 'deficient *logos*' that, according to Socrates, characterizes all inward commerce (D 184).

38 On dictation, see *The Postcard*: 'There is an other in you, who from behind dictates the terrible thing to you' (PC 125); and *Signsponge*, where the alterity of the thing is what dictates the law to us: 'Property: the *idion* of the thing which dictates, according to its muteness, in other words singularly, a description of itself' (SI 46). The contrast between these two texts produces

the sense of the thing as both active and passive, noetic and noematic, dictating and dictated.

39 This will have also been the meaning of Heidegger's attunement, which, in line with the hypostatization of hearing in *Being and Time*, has to do with the closing of the eye and the opening of the ear. On the other hand, in Heidegger, *'one opens the ear in order to appropriate for oneself the tradition of philosophy, in order to correspond to the call of being* [Ouvrir l'oreille pour s'approprier la tradition de la philosophie, pour correspondre à l'appel de l'être]' (Derrida, 'L'Oreille de Heidegger,' p. 368). Derrida's response to Heidegger will revolve around the assertion that the ear opens Dasein ('l'oreille qui ouvre le *Dasein*'), not to his ownmost potentiality of being ('à son pouvoir-être propre'), but to the exteriority of the other (p. 355).

40 Derrida's modification of Husserlian intentionality does not strive to transcendentalize it, to step behind the sense of hearing, and to register it in the extra-sensory, extra-ordinary manner. Its only goal is to show how the thing mediates all subjective auto-affective relations. This is the case, for instance, with Hélène Cixous, who recovers her eyesight after a laser surgery: 'Now here she is … and, getting her sight back, she finally hears herself *hearing* and touches *touch*' (V 51).

41 What I say is, in the first instance, 'what says me to me,' and 'what says me to me' is, in the last instance, what I say. This 'virtuous' circularity invalidates all ventures that try to distinguish the one from the other: 'But this thing which cannot be taken back, is it what the child says or is it what says the child, the desire of the child? [*Mais cette chose qui ne se reprend plus, c'est ce que dit l'enfant ou ce qui dit l'enfant, le désir d'enfant?*] You couldn't tell' (PC 167/180).

42 On a Derridian treatment of the topic of the telephone, one would need to refer to Avital Ronell's *The Telephone Book: Technology, Schizophrenia, Electric Speech* (Lincoln: University of Nebraska Press, 1991). For Ronell, the telephone, like the thing it metonymizes, presupposes a certain alterity, that is, another telephonic apparatus: 'When does the telephone become what it is? It presupposes the existence of another telephone, somewhere … To be what it is, it has to be pluralized, multiplied, engaged by another line' (p. 3).

43 'Things would be quite otherwise if one were attentive to the writing within the voice, that is, before the letter' (PC 465).

44 'Indeed the call is precisely something which *we ourselves* have neither planned nor prepared for nor voluntarily performed, nor have we ever done so. "It" calls, against our expectations and even against our will … The call comes *from* me and yet *from beyond me and over me*' (Heidegger, *Being and Time*, p. 275).

45 The text of *The Postcard* is interrupted with a blank space immediately after the words 'such is …,' *telle est*, which in French are homophonous with *télé-* (distance and the telephone).

46 With the invention of the 'wireless' telephone, the physical ligature seems to have disappeared, at the same time that the bond grows stronger and becomes almost all-encompassing. The natural artificiality of this thing comes to the fore in the appellation 'cellular,' which capitalizes on a biological or biologized discourse.

47 'Elle [la chose] est toujour *sous* et *derrière*. D'où, déjà, une première explication du caractère dissimulé, mystérieux, refusé, dérobé, terrible, anonyme, de la chose [*It* [*the thing*] *is always* underneath *and* behind. *From here one can already draw the first explanation for the dissimulated, mysterious, refused, hidden, terrible, anonymous character of the thing*]' (JDP 13/1). In talking about the 'character of the thing,' Derrida signs his own dissimulated, hidden, and so forth, name twice: *derrière* – behind – and *déjà* – already.

48 Derrida adopts the Levinasian notion of the caress, except that the caressed is a thing, not another person. For Levinas, 'the caress consists in seizing upon nothing, in soliciting what ceaselessly escapes its form toward a future never future enough, in soliciting what slips away as though it *were not yet*' (*Totality and Infinity*, pp. 257–8).

49 Conversely, touching transpires 'always by way of a figure' (OT 105).

50 This is what Derrida calls 'humanualism' (*humainism*), prevalent in the history of Western philosophy: 'Human beings touch more and touch better. The hand is properly human' (OT 152). And further: 'Things *manual* and *human(ual)* are on a par here, as they so often are … The "hand" is the very thing itself that most often extends between human touching and divine touching' (OT 256).

51 In the context of a certain invigorating, empowering amputation, we would need to reread *Glas* on the potency of castration and the Hegelian-Lacanian hypostatization of lack as a prototype for the severing of the hand: 'By first incising his glans, he defends himself in advance against the infinite threat, castrates in his turn the enemy … He exhibits his castration as an erection that defies the other' (p. 46, left). Even more pertinently, the same paradoxical logic applies to the cutting of the hand in the character of Jean Genet's Stilitano: 'The one-armed Stilitano, who promptly dominates the scene of the *Journal*, implants and repeats, in his body, the substitution that at once castrates and bands erect' (p. 137, right).

52 The injunction 'one cannot think it as a thing' refers to the thing in its objective determination, as is apparent in the qualification 'even less [*encore moins*] as an object.'

53 Heidegger is, then, the forerunner of the Derridian inversion of intentionality. For instance, in *The Fundamental Concepts of Metaphysics*, he writes,
'Above all, however, we shall never have comprehended these [basic phil-
osophical] concepts [*Begriffe*] and their conceptual rigor unless we have
first been *gripped* [ergriffen] by whatever they are supposed to comprehend' (p. 7).

54 The scenario of the self-obliterating double gesture unfolds, for instance, in
The Postcard, which repeats the earlier lesson of 'Freud and the Scene of
Writing': 'Two hands, the mystic writing pad ... He is erasing with one
hand, scratching, and with the other he is still scratching, writing' (p. 25);
'I write ... while trafficking with things a bit and with the other hand, describing, by throwing in shadows and blanks' (p. 83); 'Still scratching, I
would like to write with both hands' (p. 90). Typewriting follows the same
two-handed model: 'You do it more with the fingers – and with two hands
rather than one' (PM 21).

55 'When Our Eyes Touch' is the title of the preface to *On Touching*; in *Veils*,
Derrida uses 'diminution' as a musical term for attenuating the intensity of
the sound, and as a reduction of the knit in tactile, textile weaving (V 21-4);
and in *The Ear of the Other*, the secret name by which the other calls me is a
scent (EO 106). The inclusion of the olfactory sense further undermines the
figural appearance of the thing because olfaction signals 'dissolvability'
and 'the lack of form' (Fiona Borthwick, 'Olfaction and Taste: Invasive
Odours and Disappearing Objects,' *Australian Journal of Anthropology* 11(2),
p. 129).

56 Mairéad Hanrahan ('The Legacy of Jacques Derrida,' *Paragraph* 28(3),
November 2005) has begun to address the complexity of this specularity in
terms of the displacement of the border between the reading and the read
text: 'His touch, in other words, displaces the border – "to touch is to touch
a border, however deeply one may penetrate" – between the reading and
the read text, in a contact which neither consigns the latter to solitary (and
unread) intactness nor abolishes the difference in a gesture that would ultimately involve the assimilation of one or other text to the other' (p. 75).

57 'What is produced in the current trembling is a reevaluation of the relationship between the general text and what was believed to be, in the
form of reality [*sous la forme de la réalité*] (history, politics, economics, sexu-
ality, etc.), the simple, referable exterior of language or writing, the belief
that this exterior could operate from the simple position of cause or accident' (P 91/126).

58 The non-philosophical, non-idealizable, un-thought thing is both the secret
kernel and the cryptic container of (that is, both more and less than) the

thing the philosopher thinks and idealizes: '*The Thing which summons us here is not the Thing itself of philosophers* [La Chose même de philosophes] ... *That does not mean, however, that it is simply something other than the philosophical thing ... but perhaps that which philosophy thinks without thinking it ... the secret or the crypt of the philosophers' thing itself* [le secret ou la crypte de la chose même de philosophes]' (JDP 13/12).

59 As such, the 'principle of principles' already harbours an 'internal tension,' a 'lapse in Husserl's phenomenological vigilance' that necessitates repetition, absence, and writing in the fullness of all intuitive evidence (Lawlor, *Derrida and Husserl*, p. 32).

60 The same fold announces itself in the Husserlian definition of intentionality as the 'consciousness *of* something' (*Ideas I*, pp. 200ff). The genitive form stands at the intersection of the objective and the subjective refering to the consciousness *that belongs to* something and the consciousness *that makes sense of* something.

61 On the same page of the essay on Jabès, this circularity results in the subjectivization of the poet along with the book: 'And the book is indeed the subject of the poet [*le livre est bien le sujet du poète*], the speaking and knowing being who *in* the book writes *on* the book. This movement through which the book, *articulated* by the voice of the poet, is folded and bound to itself, the movement through which the book becomes a subject in itself and for itself [*se plie et se relie à soi, devient sujet en soi et pour soi*], is not critical or speculative reflection, but is, first of all, poetry and history' (WD 65/100). Here, Derrida operates with the double sense of 'subject' as an active agent and a theme, which means, precisely, an 'object.' The doubling of the meaning of the subject is synonymous with the 'folding' of the book and the inversion of intentionality.

62 The source of this circularity is the written quality of the thing: 'Writing is at once the condition of the fecundity of an origin and the cause of its loss. Writing makes possible the development of an original sense and also produces the loss of sense which takes place in this development' (Rudolf Bernet, 'On Derrida's "Introduction" to Husserl's *Origin of* Geometry,' in Hugh Silverman, ed., *Derrida and Deconstruction* [New York and London: Routledge, 2005], p. 144).

3. Deconstruction of Fetishism

1 For Stiegler, 'the relation binding the "who" and the "what" is invention ... The technical inventing the human, the human inventing the technical' (*Technics and Time I*, pp. 134, 137). Expressed in psychoanalytic terminology,

the indeterminate and indeterminable opening for the invention or, literally, for the in-coming of consciousness is the unconscious (as a 'bond' between the 'who' and the 'what').

2 Psyche is 'the proper name of an allegory,' 'the common name for the soul,' and 'in French, the name of a revolving mirror' (MPD 39). This is, in part, a Husserlian heritage: '"Material thing" and "psyche" are different regions of being, and yet the latter is founded on the former, and out of that fact arises the fact that psychology is founded on somatology' (*Ideas I*, p. 32).

3 It remains to be decided whether, in and of itself, Psyche's capacity to see would be enough to undermine the multifarious ways of treating her as 'dead,' or whether it would intensify such treatment by bearing witness to it with the sort of muteness with which inanimate things register events.

4 Such, for instance, is the resistance of the 'bond': 'Bonds, paradoxically, are unintelligible to the understanding because they are too subtle, and impossible to dissect. They resist the separating power of the intellect, because in principle, at least, they are in themselves ... indissoluble' (Gasché, *Inventions of Difference*, p. 177). Shortly, we shall have an occasion to return to the resistance of the bond in connection with the thing.

5 This belief can be traced back to Descartes, who writes in the Synopsis of his meditations (*Meditations on First Philosophy*, trans. John Cottingham [Cambridge and New York: Cambridge University Press, 1996]): 'We cannot understand a mind except as being indivisible. For we cannot conceive of half of a mind, while we can conceive of half of the body, however small' (p. 9). Nonetheless, in the case of Descartes himself, the *cogito* presupposes the disavowed divisibility of mental substance, inasmuch as the 'thinking thing' must first separate from itself in order to come back to and think itself.

6 I take it that Derrida retains the basic Husserlian meaning of the word 'substrate' explained in *Ideas I*, §11. There, the 'ultimate' (i.e., the lowest) substrates refer to non-formalized objects (p. 23).

7 Freud describes the remarkable, self-remarking thing in his 'A Note Upon the "Mystic Writing-Pad"' (in *On Metapsychology: The Theory of Psychoanalysis*, trans. James Strachey [London and New York: Penguin, 1991]). The 'permanent trace' retained upon the wax slab remarks the impermanent, erasable, 'vanishing' trace left on the upper, celluloid layer (p. 432). This might appear to contradict Derrida's assertion that 'remarking is remarked against the unconscious in general' (ARF 97, n19). Nevertheless, the self-remarcation of the extended psychic thing signals the encryption of a trace whose retracing (memorialization) transpires entirely within the unconscious such that it is neither lost to nor recovered by conscious remembrance.

8 On the theoretical and practical levels alike, psychoanalysis replicates the unbound bond of the thing: 'If interpretation supposes analysis, that is to say, the *analuein* of the unbinding that unties, then to *make* or *do* [psychoanalysis], on the contrary, comes down to binding, to binding oneself and allying oneself, to doing the contrary at the same time' (HC 104).

9 Note that the French *la chose* is in the feminine. That means that it shares the third person singular pronoun (*elle*) with Psyche.

10 Martin Heidegger, *Kant and the Problem of Metaphysics*, trans. Richard Taft (Bloomington: Indiana University Press, 1997). See especially §34: 'Time as pure self-affection and the temporal character of the self' (pp. 132–6).

11 Emmanuel Levinas, *Time and the Other*, trans. Alphonso Lingis (Pittsburgh: Duquesne University Press, 1987), pp. 74ff.

12 It is no longer Dasein as the clearing for being that lets things be, but the radical absence of the I. Also refer to this chapter's epigraph on the 'task' of freeing things.

13 'There is at least one spot in every dream at which it is unplumbable – a navel, as it were, that is its point of contact with the unknown' (Sigmund Freud, *The Interpretation of Dreams*, trans. James Strachey, in *The Standard Edition of the Complete Psychological Works of Sigmund Freud*, vol. 4 [London: Hogarth, 1953], p. 111 n1).

14 In each case, we will deal with the mother, or mothers, and her/their son, or sons. Besides ensuring a certain 'analytic consistency,' this reiterated situation reflects (still, unfortunately) the vestiges of philosophical phallogocentrism.

15 'The most natural flowers are the most artificial, like the virginity of the Holy Virgin' (G 54, left).

16 The homophony of *sans* (without) and *sang* (blood) is crucial to understanding both *Glas* and *The Truth in Painting*.

17 'As the possessor of the fetish, she [the mother] carries a substitute of the thing itself – that father in himself; yet as the deconstructed fetish she also carries the trace of the thing itself; through not being there she *is* – one presumes, since the verb of being is strategically suppressed in the sentence – the father in himself' (Gayatri C. Spivak, 'Displacement and the Discourse of Woman,' in Nancy Holland, ed., *Feminist Interpretations of Jacques Derrida* [University Park, PA: Pennsylvania State University Press, 1997], p. 54). In Spivak's locution, when the mother 'carries the trace of the thing itself,' she is no longer a mother, for she turns into 'the father in himself.'

18 Elsewhere, Derrida talks of the mother who is 'not replaceable,' but who 'replaces *herself* … and that is how she remains a living mother' (HC 41).

19 To complete the symmetry of the inversion, we ought to add the mother-matrix coupling to the pairing of sons and threads.

20 The phantomaticity of the mother of Derrida is expressed in her capacity to survive, to live beyond death with a memory of mortality: 'The point is that the figure of the mother ... is not only that of survival. But, inasmuch as it survives, it is also that of the ultimate addressee in the phantasm' (EO 53). The infusion of a living mother at once with the memory and a premonition of death is meant as a palliative against the Nietzschean mother, to which Derrida, perhaps, feels closely related. This mother is a 'living feminine' – the element combined with the name of the dead father in Nietzsche-the-child (cf. EO 16ff).

21 Hartman, *Saving the Text*, p. 106. Since it would be impracticable to cite *Circumfession* in its entirety here, I confine myself to a highly abbreviated account.

22 It is the mother herself who says, as though in the place of her son, 'I have a pain in my mother' (CI 23).

23 'When each text has secured the countersignature of the other thing, it merely finds itself provided with its own irreplaceable idiom, hence with a signature detached from the permanent name of the "general" author' (SI 128ff).

24 In English in the original.

25 In her *Portrait of Jacques Derrida as a Young Jewish Saint* (trans. Beverley Bie Brabic [New York: Columbia University Press: 2004]), Hélène Cixous illuminates the other side of this appropriation in her account of the castrating mother: 'I call my mother to make sure of this: how does one say "I cut" in German? *Ich schneide* says my mother, whereupon she cuts me off. They cut therefore and they are cut. Everything is fiction and everything is reality. Circumcision is all around us and we don't know it' (p. 74).

26 The three terms revolve around the Heideggerian corpus. *Ruinanz* is a recognizably Heideggerian motif that highlights the erasure/forgetting of time accompanying the factical being-in-the-world. Cf. Martin Heidegger, *Phänomenologische Interpretationen zu Aristoteles: Einführung in die phänomenologische Forschung*, Martin Heidegger Gesamtausgabe, vol. 61 (Frankfurt: Vittorio Klostermann, 1985), pp. 131–55. Cinders are the remnants of the Heideggerian inflammation of spirit (see OS 84ff). Finally, the remains are exposed, like the carcasses of small sea creatures swept to the shore, after the epochal withdrawal of Being.

27 See also P 316.

28 Psychoanalysis is always an auto-analysis mediated by the other – the auto-analysis of the other.

29 Symptomatically, Freud writes in *The Project*, 'What we call *things* are residues that evade being judged' (Sigmund Freud, *The Project for a Scientific Psychology*, trans. James Strachey, in *The Standard Edition*, vol. 1. [London: Hogarth, 1966], p. 334).

172 Notes to pages 82–6

30 'One of the great common lessons of psychoanalysis and deconstruction is the generative power of what is left out' (Alan Bass, 'The Double Game: An Introduction,' in J.H. Smith and W. Kerrigan, eds, *Taking Chances: Derrida, Psychoanalysis, and Literature* [Baltimore and London: Johns Hopkins University Press], p. 67).

31 Derrida is aware of the etymological connection between *la chose* and cause. See PC 271 for the way in which the deferral of the thing in the other thing (*autre chose*) destabilizes the notion of causality.

32 As a thing that welcomes things, the unconscious replicates the existential spatiality of 'always already' being-in-the-world, traversing the categorial and existential analytics of Dasein.

33 'Psychoanalysis is, in fact, itself the primal scene it seeks: it is the first occurrence of what has been repeating itself in the patient without having occurred. Psychoanalysis is not the interpretation of repetition; it is the repetition of a *trauma of interpretation* ... the traumatic deferred interpretation not *of* an event, but *as* an event that never took place as such' (Barbara Johnson, 'The Frame of Reference: Poe, Lacan, Derrida,' in John P. Muller and William Richardson, eds, *The Purloined Poe: Lacan, Derrida, and Psychoanalytic Reading* [Baltimore and London: Johns Hopkins University Press, 1988], p. 245).

34 Benedict de Spinoza, *Ethics*, trans. Edwin Curley (London and New York: Penguin, 1996), p. 78. The Latin version is as follows: 'Videmus deinde quod ille, qui amat, necessario conatur rem, quam amat, praesentem habere et conservare; et contra qui odit, rem, quam odio habet, amovere et destruere conatur' (*Ethica* IIP13S). In a similar vein, the earlier discussion of the extended psychic thing may be compared with the Spinozan view of modalized substance in Book I of the *Ethics*.

35 In his occasional deconstructive mood, Žižek calls this unevenness 'the parallax of the two frames [that] is not symmetrical.' He writes: 'All that has to intervene into the Real is an empty frame so that the same things we saw "directly" before are now seen through the frame. A certain surplus-effect is thus generated, which cannot simply be cancelled through demystification' (Slavoj Žižek, 'A Plea for a Return to *Différance* (with a Minor *Pro Domo Sua*),' *Critical Inquiry 32*, Winter 2006, pp. 234–5).

36 Despite the undeniable Derridian tendency to confine use-value to usefulness, in *Specters of Marx*, Derrida points out the complexity and 'underdetermination' of this taken-for-granted term (cf. SM 150ff).

37 The institution of such a regime is the target of the complaint launched by Gayatri Spivak ('Limits and Openings of Marx in Derrida,' in *Outside in the Teaching Machine* [New York and London: Routledge, 1993]): 'There is no

such thing as subtracting use-value from a thing in this sphere [Marx's species-life], for the prior mark of the material transformation with Nature is mutely testified to even by the "thing in its nudity". One can "subtract" use-value (a methodological abbreviation) only in the other direction ... to make quantitative exchange-value' (p. 105).

38 This criticism mirrors the rebuke of Lacan in 'Le Facteur de la vérité' (PC 441ff).

39 Karl Marx, *Capital I*, trans. Ben Fowler (London and New York: Penguin, 1976), p. 300.

40 Another outcome of the fallen shoes is that they are '"without" use, and also, therefore, without truth' (Jay M. Bernstein, *The Fate of Art: Aesthetic Alienation from Kant to Derrida and Adorno* [Cambridge and Oxford, UK: Polity, 1992], p. 146). Derrida will complicate both uses of the 'without,' but the same can be said about surplus value.

41 On the profit gained from an ostensibly useless play, see also PC 321.

42 This, I believe, is Derrida's tacit answer to the initial question he posed: 'To whom and to what, in consequence would one have to *restitute* them [the shoes], render them, to discharge a debt?' (TP 258).

43 Marx, *Capital I*, p. 255.

44 *Ibid.*, p. 229.

45 '*La* chose n'est rien parce que toute chose est singulière' [The *thing is nothing because every thing is singular*]' (JDP 13/1). On the other hand, robbing the things of their singularity, money as the expression of general equivalency threatens to turn the thing into nothing.

46 In French, *coupure* means, inter alia, a 'cut' and a 'banknote.' The English economic jargon has, to some extent, preserved the duplicity of the term in such expressions as 'to cut a check.' Thus, taking up Derrida's insight, Jon Stratton (*Writing Sites: A Genealogy of the Postmodern World* [Ann Arbor: University of Michigan Press, 1990]) writes: 'The universality of money is the trace of the fundamental nature of the fracture. Money is the articulation of the fracture in its economic form' (p. 186).

47 Simon Critchley, 'The Hypothesis, the Context, the Messianic, the Political, the Economic, the Technological: On Derrida's *Specters of Marx*,' in *Ethics-Politics-Subjectivity: Essays on Derrida, Levinas, and Contemporary French Thought* (London and New York: Verso, 1999), p. 168. Rephrasing Wallace Stevens, Critchley adds, on the same page, '*Money is a kind of deconstruction.*'

48 For the difference between money and currency, *argent* and *monnaie*, see N 316ff.

49 Amusingly enough, Marx 'himself,' or rather the spectrality of Marx, is unable to break either with the ghostly engenderment of money or with the

indeterminacy of the thing. In *Marx en jeu*, Derrida asks, 'Qui porte le nom de Marx, mais aussi que porte le nom de Marx? [*Who bears the name of Marx, but also what does the name of Marx bear?*]' (p. 10). The division of roles between 'who' and 'what' gives rise to a certain Shakespearean theatricality of the thing: '"*The play's the thing*" , le jeu c'est la chose même ...; donc, la chose c'est le théâtre et le théâtre dans le théâtre, la chose même [*therefore, the thing is the theatre and the theatre in the theatre, the thing itself*]' (p. 13). In this theatre, Marx's ghosts play the role of money, which plays the role of the thing.

50 I have in mind the purely economic resistance, not political-economic class alliances.

51 In the first instance, I am not citing the divergence of signifier from the signified, of the referent from the sign, but two distinct modes of signification: the quasi-transcendental and the empirical.

52 'Counterfeit money – is not a thing like any other ...; It is "something" like a sign, and even a false sign, or rather a true sign with a false value, a sign whose signified seems (but that is the whole story) finally not to correspond or be equivalent to anything, a fictive sign without *secure* signification, a simulacrum, a double of a sign or a signifier' (GT 93). Since all money may be, potentially, counterfeit, it cannot transcendentally vouchsafe commensurability. This conclusion pre-empts Hamacher's suggestion: 'Money is the transcendental of commodity-language, that form which vouchsafes all other forms of their commensurability, appearing as a copula in all the statements and postulates of commodity-language' (Werner Hamacher, 'Lingua Amissa: The Messianism of Commodity-Language and Derrida's *Specters of Marx*,' in Michael Sprinker, ed., *Ghostly Demarcations: A Symposium on Jacques Derrida's* Specters of Marx [London and New York: Verso, 1999], p. 174).

53 In Marx's view, this is particularly detrimental to the worker who gives credit to the capitalist by advancing the 'use-value of his labor-power' without being paid immediately. 'That this credit is no mere fiction,' Marx observes, 'is shown not only by the occasional loss of the wages the worker has already advanced, when a capitalist goes bankrupt, but also by a series of more long-lasting consequences' (*Capital I*, p. 278).

54 There isn't 'a thing that is *one* and *identifiable*, identical with itself, which whether religious or irreligious, we agree to call "religion"' (AR 73). Although (or because) religion is not a thing in the traditional sense of thinghood, it verges on the thinghood of the deconstructed thing that is not one and self-identical, but disseminated and disseminating, attached and absolved, and so forth.

55 This haunting is explicated in D 36ff, and SQ 65–96, passim.

56 'The concept of the world gestures toward a history, it has a memory that distinguishes it from that of the globe, of the universe, of the Earth, of the *cosmos* … For the world begins by designating, and tends to remains, in an Abrahamic tradition … a particular time-space, a certain oriented history of human brotherhood, of what in this Pauline language one calls *citizens of the world* (*sympolitai,* fellow citizens of the saints in the house of God), brothers, fellow men, neighbors, insofar as they are creatures and sons of God' (N 374–5).

57 This 'accomplishment' of religion prompts Leonard Lawlor to write, 'What makes *Specters of Marx* so uncanny is that, in a book purportedly on Marxism, Derrida seems to be reviving the political power of religious faith' (*Derrida and Husserl,* p. 224). But 'the political power of religious faith' is revived in Derrida only if we carefully isolate the precise meaning of each word in this syntagma, understanding, for instance, 'religion' in terms of a divided possibility of re-linking the world through self-affective globalization and through the hetero-affective secret community of the New International. The same applies to 'faith,' which stands for the irreducibility of credit, credibility, trust, *and* of their violation at the root of any being-with, and to 'power' that renders this re-linking both possible and impossible, and so on.

58 Heidegger, *Being and Time,* p. 65.

59 '*Notre monde* se touche,' 'our world touches itself, can be touched, is touched; our world *is in touch*' (OT 53), presupposes that it has, first, detached itself from itself and from us, and that it hetero-affects itself in its very auto-affection.

60 The book starts with the question 'What is avoiding?' and continues: '*Sein und Zeit* (1927): what does Heidegger say at that time? He announces and he prescribes. He *warns* [*avertit*]: a certain number of terms will have to be avoided (*vermeiden*). Among them, spirit (*Geist*)' (OS 1).

61 Cf. GG, passim.

62 On money as 'the *spirit* of the market,' see N 315ff.

4. On the Thing That Deconstructs Aesthetics

1 'Derrida learned from Ponge, that is, how to use style (rhetoric, rather than grammar or logic) to generalize by means of the absolutely particular' (Gregory Ulmer, *Heuretics: The Logic of Invention* [Baltimore and London: Johns Hopkins University Press, 1994], p. 184). Despite Ulmer's suggestion to the contrary, the question of style, for Derrida, is irreducible to rhetoric;

this question unfailingly inflects and internally subverts even those regions that are, presumably, 'rhetoric-free.'

2 For Derrida, the splitting of the point, its division against itself, does not result in a negation of the negation that yields a line. In its absolute alterity and divisibility, the point cannot be reflected by another point that would relieve or re-elevate it into a higher plane. For the discussion of spatiality and the point in Hegel's *Encyclopedia*, see MP 40ff.

3 '*Le punctum déchire l'espace*' (PSY 292).

4 On the impossibility of pointing out, see P 42: 'In the last analysis, it is impossible to *point* it [the new concept of writing] out, for a unilinear text, or a punctual position, an operation signed by a single author, are all by definition incapable of practicing this interval.'

5 Marian Hobson has established an analogy between the signature and the thing: 'For the law prescribed by the thing is also no law, the thing is singular, whereas a law is general and exemplary. Like "signature," it is a contradictory injunction, like "signature" it provokes the event' (*Jacques Derrida*, p. 132). However apt, this analogy misses the point that the thing itself is capable of signing or countersigning the signature of the subject.

6 Let us attempt to put two Derridian passages not just side by side, but face to face (as we do in the beginning of each chapter), and let us listen in on them communicating or whispering to one another something on the subject of the signature's giving withdrawal. First passage (1): 'Today events called "video" *can* lay bare symptoms that are far more interesting and provocative: for example, those that lead us to think the singularity of "works" and "signatures" beginning with the very thing that institutes them and threatens them at the same time' (Jacques Derrida, 'Videor,' in Michael Renov and Erika Suderburg, eds, *Resolutions* [London and Minneapolis: University of Minnesota Press, 1996], p.76). Second passage (2): 'As for the great draftsman … does he not also try in vain, up to the point of exhausting a *ductus* or stylus, to capture this withdrawal [*retrait*] of the *trait*, to remark it, to sign it finally – in an endless scarification?' (MB 56). This withdrawal of the trait, *retrait du trait*, self-iterative dissemination is characteristic of the thing that plays with the draughtsman's signature. The play of the thing is predicated on the fact that *at the same time* it institutes and threatens the signature and the work in the singularity of their style. The gravity of this instituted threat or threatened institution is inseparable from the free play of the thing: it is exhausting, it exhausts the stylus that dreams of catching up with it. How to 'think the singularity' of something ('works,' 'signatures' no longer identical or self-identical – this is what the quotation marks give us to think) beginning with the giving withdrawal of the thing that bestows and

takes away this very singularity? What does the *ductus*, or stylus, or – again – 'the thought of singularity' wound if not *itself*, when it attempts in vain 'to capture this withdrawal'? How to square its exhaustion, the finality of the signature, and the 'endless scarification' it inflicts without respite? And so on ...

7 Derrida inherits the division or the de-phasing of the instant from Blanchot and Levinas, who, in turn, inherit some version of the Heideggerian ekstasis of Dasein. For the Derridian treatment of the instant, see D 33ff.

8 The spongy absorption enacted by the thing counterbalances Nancy's emphasis on its absolute exteriority and non-relationality: 'Every thing outside all the others, every thing according to the stretching that spaces them and without which there would be just one indistinct thing gathered into the point at which it would annul itself, a thing unthinged, a de-realized *res*' (Jean-Luc Nancy, *A Finite Thinking* [Stanford: Stanford University Press, 2003], p. 315) .

9 As Krell observes, the signature 'always already' signifies the remains (and therefore, I would add, something of the thing): 'If my signature remains after I am gone ... that is because the signature always was "remains," always was a residue, always was a kind of cinder. Written in stone it may be, but the stone is calcined to powdery ash, to the barest possible trace' (David Farrell Krell, *The Purest of Bastards: Works of Mourning, Art, and Affirmation in the Thought of Jacques Derrida* [University Park: Pennsylvania State University Press, 2000], pp. 13–14). In fact, this 'barest possible trace' is none other than the thinghood of stone: what makes the stone a thing.

10 The focus on spectrality, finitude, and death leads us away from the narrowly circumscribed aesthetic sphere. Derrida's 'unjustified' expansion of the aesthetic is a subject of various critiques and, most notably and surprisingly, that of Christoph Menke. In *The Sovereignty of Art: Aesthetic Negativity in Adorno and Derrida* (Cambridge and London: MIT Press, 1998), Menke writes, 'Derrida's false development of the correct intuition of the nonaesthetic validity, or sovereignty, of aesthetic negativity is a form of "reverse romanticism": it equates aesthetic experience with a cognition of negativity that goes beyond the way nonaesthetic discourses understand themselves and their own practices' (p. 250). But, in thus lambasting the undue formalization of 'aesthetic negativity' in the 'cognition of negativity' that mediates between the aesthetic and the nonaesthetic, Menke discloses, simultaneously, 1) the reductionism implied in his notion of the 'sovereignty of art' (in which the aesthetic practice is relevant to, produces effects in, but is strictly separate from other kinds of praxis and from *aesthesis* in the broader sense of 'sensibility'), and 2) the inflated, idealist vacuity entailed in his definition of art: 'What art actually is, is contradiction, rejection, negation' (p. 3).

11 This happens only with the greatest reluctance in philosophy: 'None of them, as philosophers, will have known how to cut short, to stop or to cut, and thereby to shorten and to sign' (SI 32).

12 '[The poem] speaks *of itself*, signifying itself in speaking to the other about the other, signing and de-signing itself in a single gesture – *sealing and unsealing itself*' (SQ 67).

13 Jean-Luc Marion (*The Crossing of the Visible* [Stanford: Stanford University Press, 2004]) attributes a similar function to the work of art when, in the footsteps of Malévitch, he defines it as a 'nonobjective phenomenon' that 'carries out a "new realism of things" by liberating the thing from every subjective edifice' (p. 19).

14 In 'La Chose littéraire/La Chose plastique,' Nathalie Roelens confirms this liberation in thingly terms coinciding with Kantian indifference: 'Comme la chose chez Ponge, la tulipe n'est pas un objet … C'est en ce qu'elle participe de la *pulchritudo vaga* que la tulipe est une "chose" (*Ding*) et non pas un "objet" (*Object*)' (p. 367).

15 'Painting has clearly become the paradigm of all the arts, an art plural in itself, if not a total art' (US 89).

16 In *Of Grammatology*, Derrida famously criticizes Rousseau's account of art as mimesis, in that it presupposes the presence of the thing itself before and outside the artistic attempts to reproduce it. This account of art becomes fascinating through its effects and, especially, through Rousseau's examples privileging song and painting as the aesthetic sites of mimesis: 'The metaphor which makes the song a painting is possible … only under the common authority of the concept of imitation. Painting and song are reproductions, whatever might be their differences; the inside and the outside share them equally, expression has already begun to make passion go outside itself, it has begun to set it forth and to paint it' (OG 203). Nonetheless, the difference of the represented from the representer makes representation take the path of 'de-presentation,' tying it to 'the work of spacing' (ibid.) and, thus, accentuating painting at the expense of song.

17 On 'obscure self-showing,' see MB 9ff.

18 McCumber rightly associates transcendental vision not with the emptiness of form, but with the trace: 'Thus generalized, the object of vision is no longer presence but something which is "visible" only in transition: *as* coming-from and going-to, without any determinate things that it comes from and goes to. Such an "object" is then not form but what Derrida calls the trace' (John McCumber, 'Derrida and the Closure of Vision,' in David M. Levin, ed., *Modernity and the Hegemony of Vision* [Los Angeles and London: University of California Press, 1993], p. 240).

19 'More naked because one then sees the eye *itself* … stripped of the signification of the gaze that once came to animate it and veil it' (MB 106). Thus, the
   'purposiveness without purpose' of art resonates with the baring of the
   thing in phenomenological reduction.

20 Henri Bergson, *Matter and Memory*, trans. N.M. Paul and W.S. Palmer
   (New York: Zone, 1991), p. 34.

21 Bernstein, *The Fate of Art*, p. 153.

22 'Truth belongs to this movement of repayment that tries in vain to render itself adequate to its cause or to the thing. Yet this latter emerges only in the
   hiatus of disproportion … Restoring or rendering is the cause of the dead,
   the cause of deaths, the cause of a death given or requested' (MB 30).

23 Herman Rapaport (*Later Derrida: Reading the Recent Work* [New York and
   London: Routledge, 2002]) underscores the ambiguity of the word 'subjectile': 'The subjectile, being in the margins of French, is marginal and, as
   such, subaltern … Sub-ject-il. Couldn't one translate it as "he, the subject"?
   Or would it mean something more like a sub's torpedo?' (p. 122).

24 In the chapter of *The Purest of Bastards* titled 'Broken Frames,' David Farell
   Krell argues that 'the very notion of epoch and *epoché* is itself a kind of a frame
   or historical framework' (p. 27). We may conclude from this that, in following
   the logic of phenomenological reduction, the subjectile plays in reverse a succession of frames and frameworks in its drive to approach the thing.

25 The intrinsic opening to the extrinsic is an important feature of the Derridian critique of Husserl's 'intrinsic' or 'essential' historicity: 'Its [truth's] be-
   ing-sense would preserve its own *intrinsic* historicity, its own
   interconnections, and the catastrophe of worldly history would remain *exterior* to it. That is what Husserl means when he opposes *internal* or intrinsic
   (*innere*) historicity to *external* (*aussere*) history. This distinction, which has
   only a phenomenological sense, is decisive. It would be fruitless for him to
   object that historicity or being-in-history is precisely the possibility of being
   intrinsically exposed to the *extrinsic*, for then the historicity absolutely
   proper to any truth-sense would be missing and Husserl's discourse would
   be plunged into a confusion of significations and regions' (IOG 95).

26 This memory is in harmony with the forgetting of the self, which, in Celan's
   view, is reserved for anyone who faces art: 'Whoever has art before his eyes
   and on his mind … has forgotten himself. Art produces a distance from the
   I' (Paul Celan, 'The Meridian,' appended to Jacques Derrida, *Sovereignties in
   Question: The Poetics of Paul Celan*, trans. Thomas Dutoit and Outi Pasanen
   [New York: Fordham University Press, 2005], p. 178).

27 In this sense, Isobel Armstrong (*The Radical Aesthetic* [Oxford and Malden:
   Blackwell, 2000]) is right to suggest that Derrida's aesthetics is written from

the Kantian 'broken middle' of a suspension that is neither analytic nor synthetic: 'It [the aesthetic] has neither an independent role nor is it a re-membering, connective entity. Or, like the frame or *parergon*, it both is de-tached, disinterested, *and* sinks its identity, loses itself either to theory or to practice. Thus Kant's middle is always without, always associated with loss, and belongs with the displacement of the supplement' (p. 68). Only two remarks are in order: 1) the aesthetic is not a re-membering understood as *Erinnerung*, though it necessitates the non-synthetic *Gedächtnis*, and 2) the detachment of the aesthetic that defies and exceeds the planes of synthesis and analysis derives from the thingly bond of the bound and the unbound; the 'broken middle' is not only 'without,' but 'without *with.*'

28 Akin to the point (of style) and to the thing 'itself,' the 'subjectile is never literally what it is' (US 139).

29 'Paper is already "reduced" or "withdrawn", "sidelined" … But can we speak here about paper *itself*, about the "thing itself" called "paper" – or only figures for it? Hasn't "withdrawal" always been the mode of being, the process, the very movement of what we call "paper"? Isn't the essential feature of paper the withdrawal or sidelining of what is rubbed out and withdraws *beneath* what a so-called support is deemed to back, receive, or welcome? … *What is* paper, itself, strictly speaking? Isn't the history of the question "What is?" always "on the edge", just before or just after a history of paper?' (PM 50). On the subjectile suffering of paper, see US 122ff.

30 'The body proper becomes the living subjectile, drawing and writing' (US 100).

31 Gasché sets up a correlation between the suspension of the relation to meaning and the self-suspension of literature that, in challenging philo-sophical categorization, 'puts itself between quotation marks by opening it-self to the absolute loss of its meaning, whether of content or of form' (Rodolph Gasché, *The Tain of the Mirror: Derrida and the Philosophy of Reflec-tion* [Cambridge and London: Harvard University Press, 1986], p. 258). Gasché's insight must be read against the backdrop of Derrida's remarks on the 'suspensive withdrawal of the metaphor' that insists on the 'double writing of the *retrait*, suspension and *overabundant remaining*' (C 131). The subjectile is the name of this 'double writing' that suspends meaning and retains a non-relational relation to the thing.

32 In part, the impossibility of the thing's 'straightforward recognition and identification' stems from the fact that, despite the oneness of the thing's 'spatial corporeality,' its perceptual adumbration can never achieve the si-multaneity or the synchronicity of an 'all-sided' view of a total perspective (cf. Husserl, *Ideas I*, p. 87; *Ideas II*, pp. 42–3). But even here art has a role to

play. For instance, Cubism may be understood as a fantasy of all-sided, synchronous, post-reductive perception.

33 For a discussion of the 'jetty,' see Jacques Derrida, 'Some Statements and Truisms about Neologisms, Newisms, Postisms, Parasitisms, and Other Small Seismisms,' trans. Anne Tomiche, in David Carroll, ed., *The States of 'Theory': History, Art, and Critical Discourse* (Stanford: Stanford University Press, 1994), pp. 65ff. The commentators on Derrida's aesthetics have underscored the role of framing and parergonality in his thought, as much as they have overlooked the importance of the jetty or the subjectile.

34 'Whence the crafty outlook and the torment of the scene. We say shit to the subjectile, to this world as a subjectile or as the place of subjectiles in general ... Now what happens when the excrement becomes breath, when in a word it expresses itself thus, *shit*, throwing itself against the subjectile without describing anything else, without representing anything else than itself?' (US 118).

35 Phenomenologically understood, the dissemination of the thing is predicated on the disjunctiveness and discreteness harboured in any phenomenal unity. As the Husserl of *Ideas I* (§15) argues, any such phenomenal unity is made up of determinate qualities, each of which leads to discrete genera, such as shape and colour (p. 30). The thrust of modern art (Impressionism, Abstractionism, etc.), then, is to expose the disjunctiveness and discreteness masked by the thing's phenomenal unity and thereby to illuminate something of the thing's essence.

36 Sublimation is the silent keyword of the above passage, which quietly alludes to the aesthetic transformation of the anal stage in particular, and of the Freudian theory of art in general.

37 Neither of these figures of freedom appears *as such*. First, the freedom *of* determination is the pathway through which a self-remarked thing eludes a signifying, identifying grasp. Second, the freedom *from* determination is predicated on the sort of transcendental opacity that has no 'empirical' effects: 'When freedom does thus appear it does so in some determinate form, some particular configuration that is not freedom itself. The mark of freedom not appearing is the transcendental opacity, the tain through which and against the background of which freedom is given and reflected in the exemplary work' (Bernstein, *The Fate of Art*, p. 175).

38 Paul Ricoeur, *A Key to Husserl's* Ideas I, trans. Bond Harris (Milwaukee: Marquette University Press, 1996), p. 17.

39 Mimesis is a contentious topic, but even more contentious is Derrida's reading of it. Halliwell ventriloquizes the voices of a number of critics (such as Hilary Putnam) when he writes that Derrida 'is *almost entirely silent*

about the significance of Aristotle's non-Platonic understanding of mimesis for the tradition as a whole' (Stephen Halliwell, *The Aesthetics of Mimesis: Ancient Texts and Modern Problems* [Princeton and Oxford: Princeton University Press, 2002], p. 374). 'Almost entirely silent' betrays a certain unease, however, not only because Derrida addresses the problem (both in *Dissemination* and in a 'seminal' essay titled 'Economimesis'), but also because the 'non-Platonic solution' presupposes a radical break or a discontinuity between Plato and the rest of the tradition. In fact, when Derrida does touch upon the problem, he justifies his approach by pointing out the continuity of the thinking about mimesis in the history of metaphysics: 'Nothing ... was to change when, following Aristotle, and particularly during the "age of classicism", the models for imitation were to be found not simply in nature but in the works and writers of Antiquity ... All manner of reversals are included in the program' (D 190 n18).

40 On the same page, Derrida contends that the 'alternative wavers not only between representation and its other, a representative painting and its beyond, but between the inert and what gushes forth, the being-dead of the supine figure and the spurting force, of the projectile or the ejaculation.'

41 'Art is beautiful to the degree that it is productive *like* productive nature, that it reproduces the production and not the product of nature, to the degree that nature may once have been (was), before the critical dissociation and before a still to be determined forgetfulness, beautiful' (E 10).

42 The question of time is crucial to any account of the 'originary splitting' or doubling: 'When time begins, a monstrous doubling will already have begun; and it is only by repressing such catastrophe that one can be assured of controlling the doubling of sense' (John Sallis, 'Doublings,' in David Wood, ed., *Derrida: A Critical Reader* [Oxford and Cambridge: Blackwell, 1992], p. 131).

43 Cf. Stephen W. Melville, *Philosophy beside Itself: On Deconstruction and Modernism* (Minneapolis: University of Minnesota Press, 1986), pp. 96–7. For an explanation of the connection between the abyss and reflection, see also 'Translator's Note' by Alan Bass in *Margins of Philosophy* (MP 262 n73).

44 'In order to be abyssal, the smallest circle must inscribe in itself the figure of the largest' (TP 27).

45 Various commentaries on the 'dried flower' Derrida picked from Mallarmé's text have pointed out its relation to the trace. In an elegantly economic manner, Claudette Sartiliot ('Herbarium, Verbarium: The Discourse of the Flowers,' *Diacritics* 18(4), Winter 1998, pp. 68–81) notes that, for Derrida, 'flowers seem to occupy ... the degree zero in the chain of signification' (p. 72). Thus, while the flower 'is' an archi-trace defined as 'the degree zero'

of signification, a dried flower attempts to capture and to freeze its ephemeral state of constantly becoming other to itself. In other words, this allegory reflects the relation between the proto-signification of the thing and empirical systems of signification that wish to harness it and thrive on the rendering-static of the dynamic.

46 Observe, in this context, Derrida's reference to Novalis's aphorism, 'The book is Nature inscribed on a staff (like music) and *completed*,' in the first part of *Dissemination*. Derrida interprets the aphorism as saying that 'this identity [of nature and of the book] is not given: nature without the book is somehow incomplete ... it lacks something needed for it to be what it is, it has to be supplemented' (D 52–3). This incompletion, certainly, echoes the dried flower confined to a book and absent from every garden. But, as the missing part, as the supplement, the artifice of the book (and the flower it contains) precedes the supplemented nature and inflects all synthetic activity with the irreducible memory of the cut.

47 Immanuel Kant, *The Critique of Judgment*, trans. James Creed Meredith (Oxford: Clarendon, 1952), p. 226.

48 Irine Harvey ('Derrida, Kant, and the Performance of Parergonality,' in Christopher Norris and David Roden, eds, *Jacques Derrida*, vol. 3 [London, Thousand Oaks, and New Delhi: SAGE, 2003], pp. 139–55) is convinced that exemplarity as parergonality is deconstruction's condition of possibility (pp. 139–40). Yet this otherwise commendable conviction comes into conflict with Derrida's insistence on the – at once – aphoristic and syllogistic character of deconstruction. What Harvey overlooks is not just the 'quasi-' of the Derridian quasi-transcendental, but the fact that examples, like aphorisms, must be 'absolutely heterogeneous,' while deconstruction divides its energy between 'on the one hand the concatenation of syllogistic sequences, and on the other, but "at the same time", the seriality of aphoristic sequences' (PM 93). Recall, also, the opening of 'Economimesis,' where the point of departure *'feigned'* in exemplarity is a procedure, which 'can be neither empirical, nor meta-empirical' (p. 3).

49 '*Parergon* furnishes a frame that is a discourse on the frame for Kant's analytic of aesthetic judgments which is already framed, as Derrida's complex argumentation demonstrates, by an analytic of logical judgments, a relation to the understanding that Kant imports into his discourse on the beautiful, which contains within it a discourse on *parerga* or frames' (Shuli Barzilai, 'Lemmata/Lemmala: Frames for Derrida's Parerga,' *Diacritics* 20(1), Spring 1990, p. 9).

50 'When the (beautiful) object is a book, what exists and what no longer exists? ... Here is an example, but an example *en abîme*: the third *Critique*.

How to treat this book. Is it a book. What would make a book out of it …
Have I the right to say that it is beautiful' (TP 49).

51 Levinas is aware of this caveat. The other is 'the Most High,' but also absolutely abject and thus 'the most low.' Barzilai, too, is cognizant of this necessary 'contradiction' in her elaboration on the first plurivocal word of the
'Parergon' section – 'Lemmata': '*Lemmata* means one thing in Greek and
more or less the opposite in Hebrew … The everyday adverbial *lemmata* denotes in Hebrew: below, beneath, under, down. The topos of the Hebrew is
to the Greek as down is to up, as bottom is to top' (Barzilai, 'Lemmata/
Lemmala,' pp. 2–3).

Conclusion

1 This is the position of Timothy Mooney, 'Derrida's Empirical Realism,'
passim.

Index of Names